READING
THE BIBLE,
TRANSFORMING
CONFLICT

THEOLOGY IN DIALOGUE SERIES

Russell A. Butkus, Anne Clifford, Carol J. Dempsey, Series Editors

The Theology in Dialogue Series expresses a vision for the possibilities of theology in conversation with other academic disciplines. The series stems from two primary sources. The first is historical. To some degree Christian theology has always been in dialogue with the major elements of its social context, drawing on insights and methods from diverse knowledge traditions in order to address pressing and timely issues. The second source is the contemporary world. Given the complexity of contemporary life, its questions and struggles, books in the Theology in Dialogue Series reflect the perspective that creative dialogue and strategic collaboration between theology and other disciplines are necessary in seeking effective solutions to contemporary problems.

Yes, resolving problems is important, but our hope is that creative dialogue will result in more than problem solving, that it will make the positive contributions needed in an increasingly complex world. The overarching aim of the series is to demonstrate the creativity of theology in dialogue with various academic disciplines and, in doing so, to broaden the appeal of theology while enriching the pursuit of intellectual inquiry.

READING
THE BIBLE,
TRANSFORMING
CONFLICT

CAROL J. DEMPSEY
AND ELAYNE J. SHAPIRO

ORBIS BOOKS
Maryknoll, New York 10545

Founded in 1970, Orbis Books endeavors to publish works that enlighten the mind, nourish the spirit, and challenge the conscience. The publishing arm of the Maryknoll Fathers and Brothers, Orbis seeks to explore the global dimensions of the Christian faith and mission, to invite dialogue with diverse cultures and religious traditions, and to serve the cause of reconciliation and peace. The books published reflect the views of their authors and do not represent the official position of the Maryknoll Society. To learn more about Maryknoll and Orbis Books, please visit our website at www.maryknollsociety.org.

Library of Congress Cataloging-in-Publication Data

Dempsey, Carol J.
　　Reading the Bible, transforming conflict / Carol J. Dempsey and Elayne J. Shapiro.
　　　　p.　cm. – (Theology in dialogue series)
　　Includes indexes.
　　ISBN 978-1-57075-914-7 (pbk.)
　　1. Interpersonal relations – Religious aspects – Christianity. 2. Interpersonal relations – Biblical teaching. 3. Spirituality, 4. Spirituality – Biblical teaching. 5. Bible – Criticism, interpretation, etc. 6. Bible stories. I. Shapiro, Elayne J. II. Title. III. Series.
　　BV4597.52.D46 2011
　　220.8′3036 – dc22
　　　　　　　　　　　　　　　　　　　　　　　　　　　　　2010054109

To Leonard Shapiro (husband of Elayne)
for his constant encouragement throughout the entire project

To Mary Dempsey (mother of Carol)
for keeping us on task with her simple question
"Aren't you done with that book yet?"

To our students, who helped us shape our ideas

and to the cherished memory of Mary Travers
of Peter, Paul, and Mary
(Nov. 9, 1936–Sept. 16, 2009)
whose lyrical vision for peace all over the world
still blows in the wind
and hammers, sings, and rings in our hearts

CONTENTS

ACKNOWLEDGMENTS

No creation ever comes to life without the help and support of others who generously give of their time and talent. Thus, we would now like to acknowledge those who have helped us with the creative process of this work. To Carol Bruce, office manager for Communication Studies who helped to process the manuscript, we are most grateful. To the entire library staff at the University of Portland who were always ready to assist us in locating books and articles, for allowing us to renew needed books again and again and again, and especially to Heidi Senior, for her assistance with the manuscript documentation, we owe a debt of gratitude. We are also indebted to our wonderful students, especially those in our Theology 483 team-taught course, who read and commented on several chapters of this manuscript and helped us hone our ideas.

To our colleagues at Orbis Books who worked so carefully with us at every stage of the project, we say "thank you." Last but certainly not least, we are deeply grateful to Susan Perry, senior editor at Orbis, for believing in us as authors, in this series as a whole, and in this specific project. We are most appreciative for her insightful comments and suggestions at each stage of the writing of this project. And finally, we are grateful to you, our readers, who ponder the content of these pages with us as we work together for a new world order based on justice, truth, and right relationship.

To you, all, we offer our gratitude, blessing, and deepest hope.

January 28, 2011
Feast of Thomas Aquinas

INTRODUCTION

We live in an open universe that is forever expanding and evolving as we grow in deeper awareness and greater consciousness of the world around us. Embedded in the web of life, we no longer view life in a linear fashion because we have learned and continue to learn about the interconnectedness of all life. Our way of seeing and learning has also been affected by our understanding of life. Knowledge that was once compartmentalized is now becoming more integrated. Disciplines that were once independent of each other are now entering into conversation, resulting in new and emerging interdisciplinary dialogues that challenge old assumptions and inform traditional thought.

This book is part of a new educational paradigm that seeks to engage two distinct disciplines — biblical studies and communication studies — in conversation around a topic that has been a part of the human condition since the beginning of time. This topic is conflict. This text explores conflict by integrating the resources of biblical studies, the social sciences, and theology. It examines intrapersonal conflict, interpersonal conflict, and conflict between humans and God. It also provides an opportunity to explore a variety of skills in conflict mediation and negotiation aimed at developing "just" and transformative relationships for life in a complex world. Throughout we argue that the whole is greater than the sum of its parts — namely, that biblical studies offers an important lens, along with contemporary research in conflict transformation and communication studies, to glean relevant lessons about conflict for our time.

Overarching Focus and Content

The overarching focus and theme of this book is "right relationships" — right relationships with God, with one another, and with all creation. We hope students will understand what interferes with "right relationship" in biblical stories and in their own lives and that they will be able to apply what they have learned as they critique problematic situations.

Each of the twelve chapters studies a selected biblical narrative in detail, first from a biblical perspective and then from the perspective of conflict transformation theory.[1] The study of each biblical narrative includes relevant background on the historical period and the characters involved. The main conflicts within each narrative are highlighted, and the final section of each chapter includes a critical theological reflection that ponders the "grace in the wilderness" of the conflicts. Chapters also include questions

1

for reflection and discussion, other resources and activities, and some sug-
gested readings. Conflicts can generate powerlessness and self-absorption
and make communication difficult.[2] This is the "stuff" of the Bible and the
stuff of communication.

The first chapter, "The Bible and Conflict," presents the first account
of conflict in the Bible by describing the conflict-ridden encounter between
Adam and Eve and God in Genesis. It also introduces the concept of "right"
relationships and presents a basic understanding of conflict.

Chapter 2, "Joseph at Seventeen," provides an understanding of the historical background of families in ancient Israel. It also provides a brief
introduction to the cycle of ancestral stories about Abraham, Isaac, and
Jacob. The chapter then explores the biblical text of Genesis 37, focusing
on the text's historical, social, literary, and theological dimensions. Finally,
the story of Joseph and his brothers is studied through the lens of conflict. It considers such basic principles as the nature of conflict, how culture
contributes to conflict, and how power and self-esteem function in conflict.

Chapter 3, "Joseph and Potiphar's Wife," focuses on Genesis 39. After
examining Genesis 39 in its ancient context, this chapter uses the story of
Joseph and Potiphar's wife to explore a particular aspect of conflict, that
of "saving face." During conflict typically people pursue different types of
goals. This chapter explores what happens when questions of self-image and
identity enter into the fray, usually escalating any conflict.

Chapter 4, "Joseph Encounters His Brothers," focuses on the role of
the heart. Using the narrative of Joseph's encounter with his brothers, the
chapter explores the themes of forgiveness and reconciliation. Whereas forgiveness can be one-sided, reconciliation requires reestablishing relationship
and settling differences so that trust is again present. These concepts are
explored in the story of the reunion between Joseph and his brothers.

One of the most intriguing stories in the Bible is the story of Tamar and
Judah in Genesis 38:1–30. Chapter 5 looks at this story in detail, focusing
on power and demonstrating how power is present in all social interactions.
The chapter examines different forms of power, how they are employed by
the story's characters, and how they influence conflict today.

Chapter 6, "Susanna," explores the role of third parties in conflict, which
may involve facilitation, mediation, arbitration, and the criminal and civil
justice systems.

The historical backdrop to the book of Judith is rich both historically and
theologically. Chapter 7, "Judith," explores the world of Judith and its many
challenges, highlighting the religious views and values of the ancient Israelite
culture. The chapter then focuses on the use of different styles of conflict and
the effect of win-lose/zero-sum thinking in conflict transformation.

Exodus 32:1–35 captures the dynamic relationship that existed between
God and Moses. Chapter 8, "Moses and God," looks at the biblical image
of the golden calf and what happens after the golden calf debacle. Moses's

negotiation with God serves as a springboard for this chapter's discussion of the use of negotiation in conflict resolution.

Chapter 9, "Jeremiah," presents Jeremiah's interaction with King Zedekiah, detailing the final days of Jerusalem just before the Southern Kingdom fell to the Babylonians. This examination of the dialogue between Jeremiah and Zedekiah explores the nature of defensiveness in conflict.

Someone once said that "love is never enough,"[3] and that was certainly the case for Michal and David, whose marriage was riddled with disappointment and conflict. By examining the story of Michal and David in 1 and 2 Samuel, chapter 10 investigates interpersonal conflict in romantic relationships. A particular focus is the shifts that occur in their relationship. The chapter also highlights the assertiveness of Michal, which, in a patriarchal society, causes her to become a tragic yet noble figure.

Chapter 11, "Social Conflict in the Gospels," looks at the Sermon on the Mount (Matt. 5–7) as a basis for discussion on social conflict. Social conflict is a conflict between groups over values, status, power, and resources. This chapter explores the rhetorical means used to oppose established power and the conflict strategies used to bring about change.

Having looked at a variety of types of conflict in both the Old and New Testaments, chapter 12, "What's Love Got to Do with It?" focuses on Paul's addresses to the people in Rome and Corinth in order to understand how communication and an ethic of love can be transformative.

We have included an epilogue as a brief summary and also as a means to indicate new directions in dealing with conflict so that the vision of *shalom* becomes a deeper reality that can be lived among all peoples for the full flourishing of life, a divine gift meant for all. The Epilogue also raises several questions for further reflection.

Style, Tone, and Approach

We have attempted to use a reader-friendly, creative, critical, engaging, and sometimes colloquial style that is accessible to scholars, students, and general audiences. The book draws in its audience in a variety of ways, namely, through biblical case studies, the use of highlighted text, including significant questions and prompts to encourage the reader to examine conflict in his or her own life. The book also offers questions for further discussion, opportunities for critical theological reflection, and resources for further inquiry and discussion of the content of each chapter. Although many approaches to the Bible are possible, this book uses a text-centered approach for the analysis of the biblical stories. The biblical text is what unites the two different disciplines, biblical studies and communication studies.

The Value of Case Studies

Biblical texts, as case studies, will serve as a vehicle for learning about conflict. Case studies can enhance learning in a variety of ways. They can move students from a passive role of receiver to an active participant,[4] and they can provide opportunities for students to analyze critical incidents, applying their knowledge and considering how they might change their own behaviors.[5] Furthermore, case studies provide a springboard for discussing and understanding politically or socially charged issues.[6] Discussing case studies also has the potential to increase awareness of personal beliefs and values.

Case studies, when discussed by a group, also foster the ability to think with others, something that we are required to do in many aspects of our daily lives.[7] We are required to talk with others about problems at work, to make decisions with others in civic matters, and to process difficult challenges with significant others in their families. Using case studies to practice joint problem solving is especially valuable.

Using Biblical Narratives as Case Studies

What constitutes a good case? The criterion for a good case is its usefulness as a teaching device rather than the amount of information and realism any particular case contains.[8] The most important quality of a case is its relationship to the educational objectives. A case must effectively raise relevant issues and elicit relevant theories, and its organization and format must make the material immediately accessible.[9]

Biblical narratives have advantages on all of these counts: They are useful and effective at raising relevant issues and theories and their format makes them accessible to students.[10]

Effective cases are drawn around "big ideas" — those significant issues that warrant serious, in-depth examination.[11] Basically, a case must tell a good story. On both counts, big ideas and good narrative, stories of the Bible have an extremely long track record. Biblical narratives have sustained readers' attention for thousands of years. Thus, reframing them in the context of learning about conflict has the potential to expand our analytical and critical abilities.

We selected our cases based on the extent to which stories demonstrated concepts that we wanted to discuss. The Bible does not demonstrate that one right way exists to manage conflict. Examples of mercilessness and deception exist alongside examples of negotiation and forgiveness. In selecting stories to include, we reflected our own biases. For the most part, we concentrated on elements that contribute to interpersonal conflict, the one exception being Matthew, which we see as social conflict. We have chosen not to include biblical accounts of war. In all of our stories, we look for the glimmer of grace amid difficult conflict. We hope you will be inspired to continue learning long after the journey through our book is completed.

1

THE BIBLE AND CONFLICT
Beginning with the Creator and Adam and Eve

The biblical text as the received text of various faith communities is an ancient document that reflects many cultures and many cultural perspectives, as well as various and often divergent theologies. The text is a product of multiple authors, most of whom remain unknown. As a literary document, the biblical text does not record historical events as they actually happened, and yet the stories and poems reflect the history and historical times of a living ancient people. The text as we have it today is historically, socially, politically, and theologically conditioned, and reflects many processes that include borrowing, emending, enlarging, interpreting, and translating — all of which was done by many editors down through the ages. The final editor of the entire text is thought to have been from the priestly school of writers. Over the years the Bible has thus been shaped by culture and the Bible also has the potential for shaping culture when appropriated with skill and an informed understanding of its ancient contexts.[1]

What is important to note — as we have assumed in writing this book — is that because of this long transmission process, the Bible cannot be taken literally. Ultimately, the biblical histories, stories, and poems provide us with an insight into the ancient world and its peoples. They also offer us a vision of how to live in right relationship with God, with one another, and with all creation. Such a vision transcends time, space, cultures, and religious denominations.

The interpretation of the Bible is ongoing, and the biblical vision proclaimed by the text and embedded within the text remains transformative for all generations if only we have the eyes to see, the ears to hear, and the hearts to perceive the dynamic work of the Spirit, who can bring an ancient text to life in the midst of our ordinary comings and goings, while renewing the face of the earth.

Imago Dei: The Biblical Vision
Embedded in Genesis 1 and 2

Imago Dei is the idea that human beings are created in God's image, according to God's likeness (Gen. 1:26). As creatures embodying the image and likeness of God, human beings are to be a people of fecundity, creativity,

and fertility.[2] They have also been entrusted with the dominion of all creation (Gen. 1:28), which implies good governance — to till and to keep the
garden (Gen. 2:15) — just as God sustains all of creation (see Ps. 104).
Human beings are to bless and to be a blessing in the midst of creation and
to affirm creation just as God has affirmed creation (Gen. 1:4, 10, 12, 18,
21, 25, 31).

Imbued with the very breath of God (Gen. 2:7), human beings are called
to live compassionately and justly in the midst of all creation. This, then,
is living in right relationship: reverencing all life and working toward justice and compassion. As the entire biblical story unfolds, we see that God's
people are called to liberate all creation from the bonds of injustice (see, for
example, Isa. 58:1–14) and to maintain hospitality of heart for all, regardless of race, gender, creed, belief, status, orientation, or condition in life (see
Ps. 104:1–30).

The Torah's call for Israelites to circumcise the foreskins of their hearts
(Deut. 10:16; Jer. 4:4) describes this hospitality of heart that calls people
to welcome the poor, the widow, the stranger, the resident alien, and
the "other." Hospitality of heart is a core value in Israelite tradition and
teaching. This hospitality of heart is to flow from the knowledge and understanding that Israel was loved by God, whose heart was set upon the people
(Deut. 7:7–8). Hospitality of heart comes into full view in the two New Testament parables told in Matthew 25:31–46 and Luke 14:7–14, among other
stories. Matthew speaks of caring for those in need, and Luke describes a
meal celebration where the most unlikely people to be invited to a wonderful
feast are, in fact, welcomed to the table.

Finally, to live in God's image, according to God's likeness, is to embrace
the vision of Micah, who calls people to live life nonviolently, to use mediation instead of war to settle disputes, and to turn their swords and spears
into plowshares and pruning hooks (Mic. 4:1–5; Isa. 2:1–4). The one who
embraces and embodies God's image and likeness is the one who sees the
good in the midst of all and who works to maintain "the good," for, according to the Genesis creation account, creation is not only "good," but "very
good" (Gen. 1:4, 10, 12, 18, 21, 25, 31). The intrinsic goodness of all creation becomes the foundation and reason for acting justly, loving tenderly,
and walking humbly with God and with one another in the midst of all
creation.

Because all creation is interrelated and human beings are created in God's
image according to God's likeness, human beings are called to live together in
right relationship with one another and with all creation. Right relationship,
then, is essential to sustaining creation. This vision of right relationship
is foundational to understanding our yearning to transcend conflict and is
embedded in the first two chapters of Genesis.

Right relationship, then, is our interaction with one another and with
all the rest of creation wherein justice, righteousness, loving kindness, and

compassion are infused. Our book assumes that all of life is interrelated. From the perspective of sacramentality, all of creation has been fashioned in God's image, according to God's likeness, and this is the basis for right relationship. From the beginning of creation, all of life shared an independent yet interdependent existence. All the elements are independent insofar as they have their own identity, perhaps the reason why in many of the stories in the biblical text "right relationship" is askew. And they are interdependent insofar as the elements in creation depend on one another for their sustained existence.

For example, the two accounts of creation in Genesis, the Priestly account (Gen. 1:1–2:4a) and the Yahwistic account (Gen. 2:4b–25), both depict a wonderful relationship between the divine, human, and nonhuman worlds. For example, in Genesis 2:5, the Yahwistic writer states that no field, shrub, or grass was on the earth because God had sent no rain, and no person was present to till the soil. Interrelationship is needed in order to bring forth full flourishing. The animals and human beings were created as helpers and partners to one another (Gen. 2:18–19, 20–23).

As we journey through the biblical stories, we will see glimpses of right relationship and relationships that have gone askew. These stories can teach us about the obstacles that obscure our vision, whether based in culture, gender, family, or the history of the period. By studying the elements of conflict, we can learn to transcend these obstacles.

Justice, the Common Good, and Right Relationships

According to the biblical tradition, God entered into covenant with all of creation (Gen. 9:1–17). Covenant agreement called for the people to be in right relationship with God, with one another, and with all creation. Covenant indicates three hallmarks: *justice, righteousness,* and *loving kindness.* God's "law" — Torah — was given to the people to preserve and sustain covenant relationships, to assure "the good life" for all (Lev. 25:18–19). Torah was not only the Law but also a way of life that called people to act ethically.

Justice, a praxis central to covenant and Torah, is a quality of God (Isa. 30:18). The Israelite community was required to act with justice, especially on behalf of the poor, the widow, the resident alien, and the sojourner. Justice involves more than doing no wrong to one's neighbor and living peacefully in the midst of all (Jer. 22:3). As an ethical attitude of God (Ps. 140:12, 146:7), justice seeks solidarity and community. Justice demands not only a deep sensitivity to all life but also solidarity with those who are suffering, especially with those suffering injustice.

Justice welcomes all to the table and exists for the sake of the community — for the common good. Justice works to preserve the conditions for both individual and communal well-being. Justice establishes a sense of balance among all dimensions of creation, among all stakeholders who share life on the planet. This balance between personal and communal good is sustained only when all parties respect and nurture one another. The common life and the common good are possible only when the welfare of all members — both human and nonhuman — is given steadfast attention and regard.

> *Consider yourself, your family, your circle of friends, people who might ride the same bus as you, and people who hold up signs asking for help. What are some of the obstacles that might interfere with achieving "justice" as described above?*

Life is forever evolving, with new blessings and new obstacles, and new theory and skills need to be learned so that human beings can learn how to live authentically with integrity and in peace. Although we have the biblical texts and many volumes that interpret them from within different traditions, no precise blueprint or map exists that shows the way to live in right relationship. Like the ancient people, ours is often a journey through the wilderness as we struggle to learn how to act ethically and to live justly and in peace with one another, knowing that grace is present in the wilderness to inform us and guide us along the way.

Grace in the Wilderness

The final section of each chapter, Grace in the Wilderness, ask readers to seek glimpses of grace in the biblical stories of encounters between people. What, however, is "grace" and how does "grace" work in life?

We can look at grace from several perspectives. At its simplest level, grace is goodness, benevolence, and an attitude and action that finds and bestows favor or good will. Grace is the ability to perceive goodness, even in the midst of sordidness. Grace is elegance and beauty that deepens and enhances all dimensions of life.

From a biblical perspective, grace has multiple meanings. In Hebrew, the word "grace" is understood as the ability "to incline oneself favorably toward another." As a noun, grace literally means "favor." In the Torah, for example, God finds "favor" with Noah (Gen. 6:8), Jacob (Gen. 19:17–22, 31:5) and Moses (Exod. 33:12–13). God acts on behalf of Noah and Moses. Another example can be found in the Exodus story when God bestows "grace" on Israel by inspiring the Egyptians, Israel's foe, to show "favor" to the Israelites (Exod. 3:21, 11:3, 12:36). Grace, then, is the quality that provides others with something that they could not provide or obtain on their own.

In the New Testament, grace often takes the form of forgiveness (see, for example, Luke 7:42–43; 2 Cor 2:1–11; Eph. 4:32). Grace is a power that acts positively in one person's life and in the lives of others for the sake of the common good (Acts 24:20; Rom. 8:32). Thus, grace is transformative.

From a theological perspective, grace is the full involvement of our creator-God in the history of humankind and in the rest of the created world and its diverse communities of life. As a divine gift, grace is freely given to all; it is totally and absolutely gratuitous. Grace has life-sustaining and life-changing effects.

Grace is also the ability to acknowledge what is true. Grace offers opportunities for us to become people of understanding, compassion, comfort, healing, forgiveness, and reconciliation. Grace beckons us to look deeply at ourselves, our lives, and our world situations. Grace invites us to hear the truth about "the things that matter" — no matter how welcome or not welcome that word may be.

Grace also provides us with the ability to see people, things, and life as they *really* are and what they can become. Grace offers us the possibilities for growth, change, and transformation, and it can pave the way for faith and love. Finally, grace begs us to choose life even if that choice is going to ask us to do nothing more or nothing less than to journey through the wilderness, to go where we have never been before, and in that wilderness to discover, like our ancient ancestors, who we are, who God is, who God is in us, who we are in God, and what aspects of life are still in need of conversion and transformation as we evolve into deeper life, deeper wholeness, and deeper holiness. The moment of "grace" is always present, especially where conflict exists and even where conflict resolution seems impossible.

The intent of this book is to synthesize biblical, cultural, literary, and social scientific viewpoints to guide readers toward right relationships. Right relationships, however, will not occur simply because we want them. We need to learn how to develop them from our history, the wisdom the Bible has to offer, and knowledge from the social sciences. While this task may seem arduous or even daunting, it is work that can no longer be ignored on a planet whose communities of life are desperate for justice, righteousness, and peace. This is a challenge for all of us who have the potential to chart a new course in the history of the world for the sake of today's children and tomorrow's grandchildren. All communities of life wait in hope. We must become that hope as we work toward the vision of the promised new heavens and new earth already dawning in our midst.

Looking through the Communication Lens

While a biblical and theological lens provides a context for understanding the stories, the stories themselves provide models for us to explore some hard realities. Most people, countries, cultures, and religions say they want peace, yet peace escapes us. Early on in Genesis, trouble began to brew.

> *The* LORD *God took the man and put him in the garden of Eden, to till it and keep it. And the* LORD *God commanded the man, "You may freely eat of every tree of the garden; but of the tree of knowledge of good and evil, you shall not eat; for in the day that you eat of it you shall die.* (Gen. 2:15–17)

> *But the serpent said to the woman, "You will not die; for God knows that when you eat of it your eyes will be opened, and you will be like God, knowing good and evil." So when the woman saw that the tree was good for food, and that it was a delight to the eyes, and that the tree was to be desired to make one wise, she took the fruit and ate. She also gave some to her husband, who was with her, and he ate.*
> (Gen. 3:4–6)

> *But the* LORD *God called to the man and said to him, "Where are you?" He said, "I heard the sound of you in the garden, and I was afraid, because I was naked; and I hid myself." He said, "Who told you that you were naked? Have you eaten from the tree of which I commanded you not to eat?" The man said, "The woman whom you gave to be with me, she gave me fruit from the tree and I ate." Then the* LORD *God said to the woman, "What is this that you have done?" The woman said, "The serpent tricked me, and I ate"* (Gen. 3:9–13).

Given the way this scene unfolds, what can it teach us about the root causes of conflict and how conflict affects people?

Defining Conflict

Are all disagreements conflicts? What puts the story of Adam and Eve in the domain of conflict? In the narrative, while at first Eve believes she will die if she eats the fruit, the snake disagrees. Is this a conflict? If Adam and Eve had debated with each other about whether they should try the fruit, would that have been a conflict? If they had argued about whether God had lied to them, would that have been a conflict? Or was there conflict when they were confronted by God, and each tried to blame the other?

Some researchers identify three elements common to most definitions of conflict: disagreement, interference, and negative emotions.[3] Others go beyond the three ingredients: "Conflict is an interaction between at least two interdependent parties who perceive incompatible goals, scarce resources, and interference from others in achieving their goals."[4]

We are interdependent when we are intertwined in such a way that one person's behavior and choices impact the other's behavior. If parties are not interdependent, each can have his or her own way, and no reason for conflict exists. The more interdependent the parties are, the greater the consequences of each other's behaviors. In the story, Adam and Eve are intended to be helpmates. If Eve eats the apple and dies, Adam is again alone, so her behavior impacts him.

The second element of this definition of conflict, "incompatible goals," needs some explanation. Goals relate to what people want out of a situation, and goals can be grouped into four general categories. Sometimes a goal relates to the task or *content*. Sometimes the goal relates to an aspect of the *relationship*. Sometimes the goal relates to *identity*; in other words, how each person wants to be seen by others, and sometimes the goal relates to the *process*, how people are going to conduct the conflict.

Content goals relate to facts or the task at hand and often occur because the facts two people hold contradict each other. If we asked Adam or Eve, "What is this conflict about?" their answer would probably be about who is to blame for God's anger. Adam believes Eve is responsible for displeasing God, and Eve disagrees with Adam's "facts," asserting that the blame belongs to the snake. According to the way they frame the conflict, they cannot both be right.[5] They have a conflict about facts.

Relationship goals have to do with who has power, who is in control, and how independent or connected do the parties want to be. We often try to solve conflicts at the content level when in reality the problem is at the relationship level. Before returning to Adam and Eve, let's consider a contemporary conflict between housemates or couples dealing with the level of cleanliness in the apartment. "Cleaning up" is the obvious content goal. Less apparent may be relationship goals, including a struggle about who has the power to tell whom what to do. Don, for example, asks his roommate, Mark, to take out the garbage. Mark ignores the request and leaves without taking out the garbage. Later, their roles are reversed, and Mark asks Don to take out the garbage. Don also leaves without taking the garbage with him. Each may resist, not because the job itself is so bad, but rather because of what is implied at the level of relationship: one person has the power to tell the other to carry out a menial task. Every message that has a content or topic level also has a relationship level, a message about who is in control.[6] When two people find themselves continuously bickering over small, inconsequential behaviors, chances are the conflict is more about their relationship than any topic or content.

On the other hand, in this account from Genesis, Adam and Eve disagree about content, that is "the facts" of what occurred. At another level, however, they are each concerned about their image, and that is a conflict about *identity*. Eve wants both Adam and God to know that she was tricked and is not blameworthy. However, Adam implicitly blames Eve: "She gave me the fruit, and I ate," but the text does not say she *made* Adam eat. He could have refused the fruit. He also is concerned about his image and his identity as a good person.

A final type of conflict goal relates to *process*: how things should be done and how the conflict will be conducted. Some families institute family meetings to air grievances, others have yelling matches, and still others squelch overt conflict. How we are allowed or expected to behave during a conflict can become a conflict in itself. One business partner, for example, may want to conduct conflict by e-mail, while the other wants to talk face to face. One member of a couple may be used to saying anything in a conflict, but the other may want a rule such as "Don't say anything you don't really mean." In analyzing any conflict, all four types of goals must be considered.

Conflict and People

When a conflict occurs several things happen, but what we first experience is often *powerlessness*.[7] Conflict throws us off our game. In comparison to where we were before, we feel "off balance," momentarily vulnerable, and perhaps uncertain about how to proceed. We also become very *self-absorbed*. *Our* story, *our* account of the conflict, what happened from *our* perspective become most important. Each party wants the *other side* to accept his or her story. We may become defensive, hostile, or closed-minded. Our desire to be right consumes us. All of these emotional reactions make communication problematic.

This is clearly demonstrated in the Genesis account of Adam and Eve. When confronted by God, each word spoken by Adam and Eve is an attempt to regain balance by blame. Adam says, "The woman whom you gave to be with me, she gave me fruit from the tree, and I ate." Eve says, "The serpent tricked me." A conflict event often leads to a sense of powerlessness, self-absorption in one's own point of view, the desire to be seen as right and difficult communication. Behind these feelings often lies the fear that our needs will not be met.

A strong contributor to conflict is our perception of events. We all try to understand events that occur around us, and one way we try to make sense of behavior is by looking for causes.[8] We typically attribute cause for our own behavior differently than we do for others' behavior.[9] As already noted above, when confronted with a conflict, each party involved generally tries to shift the blame. Psychologists use the term "attribution theory" to explain this common behavior.

Typically for ourselves (if we have moderately good self-esteem), if something bad happens, we blame external causes. For example, a bad grade may be attributed to teacher weaknesses or an impossibly difficult exam rather than one's own method of studying. An argument may be attributed to the stubbornness of the other person or other reasons that have little to do with one's own shortcomings. Alternatively, if something good happens, we give credit to our internal disposition. If we do well in an interview, we conclude that the outcome is due to our own merits, our excellent résumé.

In contrast, typically when we explain the cause of someone else's bad behavior, just the opposite happens: we most often attribute the cause to that person's negative disposition.[10] For example, a teacher might infer that a late paper was due to the student's procrastination rather than to unforeseen circumstances for the student or poor planning in the course calendar. Attributing poor outcomes to another's disposition rather than to external circumstances is called the "fundamental attribution error."[11]

Putting It All Together

Eve and Adam are faced with God's questions, "Who told you that you were naked? Have you eaten from the tree that I commanded you not to eat?" The questions stir up the ingredients for conflict: disagreement, interference, and negative emotion. Eve and Adam are interdependent in that what happens to one of them will affect what happens to the other, but their goals differ at several levels. First, they perceive the facts differently. Adam points out that God gave Eve to him, the suggestion being that God has some responsibility here, as well as the fact that Eve is the one who gave him the fruit. Eve believes Adam ate of his own free will; she believes she is not at fault and that the snake who misled her ought to be punished. At the content level of this argument, these strong differences exist.

Relationship is also involved: they both want control over the version of events that gets accepted. At the level of identity, neither Eve nor Adam want their images marred as blameworthy. And negative emotions of fear and perhaps anger are implicit in the exchange.

Attribution theory also plays a part in this conflict. If both parties maintain that the incident was not caused by their character, but rather by outside forces, neither recognizes what they contributed to the transgression.

Another aspect to consider in conflict is that of *scarce resources*. Often people focus on material scarce resources, such as conflicts over land, oil, food, and water, and, indeed, conflict frequently occurs over these resources. However, resources that are not material can also be a source of conflict, for example, time. Consider a couple that has three children with both parents wanting time to go to the gym. Or a couple with a new baby, with both parents craving sleep. A project at work or school may require extra time to meet a deadline. If intangible resources such as time and power — or in some families love — are scarce, conflict may result. Perhaps in this scenario, Adam and Eve see God's favor as a scarce resource and vie to win it.

Given that conflict can arise from human interdependence, an incompatibility of goals, scarce resources, and various kinds of interference, we do need to understand the presence of conflict in our lives and how conflict can be transformed. In this book, using the lens of biblical studies, we emphasize throughout both the value and vision of right relationships, which should be the goal of all people. Biblical narratives offer powerful stories from which we can learn about both conflict and right relationships. They provide an opportunity for analysis, and they act as springboards for us to apply the theory and skills of conflict transformation so that we can learn to manage the realities of everyday life.

Reflection Questions:
Can You Now ... ?

1. Describe why the discussion of right relationship begins with *imago Dei?* What does this term mean?

2. Explain Adam and Eve's conflict in terms of content, relationship, and identity?

3. Think of an example in which you thought you were disagreeing over "facts" but in reality, identity and power were important underlying issues?

4. Think of a time when the conflict was over process, in other words, how to conduct the conflict?

5. Recall an example of a recent conflict that has touched you in which you've made use of attribution theory?

6. Describe to what extent, in your own life, you observe "right relationships" in your family? With friends? With the environment? With God?

7. Explain how useful, or potentially useful the concept of "right relationship" is as a guide for everyday behavior? Are there any limitations?

8. Identify the most common source of conflict in your own life? Has this changed over time?

2

JOSEPH AT SEVENTEEN
(*Genesis 37*)

Joseph, being seventeen years old, was shepherding the flock with his brothers; he was a helper to the sons of Bilhah and Zilpah, his father's wives; and Joseph brought a bad report of them to their father. Now Israel loved Joseph more than any other of his children, because he was the son of his old age; and he had made him a long robe with sleeves. But when his brothers saw that their father loved him more than all his brothers, they hated him, and could not speak peaceably to him.

Once Joseph had a dream, and when he told it to his brothers, they hated him even more.... But when he told it to his father and to his brothers, his father rebuked him, and said to him, "What kind of dream is this that you have had? Shall we indeed come, I and your mother and your brothers, and bow to the ground before you?" So his brothers were jealous of him, but his father kept the matter in mind.

(Gen. 37:2b–11)

A Biblical Interpretation of Genesis 37

One of the most popular narratives in the Hebrew Scriptures is the story of Joseph and his brothers, which begins in Genesis 37. This narrative describes Joseph's activities among his brothers that lead up to his brothers' throwing him into a pit and then selling him to a group of Ishmaelites for twenty pieces of silver. The brothers tell their father Jacob that a wild animal had devoured Joseph, a lie that sets in motion the rest of the Joseph cycle of stories (Gen. 37:1–50:26).

Before exploring Genesis 37 from a biblical perspective, we must look briefly at the historical backdrop and context of this narrative as well as a comment on the nature of family in ancient Israel.

The Ancestral Period and Mode of Life

Were Isaac, Jacob, Joseph, and their families actual historical persons? What is the historical time frame for the Joseph story? These questions have intrigued and engaged scholars for years, and no scholarly consensus exists as to whether or not the stories are rooted in history and in what time period

15

they would have actually taken place. On the one hand, biblical historian John Bright maintains that "the patriarchal narratives are firmly based in history."[1] On the other hand, Thomas Thompson and John Van Seters suggest that the biblical traditions are not historical, a view that has not been widely received but must still be taken into consideration.[2] Other biblical scholars such as W. F. Albright and G. E. Wright have tried unsuccessfully to create a scholarly consensus that would assign a particular historical setting to the ancestral period, which would include the Joseph stories.[3] With respect to the time frame of the ancestral stories, they typically have been assigned to the Early Second Millennium and/or the Middle Bronze Age. Victor H. Matthews, a specialist in Near Eastern history, points out that "there is a question whether actual social precedents from the Middle and Late Bronze Age (2000–1200 B.C.E.) are laid down in these stories. The characters may simply be constructs or composites whose actions represent biases, customs, and attitudes of a later period."[4] Matthews rightly concludes that, given the scholarly debate and uncertainties, "it is not possible to say with confidence that Abraham, Isaac, Jacob, and Joseph, as well as their wives and children, were real persons. They are shadowy figures as far as historians are concerned and may be composites of several persons or tribal leaders."[5] Matthews also maintains that until further evidence becomes available "it is just as useful to consider that the majority of the events, cities, and social customs described in the text do in fact reflect either authentic data or very good cultural memories edited into a coherent set of stories."[6]

With respect to the mode of life during the ancestral period, in very early times the people generally lived in tents and frequently camped near towns. Many of the people were shepherds and semi-nomadic breeders of cattle, sheep, and other small livestock, and their primary beast of burden was the donkey. They were often dressed in many-colored garments. Often they traveled throughout Palestine to find seasonal pasture for their flocks. Sometimes they even journeyed to Mesopotamia or Egypt to find pastureland. Some people settled long enough in one place to farm the land.

The Family in Ancient Israel

At the time when the Joseph stories would have taken place, the people were mostly agrarian. They were rural cultivators who had diversified farms. They were also laborers on other people's small landholdings. All of the families were connected to the land. Carol Meyers, in her study on the family in ancient Israel, notes:

> Land, like labor, was a major feature of an Israelite family household. That the family's immovable or real property (land as well as whatever is more or less permanently built on it) is the *sine qua non* for the livelihood and survival of an agrarian family need hardly be mentioned. Yet the specific identification of each family household with its inherited

domain (*nahalah,* "patrimony" or "inheritance") was exceptionally strong; family land was held in perpetuity.[7]

Furthermore, a family's identity was inextricably tied to the land and, thus, work and family were not separate from one another. Family roles and values were interrelated and connected to the land. Work on the farm was a family affair that involved not only the father and mother of a household, but also the children. Men and women worked as partners in the fields. Typically, the women in a family worked in the fields and in the house, preparing meals, making garments, and tending bread-making, among other tasks.

Many traditional agrarian families were part of a larger social structure. The "suprahousehold social unit was the *mispahah,*" a network of families that offered both support and protection.[8] Within the families, intergenerational and multigenerational accountability existed, along with various laws to protect the family members and their property. The ancient household was the basic unit of social interaction.

For economic reasons, most of the families were large. Large families also assured "the survival of the family group on its landholdings."[9] With respect to family relationships, husbands and wives enjoyed an interdependent relationship, but children were dependent on their parents and family members and, in turn, aging parents were dependent upon their children. Both fathers and sons had significant roles in the family; fathers were to provide for the families and to procreate for the sake of the family inheritance as well as the family's security. Firstborn sons were the heirs of the family inheritance. Sons were also obliged to care for their mothers in the event that their mothers became widowed. As the ancestral families developed, they became increasingly patriarchal, which was the case in the time of Joseph, whose father, Jacob, was one of Israel's greatest patriarchs of all times.

The Family Cycles of Stories

Three family cycles of stories exist within Genesis 11:27–50, with the first being the Abraham cycle (Gen. 11:27–25:18). In this collection of narratives, Abram (Abraham) is presented as an emigrant from Mesopotamia. He settled in Palestine, but lived for the most part an unsettled and semi-nomadic life. He pastured flocks, and one day while he was in the fields he was "called" by God to leave his homeland and to begin journeying to a promised land, known as Canaan (Gen. 12:1–3ff). The first patriarch, Abraham, was promised both land and offspring. His wife, Sarah, bore Isaac, and his concubine, Hagar, bore Ishmael. Isaac became the child of the covenant, and Ishmael became the child of promise. Isaac was part of the beginnings of Judaism, and Ishmael was part of the beginnings of Islam. Both were considered "brothers." In the New Testament, the opening passages of Matthew trace the lineage of Jesus from Abraham and his two sons.

The second cycle of stories is the Isaac cycle (Gen. 26:1–35). Little is known about the second patriarch, but these stories serve as a link between Abraham and Jacob.

The Jacob stories form the third cycle (Gen. 27:1–45). Jacob, the third patriarch, was one of Isaac's twin sons. Jacob was always embroiled in conflict — with Esau his twin brother, with Laban his uncle, and even with his God. His position and place in the land were never secure and always had to be defended. Known for his cleverness, Jacob tricked Esau into selling him his birthright (Gen. 25:19–34) and thus designating Isaac as his heir (Gen. 27:1–45). Later he also tricked Laban into selling him his sheep (Gen. 30:25–43) and his land (Gen. 31:1–32:3). He married two of Laban's daughters, Leah and then Rachel; of the two women the one he loved the most was Rachel, the mother of Joseph and Benjamin. And it is within the Jacob cycle of stories that we find the Joseph cycle of stories (Gen. 37:1–50:26).

According to the biblical text, Joseph was born to a woman who had been thought barren (30:1–2). The miracle of Rachel's pregnancy paralleled those of Rebecca and Sarah (Joseph's grandmother and great-grandmother). Both women were also thought to be barren. Joseph was Jacob's eleventh son, and Benjamin, Rachel's youngest, was Jacob's twelfth and last son. Joseph was born in Haran, three generations after Abraham and before the family entered Egypt. Immediately after Joseph was born, his family left Haran and returned to the land of Canaan. Although Joseph was born into a family of shepherds, his own life was not strictly nomadic.

We turn now to the story of Joseph, the longest single narrative in the book of Genesis. The first episode can be divided into eight units:

37:1–2a	The setting
37:2b–4	Joseph among his brothers
37:5–8	Joseph's first dream
37:9–11	Joseph's second dream
37:12–14a	The situation that leads up to the plot to kill Joseph
37:14b–24	Joseph's encounter with his brothers
37:25–28	Joseph's ill fortune
37:29–36	The brothers' coverup and the outcome

Biblical scholar Barbara Green observes that the family emerges onto the stage quickly and that the story is held together by discord.[10] Joseph is going to become the bane of his brothers' existence, and conflict after conflict is going to unfold.

The Setting (Genesis 37:1–2a)

The story of Joseph at seventeen opens with a simple statement that sets the stage for a family coup: "Jacob settled in the land where his father had lived as an alien, the land of Canaan. This is the story of the family of Jacob" (vv. 1–2a). This statement is the first unit of the narrative. The biblical text records that Jacob had twelve sons and one daughter, Dinah. The birth of the youngest son, Benjamin, brings pain into Jacob's family and to Jacob himself because Rachel dies during childbirth (Gen. 35:16–21). Eventually Jacob moves from Haran and settles his family in Canaan, which, generations later, becomes the Promised Land that the Israelites receive from God in fulfillment of the promise that God had made to Abraham (Gen. 12:1–3).

Joseph among His Brothers (Genesis 37:2b–4)

After the initial setting, a series of details follows that initiates a family conflict, one that will last almost to the end of the book of Genesis. In these verses, the story's second unit, the narrator provides us with a glimpse into the family's dynamics. While Joseph and his brothers are out in the fields shepherding the flocks, the reader learns of a distinction within the family that sets Joseph apart from his brothers. Joseph is a helper to the sons of Bilhah and Zilpah, his father's wives, and Joseph is also the son of Rachel, the best-loved wife. At this juncture, the narrator makes no mention of Benjamin, the younger son of Rachel. Next we read that Joseph gives Jacob a bad report about his brothers, another incident that sets Joseph apart from his brothers (v. 2). The content and reason for this bad report are not divulged. Was the report truthful or was it something that Joseph fabricated to make himself appear better than his older brothers?

In verse 3 we hear that Jacob (called Israel in the text) loved Joseph more than any of his other children because he was the son of his old age. Curiously, the narrator again makes no mention of the younger Benjamin. Perhaps the reason is that Benjamin reminds Jacob of his tragic loss, the death of Rachel, his beloved wife who died giving birth to Benjamin. This preferential, doting love that Jacob has for Joseph sets Joseph apart yet again from his brothers. Finally, we hear that because Jacob loved Joseph more than any of the other children, he made his son a special long-sleeved robe, known in the Greek translation as "a coat of many colors."

The brothers' response to Joseph is expected and understandable: "But when his brothers saw that their father loved him more than all his brothers, they hated him, and could not speak peaceably to him" (v. 4). The brothers are resentful and jealous of Joseph, experiencing two emotions that fuel their hatred for Joseph. In his analysis of the Joseph story, Victor Hamilton makes the following observations and raises an important question:

> The brothers' resentment is traditionally understood as directed against Joseph. But why take out their wrath on him? He had not placed an order for the garment. He did not solicit his father's time and gifts. So far everything Joseph has done (v. 2) and received (v. 3) serve only to alienate him from his brothers.[11]

While Hamilton's question and observations are accurate, the rift between Joseph and his brothers begins not with the multicolored tunic but with the bad report Joseph delivered to his father, which cast a shadow upon the brothers. This incident is the initial spark that ignites the series of family conflicts. Joseph had either made up a story about his brothers or had "snitched" on them. Either way, he was not "loyal" to his brothers and stoked their animosity. Hamilton states further that "dreams broaden the chasm between brother and brothers."[12] Joseph's dreams are the focus of the story's next two units (vv. 5–8, 9–11).

Joseph's First Dream (Genesis 37:5–8)

In verses 5–8, the story's third unit, we learn about Joseph's first dream. In the Hebrew Bible, dreams are significant and a vital means of communication.[13] The Joseph story (Gen. 37–50) contains several dreams, some of which are symbolic and in need of interpretation, while others are self-evident. In verses 5 through 8, Joseph's dream is symbolic, although Joseph does not come to understand its meaning until later in his life. For his family members, however, the context of the dream was crystal clear. The narrator tells us that because of his dream, Joseph is hated even more by his brothers (v. 5). Unsurprisingly so, the tension between Joseph and his brothers increases. The narrator next proceeds to tell us about the exchange that takes place between Joseph and his brothers (vv. 6–8). With a sense of boyish exuberance and without any foresight with respect to how his brothers would receive his message, Joseph blurts out: "Listen to this dream that I dreamed. There we were, binding sheaves in the field. Suddenly my sheaf rose and stood upright; then your sheaves gathered around it, and bowed down to my sheaf" (v. 7).

At this point, Joseph does not have the insight to understand the content of his dream, but his brothers are quick to comprehend as evidenced by their two rhetorical questions: "Are you indeed to reign over us? Are you indeed to have dominion over us?" (v. 8a).

In a hierarchical, patriarchal culture, having the next-to-youngest brother reign over the older brothers was completely unheard of, let alone acceptable. Thus, Joseph's dream represents the displacement of familiar hierarchy, indicating that Joseph was now favored not only by their father Jacob but also by their God. No wonder the brothers hated Joseph: first, because he delivered a bad report of them to their father (v. 2), second, because he was loved the most by his father and consequently received a special tunic as a sign of that great love (vv. 2–3), and, finally, because of his dreams and the words Joseph spoke (v. 8). God's divine favor now seems to rest upon Joseph to the exclusion of the other brothers. Of note, this dream is the first one recorded in Genesis where God does not speak directly to someone. For Joseph this silence adds to the dream's mysteriousness and ambiguity. For the brothers, however, the dream gives clarity to the fact that they will eventually become Joseph's subordinates.

Joseph's Second Dream (Genesis 37:9–11)

If disclosing the first dream were not enough, in the narrative's fourth unit Joseph tells his brothers and his father about a second dream he had. With the same lack of foresight, Joseph exclaims: "Look, I have had another dream: the sun, the moon, and eleven stars were bowing down to me" (v. 9). The sun and moon symbolize his parents, and the eleven stars represent his brothers, inclusive of Benjamin, the youngest of all the boys.[14] Upon hearing about his son's second dream, Jacob now weighs in; on behalf of himself and the rest of the family, he addresses Joseph directly. Like the brothers earlier (v. 8), Jacob poses two questions to the son he loves the most: "What kind of dream is this that you have had? Shall we indeed come, I and your mother and your brothers, and bow to the ground before you?" (v. 10).

In an earlier account in Genesis, Jacob has already bowed down to his brother Esau (Gen. 33:3), and now he hears that he will have to offer this subordinate gesture to his son. We can sense Jacob's annoyance with Joseph's dreams, a tone that comes through in the two questions he poses to Joseph. The story's narrator widens the chasm that exists between Joseph and his brothers by stating that the brothers are now "jealous" of their younger brother. As for Jacob, he keeps the matter in mind but offers no other comment to either Joseph or the other brothers (v. 11).

> *Given your experience, might Jacob have intervened in a more effective way?*

The Situation That Leads Up to the Plot to Kill Joseph (Genesis 37:12–14a)

After the brothers listen to Joseph's dreams and comment accordingly, they resume their normal daily duties (v. 12). Jacob, for his part, returns Joseph to the fields with the task of checking on the well-being of his brothers and the flocks and then bringing Jacob a report on his findings (vv. 13–14).

Given the extent of Jacob's pastureland, the fact that Jacob's flocks can graze all the way from Hebron to Shechem indicates that Jacob had a fair amount of wealth (see also Gen. 35:27). Oddly enough, Jacob seems unaware of the animosity of Joseph's brothers toward him even though Jacob was present when Joseph described his dreams, receiving a strong negative and bitter response from his brothers. This fifth unit closes with Joseph going off to Shechem in search of his brothers (v. 14a).

Joseph's Encounter with His Brothers (Genesis 37:14b–24)

In verses 14b–24, the sixth unit, Joseph arrives in Shechem only to learn from a stranger there that his brothers had gone to Dothan (vv. 14a–17). As Joseph draws near to Dothan, his brothers see him at a distance and conspire to kill him. Hatred and jealousy have escalated to premeditated murder: "Come now, let us kill him and throw him into one of the pits, then we shall say that a wild animal has devoured him, and we shall see what will become of his dreams" (v. 20).

The brothers' plot does not come to fruition as they had anticipated because Reuben intervenes on Joseph's behalf, with a plan to save his younger brother's life (vv. 21–22). Instead of murdering Joseph, the brothers strip him of his multicolored coat and throw him into a pit that contains no water (vv. 23–24). This pit is more commonly known as a cistern. Cisterns, used to store water, were hewn into deep rock. Shaped like a bottle, they had a small opening at the top. Once inside a cistern, a person's chances of escaping were relatively nonexistent. Thus, while the brothers did not lay a hand on Joseph, Joseph's fate was essentially sealed. Trapped in this cistern, he would surely die.

Joseph's Ill Fortune (Genesis 37:25–28)

A turn of events occurs in verses 25 through 28, the narrative's seventh unit. As Joseph lay in the pit, stripped of his garment, his brothers decide to sit down to eat a meal together. Their heartlessness is evident. Now Judah proposes a plan to his brothers regarding what to do about Joseph. As a caravan of Ishmaelites approaches, Judah suggests that they sell Joseph to the Ishmaelites.[15] He points out to his brothers that they have nothing to gain by killing Joseph and concealing his blood. The brothers take up Judah's suggestion and sell Joseph for twenty pieces of silver. Continuing their journey, the Ishmaelites take Joseph to Egypt.

The Brothers' Coverup and the Outcome (Genesis 37:29–36)

The narrative draws to a close in verses 29 through 36, the last unit. Unaware of the further decision of Judah and his brothers concerning Joseph, Reuben returns to the pit and is shocked not to find Joseph in it. Reuben's act of "tearing his clothes" is a common gesture of mourning. The question he addresses to his brothers admits of his own personal fear. As the eldest brother, Reuben is the one most answerable to his father for Joseph's well-being. The brothers, however, solve Reuben's dilemma. They slaughter a goat, dip the robe in blood, and bring it to their father, telling Jacob that a wild animal had devoured his son. The brothers' initial statement to Jacob reveals their deep animosity toward Joseph: "This we have found; see now whether it is your son's robe or not" (v. 32). The fact that they say "your son's robe" indicates their distance from both their brother Joseph and their father, Jacob. They do not consider themselves a "brother" to Joseph, nor do they consider themselves to be "sons" to Jacob in the way that Joseph is. Their language betrays their sentiments.

Jacob responds as would be expected. He dons sackcloth and mourns for his son, refusing to be comforted by family members and pledging to spend the remainder of his life in mourning (vv. 34–35).[16] Jacob's heart is broken. Good fortune, however, awaits Joseph, which the narrator hints at in verse

36, though Joseph's good fortune will not be without moments of peril as we shall soon see.

Looking through the Communication Lens

In introducing biblical studies, we said that the biblical text consists of stories and poems about our ancient ancestors who were of diverse traditions, cultures, religious beliefs, races, nationalities, communities, and life experiences. In this section we will explore how culture affects conflict, how family may set the stage for conflict, and how managing diversity presents a challenge for conflict.

How Does Culture Affect Conflict?

At the beginning of this chapter we briefly described the culture of this time period. Culture shapes communication, and it establishes norms and values that impact how a conflict unfolds or develops. We must consider the contribution of culture to any event of conflict before examining other variables. To understand how the conflict of Joseph and his brothers unfolds, we will first explore three ways in which cultures differ.

Low Context versus High Context

Anthropologist Edward Hall observes that cultures differ in the directness or indirectness with which they express information. In the dominant U.S. culture and other "low-context" cultures like those of Germany, Australia, Great Britain, Sweden, and France, people try to spell things out. While the context of communication helps us interpret messages, we expect feelings and facts to be communicated explicitly. Openness and directness are generally valued.[17]

In "high-context" cultures, like those of China, Japan, and many Middle Eastern countries, people are expected to gather much more meaning from the context, the actual situation. Most feelings will not be spelled out explicitly. People are supposed to understand the meaning of a situation implicitly through understanding the requirements of the circumstances, through nonverbal messages, and through people's roles. Low- and high-context cultures are strongly related to individualist and collectivist cultures.

Individualist versus Collectivist

Sociologist Geert Hofstede first described how individualist cultures differ from collectivist cultures.[18] We all experience some tension because of our opposing needs for autonomy (the need to be independent and consider our own needs) and connection (the need to be *inter*dependent with our family and community and put the needs of others before our own). Among cultures, however, differences occur in how important the group and family are relative to the individual's needs. In collectivist cultures, needs of the family and community come before self. People are expected to take care

of their relatives, their "in-group" members, and, in return, expect loyalty
from them. Success depends on contribution to the family and the group
more than individual achievement. Harmony, cohesion, and cooperation
are important values. Countries such as Guatemala, Ecuador, Indonesia,
Pakistan, Turkey, Saudi Arabia, and Taiwan score high on the collectivist
orientation.[19]

In an individualist culture, success depends on surpassing others. Competition is valued. People are supposed to take care of themselves and
perhaps those closest to them. Low-context countries, like the United States,
Great Britain, Germany and France, also score high on the individualist
orientation.

> *From what you have learned thus far about the culture of the period, do
> you think Joseph and his brothers were operating in a high-context or low-
> context culture? Did it have individualistic or collectivist orientation? Were
> its power norms high or low? Given your answers to these questions, what
> cultural violations might have contributed to the conflict in this story?*
>
> *To see how various countries score on Hofstede's individualist-collectivist
> scale, visit: www.geert-hofstede.com.*

High-Power versus Low-Power Distances

A third way cultures differ pertains to power distances.[20] Among "high-
power distance" cultures, power is unevenly distributed, and people are
taught to have great respect for authority. In high-power distance cultures, the norm is to yield to authority and to avoid direct confrontation.
In low-power distance cultures, more equality is the norm. Expression of
disagreement with authority figures is not unusual.

How Do Family Dynamics Contribute?

Family communication offers rich and complex nuances to the Joseph story.
In particular, it's important to look at favoritism and its impact on sibling relationships. Recent research has documented some of the ill effects of
favoritism. Psychologist Leslie Brody and colleagues describe favoritism as
"a family process in which parents treat, or are perceived to treat, one or
some of their children more positively than they do their other children."[21]
Alternatively, parents may single out one or more of their children for "dif-
ferential negative treatment." Brody and colleagues remark that favoritism
can contribute to lifelong rivalry, conflict, competition, and envy between
siblings. Similarly psychologists Grania Sheehan and Patricia Noller found
that unfair differences in parenting contribute to family distress throughout
the family system.[22]

> *Have you observed favoritism in a family? To what extent do the findings described above contribute to conflict in the story of Joseph and his brothers?*

Favoritism can disrupt sibling relationships. Alan Mikkelson, an expert in communication studies, identified some unique attributes of sibling relationships. In contemporary times, sibling relationships are the most longest lasting in people's lives; they are involuntary and permanent. While we may not actively engage with a brother or sister, they retain sibling status for life. We may acquire ex-boyfriends and ex-spouses, but we do not acquire ex-brothers or ex-sisters. In contemporary times and in the dominant U.S. culture, adult-sibling relationships are expected to be fairly egalitarian. Cross-culturally and historically, more hierarchy and greater power distances accompanied sibling relationships than many of us expect in those relationships today.[23]

To better understand sibling relationships in the time of Joseph, we turn to psychologist Victor Cicirelli's work comparing siblings in industrialized societies with those in nonindustrialized societies.[24] Sibling relationships in industrialized societies differ from nonindustrial societies with respect to status, role responsibilities, and rewards. Typically, in nonindustrial societies, older brothers have the highest status among brothers. Often younger siblings are expected to obey an older brother as they would a parent. Younger children are taught to respect older children and the right of older children to make decisions. In nonindustrial societies sibling solidarity is obligatory. Contrast that obligation with the expectations of industrial societies where siblings acquire much independence and commonly separate physically from the family. In nonindustrial societies, taking care of younger children is institutionalized, and younger children learn valuable information, values, knowledge, and skills from older siblings. Sharing resources is the norm because it maximizes the strength of the family.

> *While we cannot know for sure how Cicirelli's work played out in ancient, nonindustrial societies, how would you apply his findings to Joseph's conflict with his brothers?*

The Effects of Differing Goals on Conflict

In the introduction we defined conflict as "an interaction between at least two interdependent parties who perceive incompatible goals, scarce resources, and interference from others in achieving their goals." When we consider conflict in the Joseph story, whose goals might be incompatible and what resources would be available? In the best of all worlds, what would it take to manage the conflict?

Joseph P. Folger, Marshall S. Poole, and Randall K. Stutman, professors in psychology and communication, building on the work of various others, propose a model for managing conflict that relies first on acknowledging and understanding the differences in our positions and interests and then working toward an acceptable integrative solution. "Position" refers to the solution or particular goal we have in mind; "interests" relate to deeper needs that underlie the solution for which we advocate; and "differentiation" is the process of exploring differences. "Integration" means problem solving to find solutions.[25]

Because exploring differences produces stress and the outcomes are uncertain, we commonly try to avoid dealing with differences. Symptoms of avoidance include less direct interaction, active avoidance of the other party, harboring resentment or disappointment, and complaining to third parties about the other person.[26] Avoidance, however, eventually spirals into conflict escalation as well. As Folger and colleagues point out, the balancing act is that we need to explore differences without reverting either to avoidance or hostile escalation.[27]

How Does Avoidance Contribute to Conflict Escalation?

As active avoidance breeds resentment, less direct interaction, and possible retaliation, it becomes easier for other dynamics to come into play. A particularly dangerous phenomenon is "deindividuation," which occurs when people no longer see the humanness of a person, but treat him or her as part of a group without personal and human characteristics.[28] Parties may cease to use the person's name. Sometimes they will refer to the person by physical attributes or social roles. In the movie *Hotel Rwanda,* for example, the Hutus refer to the Tutsis as "cockroaches."

Is deindividuation present in the Joseph story? In what way?

Putting It All Together

Joseph lived in a nonindustrial society. We can infer that the culture was collectivistic: in order to survive families had to work together to tend sheep and goats, gather grain, and defend against outside groups. Putting one's own needs above the needs of the group would have been cause for censure. Power distances were great. We can expect that hierarchy existed in families and that oldest sons could expect respect from younger siblings and respect from parents. Collectivistic societies are generally low-context with individuals understanding a situation and knowing how to behave according to both their role and the context. Joseph apparently did not follow the norms.

Contributing to his blunder, however, was the fact that he was the son of Jacob's favorite wife, Rachel. Defying rules of good parenting, but imitating his own father, Jacob picked a favorite son, and in this case it was the youngest son, Joseph. We have seen that favoritism in families can create lifelong rivalry, conflict, competition, and envy between siblings. Indeed, Jacob's blindness to the effects of such favoritism stirs the plot. At seventeen, rather than contributing to harmony and cohesion that should characterize a collectivist society, Joseph "brings a bad report' of his brothers to his father. Later, he blithely relates his dreams that depict his family bowing down to him.

Helpful at this point is to recall the description of attribution theory in the introduction. Attribution theory predicts that in explaining the behavior of another person, we are more apt to attribute cause to the person's character rather than to the circumstances that are present. Thus, we see the brothers denigrate Joseph's character without any acknowledgement of how their parents' behavior and their culture have created a "setup" for their conflict.

Tragically, as hostility grows, none of these dynamics is discussed openly. Joseph and his brothers are part of a "high-context" culture, one in which differences are not explicitly discussed. As feelings escalate, Joseph's brothers fall prey to deindividuation: "They saw him from a distance, and before he came near to them, they conspired to kill him. They said to one another, 'Here comes this dreamer.' "

The words are important. They could have said, "Here comes Joseph" or "Here comes our brother," or "Here comes Rachel's firstborn." The words they use, however, disavow any familial connection to him: "Here comes this dreamer."

Managing conflict usually requires that we explore differences. In the Joseph story, however, culture, familial dysfunction, and escalating hostility over issues that could not be addressed spiraled out of control.

Theological Reflection on Genesis 37

The story of Joseph at seventeen is a classic example of how a parent's great love for one child over and above the other children in the family can cause pain, suffering, sibling rivalry, jealousy, and, in the case of Joseph, ill will to the point of a premeditated murder plot that was almost carried out. In turning to Jacob, we need to ask, "Why was he not more attentive to the needs and feelings of the other children?" and "Why was he not able to get beyond his own feelings of preference for Rachel in such a way as to see all of his sons as blessings to be cherished and loved differently yet equally?"

The text shows us how personal preferences within a family can and do affect the whole family.

The story also shows us the power of God, acting within the human condition throughout the normal course of history, to shape history and to effect change within history. Joseph is destined for greatness and will play a prominent role in the future life of his family. His dreams are prophetic, and in time Joseph will live himself into their fulfillment.

Finally, the story of the young Joseph offers us hope. First, through Joseph we see that God can choose ordinary human beings with whom to interact. God's presence remains constant within the human community. Second, even in the midst of human sordidness, human beings are capable of reversing ill-fated decisions concerning others. Reuben and Judah both persuade their brothers not to kill Joseph. Third, although Joseph suffers the terrible fate of being sold to strangers by his brothers, unjust suffering is not the final word of the story or the final page in Joseph's life. Justice will be served, and Joseph will die in peace at a ripe old age.

In Sum: Grace in the Wilderness

But when Reuben heard it, he delivered him out of their hands, saying, "Let us not take his life." Reuben said to them, "Shed no blood; throw him into this pit here in the wilderness, but lay no hand on him" — that he might rescue him out of their hand and restore him to his father. (Gen. 37:21–22)

Then Judah said to his brothers, "What profit is it if we kill our brother and conceal his blood? Come, let us sell him to the Ishmaelites, and not lay our hands on him, for he is our brother, our own flesh." (Gen. 37:26–27)

Earlier in the chapter, we described deindividuation as a process of dehumanizing those with whom we are in conflict. Both Reuben and Judah separate themselves from the dehumanizing frame of the other brothers and reclaim Joseph as family. He is not a mere dreamer: he is their brother. Stepping out of the pack and shifting the trajectory of the story requires integrity.

Within the story, three moments of grace in the wilderness exist. First, Joseph's dreams as divine gifts foreshadow what is to occur for the family; the dreams are prophetic and Joseph is thus a recipient of prophetic activity. How Joseph handles the dreams, however, reflects human clumsiness that contributes to conflict.

A second moment of grace occurs when Reuben speaks out on behalf of Joseph, saving Joseph's life. The third moment of grace is when Judah concurs with Reuben's thought that Joseph's life should be spared. Thus, grace has life-sustaining and life-changing effects for Joseph and his brothers. In the case of two of Joseph's brothers, grace has indeed bidden them to choose life for their brother. When the brothers abandon their murder plot against Joseph at the suggestions of Reuben and Judah, Joseph's life is spared. Grace has found its way into the crevices of human depravity, and conflict, with the most horrific of evil intents, has been disarmed.

Reflection Questions:
Can You Now...?

1. Describe any parallels among the stories in the ancestral cycles of Abraham, Jacob, and Joseph?

2. Explain how dreams functioned in the conflict between Joseph and his brothers?

3. Give examples of low- and high-context cultures in today's world? Why do you say this? Are you familiar with any high-context communities in this country?

4. Compare how being an individualist or collectivist culture might affect decision making?

5. Identify families whose family culture is based on high-power differences? Can you explain what you've seen in the family that makes you think they observe high-power differences?

6. Share any experiences of unusual sibling relationships? Have they been supportive or destructive?

7. Recognize whether you ever made use of deindividuation to devalue another person? Why? What was the result?

3

JOSEPH AND
POTIPHAR'S WIFE

A Study in Maintaining "Face"
(*Genesis 39*)

And after a time his master's wife cast her eyes on Joseph and said, "Lie with me." But he refused and said to his master's wife, "Look, with me here, my master has no concern about anything in the house, and he has put everything that he has in my hand. He is not greater in this house than I am, nor has he kept back anything from me except yourself, because you are his wife. How then could I do this great wickedness, and sin against God?" (Gen. 39:7–9)

[She] caught hold of his garment, saying, "Lie with me!" But he left his garment in her hand, and fled and ran outside. (Gen. 39:12)

Then she kept his garment by her until his master came home.
(Gen. 39:16)

A Biblical Interpretation of Genesis 39

The story of Potiphar's wife and Joseph (Gen. 39) is a novella marked by intrigue, symbolism, betrayal, and loyalty. It consists of three units:

39:1–6a	Joseph's circumstances in Egypt
39:6b–18	Joseph's encounter with Potiphar's wife
39:19–23	The aftermath of the accusation

Originally the story's intent was "a cautionary tale teaching young men to avoid powerful foreign women."[1] The narrative's theme is a common one found in the ancient Eastern Mediterranean world: a powerful woman tries to seduce a virile young man. The story also develops the notion of the woman as a "temptress," a growing tradition derived from the history of interpretation surrounding the story of Eve in Genesis 3.

The narrative is an example of subversive power. In the Ancient Near Eastern world, power was in the hands of the males by virtue of their gender. This power base was reinforced by family structures in which the firstborn male was the heir of the family assets. The social-political structure of the ancient Near Eastern world, of which the Israelite culture was a part, reinforced further the male power base, not to mention the developing monotheism of the male deity.

For women, power rested in their bodies, specifically, in their sexuality and sensuality. When Potiphar, an officer of the Egyptian pharaoh and a captain of the guard, made Joseph the overseer of his house, Potiphar put Joseph in charge of all that he had (Gen. 39:4). The difficulty for both Potiphar's wife and Joseph will be how to save face in the course of conflict. Against this social and political backdrop, the story now unfolds.

Joseph's Circumstances in Egypt (Genesis 39:1–6a)

The story of the encounter between Potiphar's wife and Joseph opens in Egypt. Joseph had been brought down to Egypt by the Ishmaelites to whom Joseph had been sold by his brothers for twenty pieces of silver (see Gen. 37:28). The Ishmaelites, in turn, sold Joseph to Potiphar (37:1). Etymologically, Potiphar's name means "he whom the god Re has given." The earliest attestation of this name is found in Egyptian texts from the Twentieth-First Dynasty (the eleventh and tenth centuries B.C.E.).[2] The narrator of the novella tells us that "the LORD was with Joseph" (v. 2). This phrase recalls the promise God made earlier with the patriarchs, a promise that included their descendants, of which Joseph is one (see Gen. 26:3, 28:15, 31:3). We learn further that because God was "with Joseph," Joseph became a successful man. Thus, God's presence becomes a blessing for Joseph that leads to prosperity.

We next hear that Potiphar "saw that the LORD was with [Joseph], and that the Lord caused all that [Joseph] did to prosper in his hands" (v. 3). Potiphar's ability to recognize the power of Israel's God working through Joseph attests to the power of Potiphar's own intuition, insight and giftedness insofar as he is able to discern the presence and nature of God's Spirit. And thus Joseph finds favor in Potiphar's sight and becomes Potiphar's attendant and trusted servant. Potiphar makes Joseph the overseer of his house and places him in charge of all that he had (v. 4). Because of Joseph, Potiphar's house, fields, and all that Potiphar possessed was blessed by God (v. 5). Significant here is the point that through Joseph, a non-Israelite person is able to receive the beneficence of Israel's God, whose graciousness is not limited to one group of people but includes all the families of the earth, as was promised to Abraham (Gen. 12:3) and extended to Ishmael, Abraham's firstborn son and his descendants (Gen. 17:20).[3] In verse 6 the narrator re-emphasizes Potiphar's complete trust in Joseph: "So he left all that he had in Joseph's charge; and, with him there, he had no concern for anything but the food that he ate (v. 6a).

Victor P. Hamilton makes an astute grammatical observation: "The completeness of Joseph's dedication to Potiphar, the completeness of Potiphar's trust in Joseph, and the completeness of Yahweh's blessing on the household are underscored in this last unit by the fivefold repetition of *kol* (all)."[4] This repetition is borne out in verses 3 through 6. In the text we see that the Lord caused "all" that Joseph did to prosper (v. 3), that Joseph was put in charge of "all" that Potiphar had (v. 4), that Joseph became the overseer of "all" that Potiphar had (v. 5), that God's blessing was on "all" that Potiphar had (v. 5), and that Potiphar left "all" in Joseph's charge (v. 6a). Such attributes of complete trust shed light on Joseph's status in Potiphar's household and establishes Joseph as an upright, loyal, trustworthy, and noble human being, all of which sets the stage for the next part of the narrative.

Joseph's Encounter with Potiphar's Wife (Genesis 39:6b–18)

Joseph is not only virtuous but also physically attractive: he is "handsome" and "good-looking" (v. 6b). (In the Hebrew text Joseph's mother, Rachel, is described in exactly the same way [see Gen. 29:17].) In verses 6b through 18 the action of the novella begins and the conflicts unfold when Potiphar's wife "[casts] her eyes on Joseph" and says "Lie with me" (v. 7). Joseph's refusal to accommodate Potiphar's wife and his verbal response to her overtures are clear signs of his unwavering integrity and his uncompromising loyalty not only to Potiphar but also to the God of Israel against whom Joseph will not sin (v. 9). Joseph's rhetorical question that he poses to Potiphar's wife ("How then could I do this great wickedness, and sin against God?") clearly states his unequivocal intentions. Had Joseph consented to Potiphar's wife, he would be committing adultery, a sin against both a spouse and a deity, of which the punishment incurred would normally be stoning to death (Lev. 20:10; Deut. 22:22). Adultery violates not only a spouse but also the divine boundaries placed on sexual expression.

Verses 10 through 12 reveal the insistent, aggressive, and conniving personality of Potiphar's wife who, by her sexual prowess, tries to "overpower" Joseph and thus prove him weak in strength and flawed in character. First, she speaks with him "day after day," but gets nowhere with him (v. 10). Unsuccessful, she then makes further advances toward him. This time, her advances are even more aggressive than her first efforts. The narrator tells us: "One day, however, when he [Joseph] went into the house to do his work, and while no one else was in the house, she caught hold of his garment, saying, 'Lie with me!' " (vv. 11–12a). This request is the same one she made of Joseph earlier (v. 7) and, just as before, Joseph refuses to comply with Potiphar's solicitations (v. 12b). This time, Joseph flees from the woman, leaving his garment that she had caught hold of in her hand. Tension mounts and conflict increases as the plot thickens.

Joseph's garment, now in the possession of Potiphar's wife, becomes the impetus and evidence she needs to concoct a false story about Joseph (vv. 13–18). Her fabricated story is her chance to seek revenge against Joseph because he refused her advances.

Joseph is now in conflict with Potiphar's wife, a conflict that she created by her own ill will toward Joseph. Potiphar's wife involves others in this conflict as well, as she begins to weave her fabricated story. First she speaks ill of Joseph to her servants, thus trying to set a wedge between Joseph and the other members of Potiphar's household. To the servants Potiphar's wife blurts out: "See, my husband has brought among us a Hebrew to insult us! He came in to me to lie with me, and I cried out with a loud voice; and when he heard me raise my voice and cry out, he left his garment beside me, and fled outside" (vv. 14–15).

The servants' response is silence. In the Hebrew text, the phrase "my husband" is omitted and only the masculine singular third person pronoun "he" is used. Hamilton notes that by speaking about her husband indirectly as "he" (v. 14), Potiphar's wife is "attaching primary blame to Joseph and secondary blame to Potiphar, her husband." After all, Potiphar is the one who brought Joseph into the household. Thus her use of "he" instead of "Potiphar" or "husband" is an expression of contempt for him."[5]

In calling Joseph a "Hebrew" (v. 14), Potiphar's wife reminds her listeners then and now that even though Joseph has the trust of Potiphar, Joseph is still an "outsider." Potiphar's wife has now instilled in the servants' minds that Joseph attempted to rape her. If she cried out in a loud voice, however, then why did the servants not come running? Why did they remain silent when she told them what had happened? Perhaps they "wondered" about her story, having not heard her cry of distress, which she never emitted in the first place.

Joseph's garment remains in Potiphar's wife's possession, which allows her to continue fabricating her story, only this time she tells it to Potiphar, her husband (vv. 17–18). The narrator next introduces Potiphar into both the house scene and the ensuing conflict. Potiphar's wife repeats the same tale about Joseph that she had told the servants.

The Aftermath of the Accusation (Genesis 39:19–23)

Potiphar is gullible; he believes his wife without hearing Joseph's side of the story — the Joseph whom he had respected and trusted beyond doubt — without doing any further investigation into the alleged rape attempt. Potiphar's response, however, is not atypical of a husband's response to a wife in distress. Because she *is* his wife, Potiphar believes her and becomes enraged with Joseph (v. 19). Here the marital bond of unconditional trust comes to the fore, but little does Potiphar realize that he is being deceived by his wife. She now has his full attention. She has been successful in discrediting the other "male" in the household, she has put a wedge between Potiphar and Joseph, and she has her husband "in her pocket."

In verses 20 through 23 the narrator describes the outcome of events that follow the accusations of Potiphar's wife against Joseph. Potiphar imprisons Joseph (v. 20), but that is not Joseph's final fate. Verses 21–23 indicate a turn of events for Joseph:

But the LORD was with Joseph and showed him steadfast love; he gave him favor in the sight of the chief jailer. The chief jailer committed to Joseph's care all the prisoners who were in the prison, and whatever was done there, he was the one who did it. The chief jailer paid no heed to anything that was in Joseph's care, because the LORD was with him; and whatever he did, the LORD made it prosper.

The story has come full circle. The God of Israel who was with Joseph earlier (v. 2) remains with Joseph (v. 21), continuing to prosper his deeds (vv. 3, 23). Joseph, once having had the trust of Potiphar until Potiphar turned on him on account of his wife's "story," now has the trust of the chief jailer, a trust that mirrors the trust he once had with Potiphar (v. 22; see v. 4). Joseph is not acquitted of his false accusation. He remains a man accused yet graced.

Looking through the Communication Lens

The story of Joseph and Potiphar's wife provides a good example of how different goals can create and influence the course of conflict. In addition, the story highlights the challenge of maintaining "face" or social image in a conflict. To understand the story, we will first conceptualize different ways of thinking about goals. Next we will describe face theory and its relevance to conflict.

How Do Goals Contribute to Conflict?

Recall that in situations of conflict, people not only want different things but believe that the goals of another person or a group of people interferes with their goal. There are a variety of ways to think about goals. In the same way a camera lens can zoom in and out, Kathy Domenici and Stephen Littlejohn, communication and conflict scholars, point out that the focus of our attention on goals can be at the personal, relationship, or system level.[6]

When our attention is at the *level of personal goals*, we aim at influencing one person and his or her perception or behavior. In this story, Potiphar's wife wanted to get Joseph to "lie down with her." In everyday life, we try to get others to change their behaviors and perceptions in a myriad number of ways. For example, Julie wants to change her sister's behavior. Her sister always borrows her clothes and doesn't return them. They fight constantly over this, and Julie wants to change her sister's behavior. In another example, Justin wants his wife to be less timid about trying new things, and they sometimes argue about trying out new restaurants or visiting new places. He wants her to be more open to new experiences. Chris and Pat are business partners. Pat always comes late to work, and Chris wants Pat to come on time to be a good example for other workers. In these examples, one party wants to affect the other individual's behavior.

When our attention is at the *relationship level,* our goals aim to change or improve a relationship. Again in the case of Potiphar's wife, she wanted to change their relationship so that she and Joseph would become lovers. Many examples of conflict result from one person trying to change the nature of a relationship. For example, John wants his father to stop trying to control so many aspects of John's life. Conflict ensues when John addresses these issues. In another example Shawn feels his wife interferes when he tries to discipline their children. He wants to be able to handle the children in his own way. And Jean thinks that Bob disregards her input at work, and she wants him to listen to her ideas more openly. In these instances, one party wants to change something about the relationship and his or her connection to the other person.

Our attention may also focus on the *level of a whole system or community.* Joseph recognized that an illicit relationship with Potiphar's wife would alter his relationship with his own community (with God) as well as his relationship to Potiphar. Many conflicts can result as one individual tries to impact a group, organization, or society. Sheryl wants Chris to participate in group decision making to get a commitment for the group's project. Dan wants the group to make decisions by consensus so no schisms develop in the community. In these examples, the individual's attention is focused on a goal for a whole system.

> Compare the levels of attention for Joseph and Potiphar's wife. How do you perceive their goals at the personal, relationship, and community levels? Have you ever experienced a conflict where one party was concerned about a personal goal and the other party was concerned about a relationship goal? In what ways do Joseph and Potiphar's wife interfere with each other's goals?

We may find ourselves in conflict because one party looks at a situation from the personal level, while the other is working at a relationship or systemic level. For example, Potiphar's wife was focused on the personal level, on persuading Joseph to satisfy her own immediate need for pleasure. Alternatively, perhaps she thought making her husband jealous might improve their relationship. Joseph might have been thinking at the relationship level with respect to the impact of betrayal on his relationship with Potiphar, or he might have been thinking at the system level — the implications for a community if people cannot trust one another — or the implications for his relationship with God.

In a divorce, couples who focus on their individual goals might think about their own grievances, attempting to get everything they can from their spouse and seeking a lawyer who will "play hardball." Alternatively, they might look ahead to future years of family occasions, realizing that they want family events to be harmonious. By attending to system goals, they may choose someone to mediate the divorce so that each person has security and so their relationship does not spiral into greater hostility. Thinking systemically about the whole family and the future can impact the conflict style they adopt as separation begins.

How Do Types of Goals Affect Our Approach to Conflict?

In the introduction, we pointed out that people in situations of conflict pursue four different types of goals: content, relationship, process, and identity. *Content goals* relate to the topic under discussion. When someone asks, "What was the fight about?" we typically talk about the surface issues. *Relationship goals* (note "relationship" is being used in a different way than above) have to do with who has power, who is in control, and how independent or connected we want to be. When housemates fight about the level of cleanliness in the apartment, "cleaning up" is the manifest content. Less apparent may be relationship goals. Often we try to solve conflicts at the content level when in reality conflict lies at the relationship level.

> What is communicated at the content level and the relationship level in the scene between Joseph and Potiphar's wife? The story does not refer to Potiphar's wife by her name. Does that contribute to our understanding of power and her behavior? Can you think of a recent conflict of your own that appeared to be at the level of content, but was actually about relationship?

A third type of conflict goal relates to *process*. How are we going to conduct this conflict? Joseph tried to resolve the conflict using persuasion. Potiphar's wife, by grabbing hold of his garment and keeping it next to her, used a nonverbal tactic. Process can also be a source of conflict. Some organizations use suggestion boxes to handle employee grievances. Religious organizations or other community groups may hold annual meetings to explore problems. One partner in a couple that is having marital problems may want to sit down and air things out as they develop; the other may prefer to seek the assistance of a marriage counselor. In conflict management, we need to be aware that goals can relate to *how* we will conduct the conflict and that participants may argue over the process to be used.

The fourth type of conflict goal pertains to *identity*. Identity has to do with our self-image, how we perceive we are seen by others, and how we want to be treated. Identity is closely related to the concept of face. *Face* is "the conception of self that each person displays in particular interactions with others."[7] Joseph P. Folger, Marshall S. Poole, and Randall K. Stutman, communication scholars, claim that when face is threatened, work on task ceases.[8]

Penelope Brown and Stephen Levinson identify two types of face: positive face and negative face.[9] *Positive face* is the need to have a good self-image reinforced by others. We want people to respect us and reinforce our identity. When Potiphar's wife propositioned Joseph, Joseph's refusal threatened her positive face. At the same time, participating in an illicit affair threatened Joseph's *positive face*. "Look, with me here, my master has no concern about anything in the house, and he has put everything that he has in my hand. He is not greater in this house than I am, nor has he kept back anything from me except yourself, because you are his wife. How then could I do this great wickedness, and sin against God?" (Gen. 39:8–9). Although Joseph did not call Potiphar's wife wicked or sinful, the implication was there, and it threatened her positive face. And the insult was multiplied when she repeatedly approached him: "And although she spoke to Joseph day after day, he would not consent to lie beside her or to be with her" (Gen. 39:10). To get even, Potiphar's wife told her household and Potiphar "See, my husband has brought among us a Hebrew to insult us! He came in to me to lie with me, and I cried out with a loud voice; and when he heard me raise my voice and cry out, he left his garment beside me, and fled outside" (Gen. 39:14–15).

> *Can you think of an example where loss of face mattered more than losing ground on the subject itself?*

Examples abound in everyday life where a perceived attack on competence or positive face results in conflict. Ellen complained that a teacher had given her an undeserved low grade. Getting a poor grade in and of itself damaged her positive face. When her friend questioned how thoroughly she had actually studied, a fight ensued. By questioning Ellen's competence as a student, Ellen's positive face was further threatened.

Negative face is the desire for autonomy, for the ability to control one's life and to be free from imposition by another. When Potiphar's wife told Joseph to lie down with her, she clearly threatened his negative face. Sometimes imposing on negative face sets the stage for conflict. As an example, Mary hung out in Joann's apartment and endlessly complained about her relationship with her boyfriend. A conflict ensued when Joann tried to get Mary to move on. By impinging on Joann's time, Mary was impacting Joann's negative face, her sense of autonomy. Perhaps you've had an experience in which a friend has asked you for advice. Yet when you told the friend how to handle the situation, the friend started arguing with you about your approach. Sometimes advice-giving goes awry because in telling another what to do, we impinge on the other person's sense of autonomy, their negative face.

In conflict, people may pursue different types of goals. One person may be concentrating on the content issues while the other person is concentrating on regaining lost face. In managing conflict, we need to be cognizant of all four types of goals: content, process, relationship, and identity.

> Think back to the story of Joseph and his brothers. In what ways might positive and negative face have contributed to that conflict?

What Is a Face Threat?

In the story of Joseph and Potiphar's wife, face was clearly an issue. A *face threat* occurs when the way a person wishes to be perceived is threatened. When a person's face is threatened, a cascade of events may follow. First, a face threat may elicit emotion: fear, anger, or shame. Second, after the emotional arousal, action, such as revenge or retaliation, may follow. Sally Planalp, a professor of communication, points out that we may respond with anger when our sense of security is threatened, our self esteem is damaged, or our feelings are hurt.[10] When we feel wronged or threatened, anger may generate the desire for revenge; then conflict escalates and the outcome is destructive. Damaged self-esteem can be a strong motivator. If you've ever witnessed a teacher using sarcasm against a classmate, you have probably experienced or witnessed the fear, anger or embarrassment that results.

What Is Facework?

Facework is communication undertaken to counterbalance threats to one's face or self-image. Facework can be used to maintain or restore one's own face or someone else's face. Sometimes facework is unilateral or brought about by just one party in a conflict. For example, avoidance, not drawing attention to the threat or ignoring it, may smooth a social interaction. Josh may tell a story that embarrasses Heather. Heather might ignore the affront or she may choose involve others. Or friends who are present may simply go on with the conversation and not comment on Josh's remark, thereby helping Heather to maintain face. Heather, or others present, may also make use of humor to release some of the tension and emotion engendered by this threat to her face. Someone might also proffer excuses to justify Josh's bad behavior.

Facework may involve talk about a personal relationship. Heather might raise this issue with Josh. An apology might mitigate the effect of face threat, and a conversation about their relationship may ensue.

> What kinds of facework can you identify in the story of Joseph and Potiphar's wife?

The story of Joseph and Potiphar's wife is a good example of how different goals can create and influence the course of conflict. The story permits analysis using multiple perspectives. By exploring goals at various levels (personal, relationship, and system), we can see how complicated managing conflict becomes when one person sets her sights on her relationship with God and community, while the other person focuses on achieving a personal goal. By examining content, process, and identity goals, we can see that managing conflict means being aware of several domains and addressing people's needs from a variety of perspectives. Understanding face theory, with its emphasis on both positive and negative face needs, helps to clarify how central identity issues are to this particular example of conflict and to conflict in our own lives.

Theological Reflection on Genesis 39

In viewing Genesis 39:1–23 as a whole, we see the conflicts that exist between Joseph and Potiphar's wife and between Joseph and Potiphar because of the behavior of Potiphar's wife. We also see how power and gender interact with one another negatively. It seems likely that Potiphar's wife is a "kept woman" under the thumb of her husband. Perhaps she employs the only power available to her: her sexuality. Even her sexual power, however, is compromised in the midst of her encounter with Joseph and the resulting fallout. Joseph becomes a victim of injustice and is imprisoned for a crime he did not commit. A relationship of trust between Potiphar and Joseph now lies in shambles on account of a falsehood that also compromises whatever integrity Potiphar's wife may still have had.

Interestingly enough, this story does not involve a portrait of God intervening directly into the situation to inform Potiphar of the truth of the circumstances. This did happen in the earlier story of Abraham, Sarah, and King Abimelech (see Gen. 20:1–18) when in order to protect himself Abraham attempted to pass off Sarah as his sister and not his wife. Abimelech almost took Sarah for himself, not realizing, until God informed him, that she was Abraham's wife and that his action would be sinful. Instead, in this story we see God working through the course of human events to bring about good in Joseph's life.

Although Joseph is not acquitted by Potiphar, he is "acquitted" by God and eventually finds favor in the sight of the Pharaoh (Gen. 41:39). This favorable relationship leads to Joseph's family being welcomed into Egypt, Joseph being reunited with his family, and the family of Jacob being saved from starvation and death from the plague in Canaan (see Gen. 41:42–50).

In Sum: Grace in the Wilderness

In the story of Joseph and Potiphar's wife, the Spirit of the Lord remains with Joseph and gives him success (v. 2). God's grace remains constant in Joseph's life, with grace working through the life of the chief jailer, whose trust in Joseph affirms and deepens Joseph's unwavering integrity and loyalty. Joseph remains a person graced, and his life remains on course despite the unjust hardships he has to bear because of another's dishonesty.

With respect to conflict, we observe Joseph's valiant attempt to maintain his own integrity and meet the face needs of Potiphar's wife. When she propositions him, rather than cast aspersions on her character (which would have been a bald threat to her positive face), Joseph cast aspersions on his own character by saying, "How then could I do this great wickedness?" As is often the case in our own lives, even adept facework may be insufficient when dealing with vindictive people. Potiphar's wife damages both his positive face by accusing him of near rape and his negative face by having him arrested. Joseph, however, acts with grace despite the consequences to himself.

Reflection Questions:
Can You Now ... ?

1. Explain the relationship between sexuality and power?

2. Give an example of how applying concepts of personal, relationship, and system goals would alter a story of conflict?

3. Explain how these three types of goals affect your interactions with others?

4. Define the concept of face? Describe a situation of conflict in which you have either lost or gained face?

5. Identify instances of losing face and gaining face in the story of Joseph?

6. Consider a situation of conflict you've experienced recently. How could you apply face theory to resolving it?

JOSEPH ENCOUNTERS
HIS BROTHERS

Forgiveness and Reconciliation
(*Genesis 42:1–47:26*)

Then Joseph could no longer control himself before all those who stood by him, and he cried out, "Send everyone away from me." So no one stayed with him when Joseph made himself known to his brothers. And he wept so loudly that the Egyptians heard it, and the household of Pharaoh heard it. Joseph said to his brothers, "I am Joseph. Is my father still alive?" But his brother could not answer him, so dismayed were they at his presence.

Then Joseph said to his brothers, "Come closer to me." And they came closer. He said, "I am your brother, Joseph, whom you sold into Egypt. And now do not be distressed, or angry with yourselves, because you sold me here; for God sent me before you to preserve life. For the famine has been in the land these two years; and there are five more years in which there will be neither plowing nor harvest. God sent me before you to preserve for you a remnant on earth, and to keep alive for you many survivors. So it was not you who sent me here, but God."

(Gen. 45:1–8)

A Biblical Interpretation of Genesis 42:1–47:26

The family of Joseph is suffering pain and hardship. Jacob, thinking he has lost his beloved son Joseph to a wild animal, grieves. Joseph's brothers, living in Canaan with their father Jacob, are about to starve to death because a great and severe famine has struck the land (Gen. 37:33–36, 41:53–57). The occasion of the famine sets in motion Jacob's command to his sons to go down to Egypt, where grain is plentiful (Gen. 42:1–3). The brothers' descent into Egypt is a pivotal move because it leads to the reunion between the brothers and Joseph and eventually to Jacob's reunion with Joseph. Genesis 42:1–47:26 is a heartwarming story about forgiveness and lessons learned along the way.

Before discussing the story in detail, it will be helpful to explore the concepts of forgiveness and reconciliation, noting their similarities and differences, and then determining which virtues are prominent in the story about Joseph and his brothers.

Forgiveness

In the biblical tradition, forgiveness is primarily an act of God whereby God, acting with divine compassion, removes the obstacles and boundaries to being in right relationship with God, with one another, and with all creation. Forgiveness can renew or restore relationships. Throughout the Hebrew Scriptures, we see that Israel's God is often a merciful God (see, for example, 1 Kings 8:23; Ps. 13:5; Isa. 60:10; Mic. 7:18–20), who takes no pleasure in the death of a sinner. Covenant is the sign of God's steadfast love (Ps. 106 and Ps. 107), and through the covenant made with Israel God offers continued mercy and compassion. The divine virtues are based solely upon God's graciousness and God's righteousness and reliability (see 1 Kings 8:30; Ps. 130:3–4; Jer. 31:34). In the New Testament, forgiveness of one's neighbor becomes central to the teachings of Jesus. When sins are forgiven, reconciliation is possible, but forgiveness can take place independently of reconciliation.

The final word and act of God is not wrath or devastating judgment. The final word is mercy, favor, compassion (Hos. 11:8–9), and the deepest expression of forgiveness is not necessarily verbal. When forgiveness comes from the heart, then peace can abide.[1] In order to forgive another from the heart, however, the one doing the forgiving needs to have a heart that has been transformed (Ezek. 36:16–38) and that remains a challenge for and an invitation to all people today.

Reconciliation

In the Hebrew Scriptures, reconciliation is associated with cultic purity rituals that involve the cleansing of someone or something deemed "unclean" or unworthy. Usually some sort of restitution has to occur before reconciliation can take place (see, for example, 1 Sam. 12:3). In Hebrew the root word for reconciliation is *kaphar,* which means "to cover," or "to make atonement" (Lev. 6:30, 8:15; Ezek. 45:15, 17, 20). The term *ratsah* can also be translated as "to reconcile" (see 1 Sam. 29:4).

In the New Testament, reconciliation pertains to right relationship among people and with God. The ability to be reconciled one with another is a grace given by God. Not all people have the openness or capacity to receive this grace, and thus not all people have the openness or capacity for reconciliation, which is itself a gift. For Christians, this gift of reconciliation comes to its fullness through Jesus, who made intercession for all the transgressors of his day, for all those who hated him and one another, and for all those guilty of injustices down through the ages. Paul reminds us that God remains reconciled to all (Col. 1:15–20).

Thus, reconciliation is a grace and a gift that may or may not flow from forgiveness. Reconciliation involves two parties, whereas forgiveness can be only one way. Like forgiveness, reconciliation renews relationships and draws those being reconciled into deeper union and communion with each other.

The story of Joseph and his brothers in Genesis 42:1–47:26 is a story that focuses on forgiveness. After all that the brothers have done to Joseph, he forgives them. The narrative consists of ten units:

42:1–5	Jacob's sons sent to Egypt
42:6–25	First encounter between Joseph and his brothers
42:26–38	Joseph's brothers return to Canaan
43:1–34	Second encounter between Joseph and his brothers
44:1–17	Joseph detains Benjamin
44:18–34	Judah pleads for Benjamin's release
45:1–28	Joseph reveals himself to his brothers
46:1–27	Jacob and the entire family go to Egypt
47:1–12	Exchange between Joseph and Pharaoh
47:13–26	Famine strikes Egypt

Jacob's Sons Sent to Egypt (Genesis 42:1–5)

The story of Joseph and his brothers begun in Genesis 37 now continues in Genesis 42. Having suffered the supposed loss of his son Joseph and having grieved over that loss (Gen. 37:29–36), Jacob, the parent, now confronts his other sons. Faced with the famine that has now reached Canaan, Jacob learns of grain in Egypt, and says to his sons, "Why do you keep looking at one another?" He then sends them down to Egypt to buy grain. Biblical scholar Victor P. Hamilton notes that "as father, Jacob retains authority over even married, grown sons. He speaks and mandates; they obey and cooperate." Hierarchy and patriarchy are core to the ancestral familial relationships.[2] One brother, however, will not be going with the others. Jacob does not send Benjamin. Benjamin is also the son of Rachel, whom Jacob loved more than any of his other wives. This first scene closes with the brothers' arrival into Egypt.

First Encounter between Joseph and His Brothers (Genesis 42:6–25)

With the geographic setting now in place, the narrative quickly switches its focus to Egypt, where Joseph is governor over the land (see Gen. 41:37–49). The central literary technique that brings the tale to life is irony. Upon seeing Joseph, the brothers all bow down before him, acting as "servants," which also happened in one of Joseph's earlier dreams, and in the same dream that so incensed his brothers once Joseph told them about the dream (see Gen. 37:5–8). Joseph recognizes his brothers immediately, but, surprisingly, they do not recognize him. Hamilton points out many reasons why the brothers would not recognize Joseph: "They assume he is dead; he is probably clean shaven; he speaks to them in Egyptian through an interpreter (v. 23); he is wearing the trappings of his Egyptian office; he has an Egyptian name (41:45).... The brothers are lacking in both recognition (ch. 42) and insight (ch. 37)."[3] Thus, to his brothers, Joseph is an "Egyptian."

Joseph puts his brothers through several trials. When he accuses them of being spies, the brothers respond by telling Joseph their family story, including that one of the brothers "is no more" (v. 13). Joseph imprisons all of the brothers but one as spies, demanding that that brother go back home and bring the youngest brother, Benjamin, back to Egypt; if not, the rest of the brothers will never be set free (vv. 15–17). The brothers remain in prison for three days (v. 17).

In verses 18 through 25 Joseph reverses course. Instead of keeping all the brothers imprisoned, he releases all but Simeon, sending the others back to Canaan, stocked with grain for their households and commissioned to bring their youngest brother back to Egypt. The brothers now reflect with a new awareness on the task they are to perform: "They said to one another, 'Alas, we are paying the penalty for what we did to our brother; we saw his anguish when he pleaded with us, but we would not listen. That is why this anguish has come upon us' " (v. 21).

Reuben, for his part, reminds the brothers that he had told them not to wrong Joseph, and because they did not listen, a "reckoning of his blood," a price will have to be paid, or so he thinks (v. 22). With grain bags filled without charge and provisions for the journey, the brothers set out to return to Canaan to carry out Joseph's wishes (v. 25).[4]

Joseph's Brothers Return to Canaan (Genesis 42:26–38)

The third unit of the narrative opens as Joseph's brothers depart. One of the brothers is shocked to find that his money, which lies on top of a sack, has been returned to him. This situation causes them to fear God: "What is this that God has done to us?" (v. 28). In the ancient worlds, everything good that happened was attributed to God, and everything bad that happened was also attributed to God.

Upon arriving home, the brothers relay the entire story to Jacob, and we hear that they are worried about their fate after being labeled "spies" by Joseph (vv. 29–34). Jacob is now faced with the gut-wrenching decision of whether or not to send Benjamin to Egypt. At first, he is strongly reluctant to do so. Jacob expresses his great love for his sons and especially for Benjamin: "I am the one you have bereaved of children: Joseph is no more, and Simeon is no more, and now you would take Benjamin. All this has happened to me!" (v. 36). Jacob indirectly accuses his sons of the loss of Joseph, Simeon, and now possibly Benjamin. Reuben tries to persuade Jacob to entrust Benjamin to him (v. 37), but Jacob remains steadfast in his refusal (v. 38). Thus, the narrative reaches a stalemate.

Second Encounter between Joseph and His Brothers
(Genesis 43:1–34)

As the famine has become more severe, Jacob's family has devoured all of the grain that the brothers brought from Egypt. Jacob now beckons his sons to return to Egypt to buy more grain (v. 2), and once again one of the brothers reminds his father that Joseph has told them to bring Benjamin to Egypt (vv. 3–5). Jacob upbraids Judah and all of the brothers for having let on that there was another brother who remained at home (v. 6). Judah and Reuben both plead with their father to entrust Benjamin to them, indicating they will bear full responsibility for the situation if it turns out badly (v. 9). Judah adds one final persuasive comment: "If we had not delayed, we would now have returned twice" (v. 10). Jacob finally concedes to let Benjamin go to Egypt with his brothers and sends them all off with a gift of assorted foods for Joseph and twice as much money as before (vv. 11–12). Saying goodbye to Benjamin, he utters a prayer to God on their behalf as they get ready to leave: "May God Almighty grant you mercy before the man, so that he may send back your other brother and Benjamin. As for me, if I am bereaved of my children, I am bereaved" (v. 14).

Jacob has entrusted the entire situation to God and the brothers and, in essence, he has reconciled himself to whatever might be the outcome. He has let go. With gifts, money, and Benjamin in tow, the brothers set out for Egypt (v. 15).

What follows is a description of Joseph's second encounter with his brothers. The brothers, including Benjamin, arrive in Egypt and stand before Joseph (v. 16). Joseph then orders a meal prepared for all the brothers, who will be brought into Joseph's own house (v. 17). This entire situation makes the brothers exceedingly uncomfortable (v. 18) to the point that they blurt out their story to the steward (vv. 19–20), who offers them a reassuring word and reunites Simeon with them (v. 23).

With the preparations completed, Joseph returns home to dine with his brothers, who then present him with their gifts, bowing down once again to Joseph. When Joseph asks them a series of questions pertaining to their family, the brothers respond positively and then, bowing their heads once more, do "obeisance" (vv. 26–28). On seeing Benjamin, Joseph is overcome with emotion and leaves the room to weep in private (vv. 29–30). Here the narrator stresses Joseph's love for and bond to Benjamin by noting that Benjamin is "his [Joseph's] mother's son" (v. 29). After this poignant moment, Joseph returns to his brothers and has their meal served. Interestingly, Joseph is served separately, as are his brothers and the Egyptians present, as the act of eating with Hebrews was considered an "abomination" or a cultic taboo from the Egyptian perspective (vv. 31–32). Hamilton notes:

> For a second time Joseph is separated from his brothers at meal time (see 37:25 for the first). But he is no helpless occupant of an empty cistern this time. At the first meal separation he was the victim. Here

he is the victor. At least he does not deprive his brothers of food, as they once deprived him.[5]

Seated at different tables, all enjoy the meal, and portions from Joseph's table are shared with his brothers, with Benjamin receiving five times as much as anyone else. However, the brothers fail to pick up on the hint that Joseph is giving them: just as he received a special coat, so Benjamin, the "youngest brother," now receives a special portion. Although the meal is more like a banquet than an ordinary dinner, the merriment on the brothers' part is soon to turn to bewilderment.

Joseph Detains Benjamin (Genesis 44:1–17)

Following the dinner, Joseph prepares his brothers to return to Canaan, loading them with grain and returning their money to them. He commands his steward to put his silver cup in the top of Benjamin's sack (vv. 1–2) and then the brothers are sent away. Before they have traveled a great distance, Joseph has his steward follow them and then round them up for questioning. Joseph had asked his steward to accuse the brothers of stealing Joseph's silver cup (vv. 3–5). After the accusation and the discovery of the cup in Benjamin's sack, the brothers, who are quite shaken, return to Joseph, who confronts them with the theft. As punishment, Benjamin is to remain to serve as Joseph's servant (vv. 14–17) while the rest of the brothers return home.

Judah Pleads for Benjamin's Release (Genesis 44:18–34)

Faced with the threat of losing Benjamin, Judah challenges Joseph. Pleading with Joseph, he reminds him of all that has transpired thus far (vv. 18–34), including only those details that will possibly obtain Benjamin's release. Judah's appeal is quite moving and poignant and, in the end, he offers to stay, taking the place of Benjamin. Hamilton observes that this speech reveals a spiritual transformation that Judah has undergone:

> His speech to Joseph in ch. 44 represents a profound advancement over his speech about Joseph in 37:26ff. He who once callously engineered the selling of Joseph to strangers out of envy and anger is now willing to become Joseph's slave so that the rest of his brothers, and especially Benjamin, may be freed and allowed to return to Canaan to rejoin their father.[6]

Joseph Reveals Himself to His Brothers (Genesis 45:1–28)

Totally overcome with emotion, Joseph reveals himself to his brothers, shocking them all (vv. 1–3). Immediately he tells them that his fate had been destined by God to save them and their father. Joseph expresses no animosity toward his brothers, but instead weeps with Benjamin at their happy reunion and then kisses all his brothers without restraint (vv. 14–15). He also has a gracious word for them to deliver to Jacob. In the end all of the brothers are reunited with no animosity among them. The symbolic gestures in Joseph's dream (see Gen. 37:1–11) have been played out, and Joseph preserves the family, saving its members from starvation. His ill fate has turned into good fortune for himself and for his family.

The gracious hospitality that Joseph extends to his brothers continues as Pharaoh, the king of Egypt, offers the family rich provisions. Pharaoh, delighting in the fact that Joseph's brothers are in Egypt, opens wide the doors and resources of Egypt not only to the brothers but also to Jacob their father (vv. 16–18). Pharaoh tells Joseph to send the brothers back to Canaan so that they can gather their wives, children, and father together and bring them all down to Egypt (v. 18). He also tells Joseph to offer his brothers wagons to transport their households (v. 19). Furthermore, they are to have no concerns about their possessions because in Egypt, they will be given the best of all the land (v. 20).

Such news is wonderful for Joseph and his family, but it is also interesting to note how welcoming the pharaoh is to an alien people. The pharaoh's benevolence helps to facilitate the reunion of Joseph's family and, in fact, makes the reunion an enduring one because now the entire family will be gathered together in one place with few worries.

The following verses describe Joseph carrying out the pharaoh's orders and giving his brothers advice for the journey: "Do not quarrel along the way" (v. 24). As this section of the narrative closes, the brothers return to Canaan to gather their families and their father for the move to Egypt. Jacob is jubilant at hearing the great news about Joseph and wants to go at once to see him (vv. 25–28); Jacob, however, has not yet been told the real story of how Joseph ended up in Egypt.

Jacob and the Entire Family Go to Egypt (Genesis 46:1–27)

The next part of the narrative opens as Jacob and all of his family travel to Egypt. At Beersheba, the site where God appeared to Isaac (Gen. 26:23–25) and where Isaac built an altar (Gen. 25:25), he offers sacrifices to God (v. 1). This spontaneous act of worship on Jacob's part is a sign of deep gratitude to God for extending divine benevolence to the family through Joseph and Pharaoh.

In addition, Jacob is gifted with an experience of God, who speaks to him in "the visions of the night" (v. 2), although this encounter was not Jacob's first experience of God (see also Gen. 28:10ff, 32:21ff). The repetition of a person's name, "Jacob, Jacob" (v. 2), is often used throughout the Bible (see Gen. 22:11; Exod. 3:4; 1 Sam. 3:10; Acts 9:4). What follows the divine address to Jacob is a statement of confidence to reassure him: "I am God, the God of your father; do not be afraid to go down to Egypt, for I will make of you a great nation there. I myself go down with you to Egypt, and I will also bring you up again; and Joseph's own hand shall close your eyes" (Gen. 46:3–4). Thus, Jacob now lives under a divine promise.

With a buoyed spirit, Jacob and his entire family set out for Egypt, carrying with them their livestock and possessions (vv. 5–7). Verses 8 through 27 catalogue the names of the entire family of Jacob entering the land of Egypt.

Verses 28 through 34 describe the wonderful encounter between Jacob and Joseph at Goshen. Upon seeing his father, Joseph falls upon him, weeping tears of joy, and Jacob, happy to be with his beloved son once again, is now content to go to his grave (vv. 28–30). As for his other brothers and their households, Joseph now makes plans to announce their arrival to Pharaoh. The family will reside in Goshen since they are shepherds, an occupation unwelcome among the Egyptians (vv. 31–34).

Exchange between Joseph and Pharaoh (Genesis 47:1–12)

Having instructed his brothers and their household about what they should say and do when Pharaoh calls them, Joseph now informs Pharaoh that his family has arrived in the land (v. 1). As promised, Pharaoh gives the family the best land in all of Egypt — Goshen — and there the family remains (v. 6). Readers may puzzle as to why preferential treatment is being given to one family over and above what is given to other families, whether they be Hebrew or Egyptian (vv. 5–6).

A lively, informational exchange takes place between Jacob and Pharaoh and then after Jacob blesses Pharaoh twice (vv. 7 and 10), Jacob and his household settle in the land of Goshen, also referred to as the land of Rameses (vv. 11–12). Jacob's family, once separated physically and emotionally from one another, is reunited, graced, and blessed. A leader who does not even worship Israel's God has wholeheartedly welcomed a group of immigrants into his land.

Famine Strikes Egypt (Genesis 47:13–26)

The famine that struck Canaan earlier now spreads to Egypt (v. 13). The Egyptians suffer terribly while Joseph's family enjoys plenty. As governor of the land and people, Joseph strikes a deal, taking from the Egyptians their money, livestock, and land in exchange for food. Having amassed such treasures for the Pharaoh, the penniless Egyptians are enslaved "from one end of Egypt to the other" (v. 21). Thus, through Joseph, Pharaoh has amassed even more power and wealth. The Israelites are then encouraged to tithe one-fifth of their goods, and to offer this fifth to Pharaoh. They do so and then promise, unfortunately, to be Pharaoh's slaves: "You have saved our lives; may it please my lord, we will be slaves to Pharaoh" (v. 25). Thus, the choice for life is a costly one for the Israelite community, with only the priests being exempt from the tithe.

As we have seen, the story of Joseph becoming reconciled with his brothers and father has many layers, with the most important one being serious conflict and betrayal within Jacob's family. Before any reconciliation can occur, forgiveness needs to take place. How we understand forgiveness is crucial not only to the Joseph story but also to everyday life.

Looking through the Communication Lens

Before returning to the story of Joseph, let's consider a recent incident. On July 10, 2008, Ingrid Betancourt, a French Colombian citizen, addressed a group of reporters to talk about her experience as a hostage. She had been held for more than six years, chained, physically tortured, and humiliated by the Revolutionary Armed Forces of Colombia. In an interview, she said, "The only thing I've settled in my mind is that I want to forgive, and forgiveness comes with forgetting."[7] Betancourt, a Roman Catholic, has a personal meaning for the word "forgiveness," but in ordinary discourse, much disagreement exists about the meaning of forgiveness.

> *In your opinion, what is involved in the kind of "forgiveness" Betancourt refers to? How is she defining forgiveness? To what extent does it match your own idea of forgiveness?*

What Is Forgiveness?

Scholars note that we use the term "forgiveness" in at least two ways.[8] Much like Ingrid Betancourt, many of us conceive of forgiving as an individual experience, something we can do *unilaterally* without any apology from the other party, remorse on his or her part, compensation, or assurance the offense will not happen again. Another way of thinking about forgiveness, however, involves *interpersonal* interactions. *Bilateral forgiveness* means the offender and the victim are involved or engaged with each other in some way. The offender recognizes that he or she has done something wrong, expresses regret, acknowledges out loud the wrongdoing and the harm inflicted, resolves not to repeat the error, and offers some sort of restitution. After the offender makes amends, the injured party relinquishes the grudge that stemmed from the offense.

Another feature of our understanding of "forgiveness" is the notion of *unforgiveness*. When psychologists Everett L. Worthington and Nathaniel Wade consider unforgiveness, they define it as "a 'cold' emotion involving resentment, bitterness, and perhaps hatred."[9] Residual anger characterizes unforgiveness, and rumination can intensify it. In our hostage example above, relinquishing unforgiveness may be the first step toward forgiveness, but forgiveness is not the only way to lessen unforgiveness. One can seek social justice and try to correct the situation that contributed to his or her own grievance. People can retaliate, however, so, for example, if one dating partner or spouse flirts with someone new, the other partner may do the same, and the situation is exacerbated. One can also seek revenge or use psychological defenses such as denial to reduce unforgiveness.[10] Forgiveness may be viewed as "a choice either unconscious or deliberate to relinquish unforgiveness."[11]

Researchers distinguish forgiveness from pardoning, condoning, reconciliation, and forgetting.[12] *Pardoning* implies sparing the offender from the legal consequences of action. *Condoning* suggests that the offender had a reasonable excuse for the behavior. In a sense, Joseph provides a reasonable excuse for his brothers when later in the story, after revealing his true identity, he tells his brothers not to be distressed or angry with themselves, that God's hand was at work in bringing him to Egypt (Gen. 45:5). *Reconciliation,* on the other hand, means renewing the relationship, and *forgetting* means the transgression is no longer remembered.

As you consider the passage below from the story of Joseph, can you apply these definitions to the story as it has unfolded?

> When Joseph saw his brothers, he recognized them, but he treated them like strangers and spoke harshly to them. "Where do you come from?" he said. They said, "From the land of Canaan, to buy food." Although Joseph had recognized his brothers, they did not recognize him. Joseph also remembered the dreams that he had dreamed about them. He said to them, "You are spies; you have come to see the nakedness of the land! . . . " Here is how you shall be tested: as Pharaoh lives, you shall not leave this place unless your youngest brother comes here!" (Gen. 42:7–15).

Defining Forgiveness from a Communications Perspective

For our purposes, forgiveness is both an experience of transformation from a negative to a positive state and an interaction in which harmful conduct is acknowledged by one or both parties and the harmed party relinquishes any grudge. As we consider forgiveness in the context of conflict, we need to keep in mind some of the issues concerning attribution theory that were referred to in the introduction. Attribution theory addresses how we see "cause." Do we attribute cause to the character of the person involved or to external circumstances? What is known as the "fundamental attribution error" says that when we are judging others, our tendency is to attribute the cause of a transgression to the other person's character or disposition. The offender, however, using *self-serving bias* will likely emphasize the external, mitigating circumstances. As we think about forgiveness, we should keep in mind these perceptual differences between offender and victim. Whereas the accuser focuses on the person, the accused may be focusing on extenuating conditions. In conflict, each party may see himself or herself as the victim.

> *Given what we know about attribution theory, how might we expect Joseph to explain his being thrown into the pit and sold? How would his brothers explain it?*

Context Matters

Different contexts, which can include the quality or type of a relationship, create different challenges for forgiveness.[13] If the *quality* of a couple's relationship has been excellent and one partner transgresses, the process of forgiveness will be different than if they had a poor relationship prior to the offense.

Differing *types* of relationships, which require differing approaches, can be illustrated by examples in international settings, conflicts at work, conflicts with friends and romantic partners, and within families. The steps that are required for forgiveness in each of these instances will vary widely. For example, several times while intending to target terrorists, the U.S. Armed Forces have killed and wounded innocent civilians. Typically, the government has offered apologies, explanations, and monetary remunerations. Does this earn forgiveness? Some of the victims' families do not think that monetary compensation is sufficient. What would be required for a just response that would initiate and implement a process of forgiveness? For them to begin to forgive, the people behind the bombing would also need to be put on trial.[14] If the countries are allies, the process of forgiving will likely be different than in conflicts where the countries are already antagonists.

Consider possible settings at work. If a manager takes credit for a report you have prepared, would you harbor feelings of anger and resentment or express your anger directly to the boss? The norms and culture of your workplace would naturally impact the behaviors of both your boss and yourself.

Consider a conflict with a friend. Right after a breakup with your significant other, your good friend starts dating that person. You find this very disloyal on the part of your friend. Can you maintain the friendship without forgiving your friend for this transgression? As with the workplace, the norms of your relationship will govern how forgiveness is enacted. If your romantic partner went out Friday night with a group of friends instead of keeping your regular Friday night date, would you give your partner the silent treatment or retaliate?

If a parent consistently and harshly berates a child, how should the child react? What issues of forgiveness are involved? As Cynthia Battle and Ivan Miller have pointed out, family relationships differ from other relationships with respect to forgiveness: family relationships are involuntary, longer term, and more intimate than other social relationships.[15] Interactions are typically more frequent than in other relationships, and offenses can be minor but repeated. Moreover, multiple family members may be affected by the actions of another member, setting off a complex series of reactions.[16]

Culture Matters

We mentioned in chapter 1 that every culture has its own filter or means of dealing with conflict. Culture influences forgiveness in fundamental ways as well, as is shown in the work of Steven Sandage and Ian Williamson, who have demonstrated how individualistic worldviews and collectivist worldviews lead to different appropriate communication behaviors. Individualists see themselves as independent, and the primary concern is one's own face. Forgiveness is distinct from reconciliation, and the central goal of forgiveness is one's own personal well-being. Tools for forgiveness include psychotherapy, self-help, and individual coping skills.

> Recall the account in Genesis 37:18–28 that tells of Joseph's brothers selling him to the Ishmaelites. Consider the description above (Battle and Miller) of how family transgressions are different than other social relationships. To what extent do those differences apply to the story?

Collectivist cultures, on the other hand, emphasize social *inter*dependence. Primary face concerns include both self and the other. Forgiveness and reconciliation are closely related. While self-forgiveness has a low-value, social well-being is the central goal. Primary tools in any search for forgiveness include mediators, healers, and the use of narratives. The table below contrasts the differences outlined by Sandage and Williamson between individualistic and collectivistic cultures regarding forgiveness.

Comparison of Individualistic and Collectivistic Worldviews in Relation to Forgiveness[17]

Factor Viewed	Individualistic Worldview	Collectivistic Worldview
View of self	Independent, self-reflexive	Interdependent, socially embedded
View of relationships	Exchange/contractual	Communal/covenantal
Primary face concern	Self-face	Other-face and self-face
Forgiveness and reconciliation	Sharply distinct	Closely related
Value of self-forgiveness	High	Low
Central goal of forgiveness	Personal well-being	Social well-being
Primary tools for forgiveness	Professional psychotherapy, self-help resources, and individual coping skills	Communal mediators/healers, narratives, rituals, and symbols

In chapter 2 we introduced the topic of facework. Recall that face is the image we hold of ourselves and that we want others to reinforce. Losing face and saving face may strongly influence how forgiveness is enacted. Our need to feel approval, inclusion, and competence may enhance or impede the forgiveness process, and the strength of each of these may be influenced by whether we belong to an individualistic or collectivistic culture. As we see in the table on the facing page, our culture lays the ground rules for what is normative. Whereas personal well-being may be central for an individualistic culture, social well-being may prevail for a collectivist culture, and facework would then have to take that into consideration.

How Do Different Religions View Forgiveness?

Each religion has its own rules and traditions for forgiveness. In Hinduism, forgiveness is described as "tolerance and as absence of agitation of the mind."[18] Traditionally, people suffering an illness would ask themselves if they had done anything wrong in the present or in a previous life. Before reaching the equanimity of forgiveness, however, the individual would likely experience anger, unfairness, and a feeling of unforgiveness toward the persons responsible for the situation.

In the New Testament, two words are commonly used to denote forgiveness: *eleao* (and cognate nouns) meaning to show mercy (seventy-eight times), and *aphiemi* — meaning release, discharge, or put away (sixty-four times). A third word is also used, *splanchnizomai*, which means "feeling sorry for or having compassion on."[19] Throughout the New Testament, forgiveness is associated with having compassion.

In the Jewish tradition, common words for forgiveness include *mehillah* and *selihah*. Sometimes these words are used interchangeably, but classically *mehillah* referred to "wiping away of a transgression," and *sehillah* connoted reconciliation.[20]

Islam uses three terms for forgiveness: *'afw,* which is used 35 times in the Qur'an and means to pardon, to excuse for a fault, a waiver of punishment; *safhu* (8 times), meaning to turn away from a transgression; and *ghafara* (234 times) meaning to cover, forgive, or remit.[21]

Buddhism, as a global religion with wide linguistic diversity, makes a single definition of forgiveness difficult to translate. Compassion, pity, and forbearance are all concepts that contribute to forgiveness in the Buddhist tradition.[22]

The Process of Arriving at Forgiveness

Douglas Kelley found three forms of forgiveness-granting communication: direct forgiveness, indirect forgiveness, and conditional forgiveness.[23] *Direct* forgiveness means openly telling the offender that he or she is indeed forgiven. *Indirect* forgiveness is not verbalized but conveyed by acting normally to the offender, by using humor, hugging, or downplaying the impact of the transgression. *Conditional* forgiveness involves "if-then" statements, such as "I will forgive you if you promise. . . ."[24] Conditional forgiveness conveys the idea that repetition of the offending behavior will not be tolerated.[25]

Andy Merolla found that among friends and dating relationships most respondents used indirect methods to communicate forgiveness and that conditional methods were used the least.[26] However, when *conditional* forgiveness was used, it occurred most frequently in dating relationships. Why would this be? Merolla speculates that in a dating relationship, the offense might not be worth forgiving if the romantic partner is not willing to make changes.

What elements of direct, indirect, and conditional forgiveness were demonstrated among Joseph and his brothers?

Wanda Malcolm and Leslie Greenberg describe a process that a victimized individual can employ when he or she wants to experience forgiveness. First, the victim recognizes the strong emotions such as anger and sadness that are a consequence of the offending actions. Second, the person lets go of unmet needs from the offender. If we go back to Ingrid Betancourt, for example, "letting go of unmet needs" would mean that Betancourt, a victim, recognizes that if she is going to forgive the offenders, she will do this without getting an apology or compensation from them.

Next, a shift occurs in the victim's view of the offender. An understanding of the offender's perception, a kind of empathy, enters the victim's thinking. Finally, the victim creates a new understanding of himself or herself as well as of the relationship with the other.[27] If we apply this process to the Betancourt example, it might mean that she would begin to empathize with her captors. She might rethink their motivations to better understand why events occurred as they did. This process might help her relinquish her unforgiveness.

Communication professors Vincent Waldron and Douglas Kelley identify seven tasks that need to be undertaken in the process of forgiveness leading to reconciliation. The tasks need not be accomplished sequentially.[28] They comprise:

1. Confront the transgression. Both parties must acknowledge that wrongdoing has taken place and that at least one partner has been badly hurt. Responsibility for the transgression must be taken and (sometime) shared.

2. Manage emotion. Strong negative emotion must be expressed, labeled, acknowledged, legitimized, accepted, and de-intensified. Emotions may include shock, anger, and fear.

3. Engage in sense-making. The wounded partner invites information-sharing about motives, details of the situation, and explanations in an effort to manage uncertainty and assess the magnitude of the offense. The offender provides an honest explanation. The parties jointly construct the meaning of the offense by considering it in the context of past behavior, current relational understandings, and implications for the future.

4. Seek forgiveness. The transgressor convincingly apologizes, expresses regret, and (where appropriate) offers to make amends. The forgiver assesses the request for forgiveness, develops empathy, and communicates openness to the possibility of forgiveness.

5. Grant forgiveness. The wounded partner indicates a willingness to forgive. Forgiveness may be extended immediately and unequivocally or a long-term process may be initiated. To reduce risk, conditional forgiveness may be offered and third parties may be involved.

6. Negotiate values and rules. Clarify the values and rules that will govern the relationship during the post-forgiveness period. Renegotiate the "relational covenant." Create the moral structure that ensures fairness and justice in future interactions.

7. Transition: monitor, maintain, or renegotiate. Monitor and maintain relational agreements; build trust, confidence, and hope; derive meaning from the experience; focus on the future; consider a redefined relationship if the process fails.[29]

Putting It Together

The very complex story of Joseph begins with the dire circumstances in which Joseph found himself at the age of seventeen. His brothers, out of jealousy for the favored son, threw him into a pit with the intention of killing him. When Reuben sought to intervene and then Judah reminded the brothers that Joseph was of their own flesh, the brothers ended up selling Joseph to the Ishmaelites. Joseph had years in which to ruminate over the treachery of his brothers. We can imagine the cascade of emotions with which he had to contend during that period of time: fear, anger, hurt, vindictiveness, a desire for revenge. As the account continues and the brothers journey to Egypt, Joseph recognizes them and after accusing them of being spies, he manipulates them into fetching Benjamin.

Joseph's behavior can be interpreted in several ways. His actions might be seen as a way of diminishing the absence of forgiveness. In his dreams in Canaan, all the brothers had bowed down to him. Having Benjamin as well in Egypt and then making himself known to the brothers might give Joseph the satisfaction of having them all witness his "dream fulfilled."

Joseph could also reestablish his loss of face of many years before, gaining the satisfaction of being right. Roy Baumeister and his associates explain some of the benefits of holding a grudge.[30] People may carry a grudge because of wounded pride, because they continue to suffer the consequences of the transgression, because it may help prevent a repeat of the original occurrence, because they want to get concessions from the offender, and because their moral principles would be compromised by forgiving the transgressors.[31]

Joseph's behavior can also be interpreted by referring back to some of the steps involved in communicating forgiveness by Waldron and Kelley:

confronting the transgression, managing emotion, and engaging in sense-making.[32] The text tells us that in talking to one another the brothers admitted that they had transgressed: "we saw his anguish when he pleaded with us, but we would not listen." The brothers did not try to justify or rationalize their actions. They recognized they had wronged Joseph. The text notes that "They [the brothers] did not know that Joseph understood them, since he spoke with them through an interpreter. He turned away from them and wept." We do not know whether Joseph wept, remembering the pain he had suffered; whether he wept because he could let go of the burden of his resentment; whether he wept because he knew they now empathized with what he had experienced; or for some other reason. Everett Worthington and Nathaniel Wade maintain that "to regain a positively valenced relationship, the victim needs to experience an emotion-arousing event that is incongruent with the cold emotion of unforgiveness."[33]

Judah, who intervened in the beginning so Joseph would not be killed, spoke in a way that revealed empathy for Jacob, their father — something that the brothers never displayed years before, and Judah also tried to protect Benjamin, Joseph's brother by Rachel. In all of these behaviors, the brothers acknowledged their guilt both implicitly and explicitly, which might have made it easier for Joseph to forgive them.

In fact, after revealing himself to them, Joseph engaged in "sense-making" by explaining to the brothers that God's purpose was enacted by the events that had happened long before. Later on, after Jacob died, the following scene occurred:

> Realizing that their father was dead, Joseph's brothers said, "What if Joseph still bears a grudge against us and pays us back in full for all the wrong that we did to him?" So they approached Joseph, saying, "Your father gave this instruction before he died, 'Say to Joseph: I beg you, forgive the crime of your brothers and the wrong they did in harming you.' Now therefore please forgive the crime of the servants of the God of your father." Joseph wept when they spoke to him. Then his brothers also wept, fell down before him and said, "We are here as your slaves." But Joseph said to them, "Do not be afraid! Am I in the place of God? Even though you intended to do harm to me, God intended it for good, in order to preserve a numerous people, as he is doing today. So have no fear; I myself will provide for you and your little ones." In this way he reassured them, speaking kindly to them. (Gen. 50:15–21)

This passage indicates that the brothers still distrusted Joseph, fearing that his earlier forgiveness had been insincere and that he would now punish them. Baumeister and his colleagues have addressed the topic of various types of forgiveness. Between the poles of no forgiveness and total forgiveness, lie hollow forgiveness and silent forgiveness.[34] *Hollow forgiveness* involves expressing forgiveness but not really meaning it. Indeed, the words, "I forgive you," from the victim may mark only the beginning of forgiveness, although the receiver may interpret the words to mean "all is forgiven." Clearly, the behavior of the brothers indicates that they found it hard to accept that Joseph had, indeed, relinquished his "unforgiveness" and moved on.

In *silent forgiveness* the victim no longer feels angry but does not convey any change of heart to the offender. Sometimes victims "hold out" because they genuinely worry about a recurrence of the transgression. Sometimes silent forgiveness can be manipulative in order to extract further concessions. What Joseph revealed, however, was that he found meaning in his suffering as a plan of God. Ingrid Betancourt, introduced at the start of this chapter, went a step further, resolving to work for the liberation of other hostages, thereby using the experience to give her renewed purpose in life, bolstering the relinquishment of unforgiveness toward her captors.

The Joseph story does leave many dangling threads. Did Joseph owe his brothers any apology for his behavior as a youth? Perhaps during the long period away from his family, Joseph might have empathized at some point with his brothers' lot and acknowledged that his own behavior had fed their hatred. Research suggests that people can be more forgiving if they have an empathetic understanding of the offender.[35] Similarly, did Jacob owe his other sons an apology for his favoritism of Joseph and Benjamin? In the context of the culture of the times, these questions may be moot. In our own culture and times, however, they are questions we can ponder.

Theological Reflection on Genesis 42–47

The story of Joseph and his brothers with their painful separation and their jubilant reunion is a familiar one in both ancient and contemporary times. The unconscionable deed done to Joseph by his brothers put Joseph in the hands of strangers and left Jacob completely distraught and the family in shambles (see Gen. 37). Even though Joseph was not tactful in describing his dreams to his brothers and even though Joseph was a favored son, the brothers' decision first to kill Joseph and then to sell him to the Ishmaelites, lying to their father about his whereabouts, was ruthlessly unjust.

Amazingly, Joseph's fate turned into good fortune, and despite his brothers' harsh treatment, he never turned his back on them especially when they were in need and about to die of hunger. Just as Pharaoh treated Joseph benevolently, so Joseph treated his kin benevolently. His test of them was not malicious, nor was it at attempt to "get even"; instead, his test was to discover whether or not they had actually changed. In the end, Joseph appeared to hold no animosity toward his brothers. Although he never voiced "I forgive you," his hospitality and benevolence toward them indicated his forgiveness. It is quite clear that in fact Joseph forgave his brothers and was reconciled to them and they to him.

One aspect of the story merits examination, and that is Joseph's treatment of the Egyptians. As governor "over them," he acts in Pharaoh's interests even though the people are struggling through an extreme famine. He takes all that they have in exchange for providing them with food and, finally, enslaves them for Pharaoh. Although he provides them with seed for growing crops, the land now belongs to Pharaoh. The "tenant farmers" must give one-fifth of all they produce to Pharaoh. They have lost their independence and ownership of their land and money. Might Joseph have handled their dire situation differently? The discussion needs to continue.

In Sum: Grace in the Wilderness

The story of Joseph and his brothers demonstrates how grace can turn difficult situations into positive experiences. Even though the brothers seriously wronged Joseph, had he not been sold to the Ishmaelites, he quite possibly would never have found his way into Egypt where, because of his talents, he was befriended by Pharaoh. Had he not been favored by Pharaoh, he would never have been in a position to help his brothers, their families, or their father, Jacob. He would not have been in a position to help Egypt prepare for the famine that was to come.

Grace thus worked through a horrible situation to bring about good, not only for one individual but for an entire household of people. Grace also allowed Joseph to forgive his brothers, which in turn allowed reconciliation among all the family members. Grace also transformed the brothers. Although they were once envious of Joseph, they acted to protect Benjamin, the other beloved son of Jacob and Rachel. Grace worked through Pharaoh, who acted kindly toward Joseph and his family even though they were strangers in the land. And finally, grace worked through Joseph who, in the end, received his brothers as his own once again, saved his family from starvation, and turned the grief of separation into the joy of reunion.

Through the lens of communication we see that people can change. The brothers confronted their transgressions. Joseph helped them all make sense of what had happened. All relinquished their grudges. Each was able to forgive the trespasses of their youth. While none of the participants forgot what had happened, they were able to move beyond the transgressions to reconciliation.

Reflection Questions:
Can You Now...?

1. Identify instances of sibling rivalry in your family or that of a good friend in which parental favoritism contributed? To what extent did the rivalry escalate? Did reconciliation ever come about? If so, how?

2. Explain why Joseph or anyone might want to relinquish unforgiveness?

3. Explain how attempting reconciliation after a conflict in the workplace would differ from that in a family? How do context, culture, and religion affect reconciliation?

4. Distinguish between forgiveness and reconciliation? Understand that forgiveness does not always lead to reconciliation?

5. Understand Waldron and Kelley's seven steps in the process of seeking reconciliation: confront the transgression, manage emotions, engage in sense-making, seek forgiveness, grant forgiveness, negotiate rules, and maintain agreement. Which steps would be hardest for you? Consider the story of Joseph: can you find evidence in the text of these steps? Were any missing?

6. Remember holding a grudge? What were your reasons or your rationalizations?

7. Consider when you needed to ask another person for forgiveness? How difficult was it to do? Is asking another for forgiveness easier or harder than asking God for forgiveness?

Additional Resources

♦ Martin Doblmeier's documentary film *Power of Forgiveness* explores the psychology, spirituality, and communicative aspects of forgiveness.

♦ In *Amish Grace: How Forgiveness Transcended Tragedy*, Donald B. Kraybill, Stephen M. Nolt, and David L. Weaver-Zercher (San Francisco: Jossey Bass/John Wiley, 2006) explore how an Amish community in Nickel Mine, Pennsylvania, reached out to the family of a shooter who went to their school and shot ten children, killing five.

♦ Simon Wiesenthal's *The Sunflower: On the Possibilities and Limits of Forgiveness* (New York: Schocken Books, 1998) challenges readers to think about vengeance and forgiveness.

♦ In *Joseph and His Brothers*, trans. John E. Woods (New York: Everyman's Library, 2004), Thomas Mann follows the story of Joseph with great fidelity and yet imaginatively expands it, filling in details of how the people lived and viewed the world. Mann augments the tale with myths of Egypt and Mesopotamia.

♦ A much lighter treatment of the Joseph story can be found in Andrew Lloyd Webber's *Joseph and the Amazing Technicolor Dreamcoat*.

TAMAR AND JUDAH

Leveling the Playing Field

(*Genesis 38*)

Then Judah said to his daughter-in-law Tamar, "Remain a widow in your father's house until my son Shelah grows up" — for he feared that he too would die, like his brothers. So Tamar went to live in her father's house.

In course of time the wife of Judah, Shua's daughter, died; when Judah's time of mourning was over, he went up to Timnah to his sheepshearers, he and his friend Hirah the Adullamite. When Tamar was told, "Your father-in-law is going up to Tumnah to shear his sheep," she put off her widow's garments, put on a veil, wrapped herself up, and sat down at the entrance to Enaim, which is on the road to Timnah. She saw that Shelah was grown up, yet she had not been given to him in marriage. When Judah saw her, he thought her to be a prostitute, for she had covered her face. He went over to her at the roadside, and said, "Come, let me come in to you," for he did not know that she was his daughter-in-law." (Gen. 38:11–16)

A Biblical Interpretation of Genesis 38

The story of Judah and Tamar in Genesis 38 is a rich text involving culture, deception, power, and family politics. In this text, the biblical writer tells the story of two people who are victims of their social and religious culture. Judah, the father of three sons, is obligated by law and culture to provide one son and then another son to his twice widowed daughter-in-law, Tamar. Bound by strict cultural traditions, Tamar is a young woman who has no future and no choice for marriage outside of her dead husband's family. Because of the "levirate law" (Deut. 25:5–10), she is not free to marry outside the family until no more brothers-in-laws are available to become her spouse. Against this background, the story of Judah and Tamar takes place.

Three themes embedded in the story of Judah and Tamar include the levirate law of marriage, prostitution, and power.

The Levirate Marriage

The first theme, the law of the levirate marriage, is described in Deuteronomy 25:5–10. Under this law, if two brothers live together and one of them dies without a child, and especially without a son, then one of the surviving brothers must take his widowed sister-in-law as a wife. The firstborn child of this new marriage is regarded by law as the son of the deceased husband (brother). The brother-in-law, however, can decline this obligation by making a declaration before the elders of the town. His choice not to uphold the levirate marriage would be considered dishonorable. The widow, in turn, would take off her brother-in-law's shoe and spit in his face because he is not continuing to raise up his brother's house. Only twice in the Hebrew Scriptures, specifically in the story about Judah and Tamar and the story of Ruth, do we see the law of the levirate marriage coming into play.

In the story of Judah and Tamar, Judah's first born son, Er, dies without having a child by his wife, Tamar (Gen. 38:6–7). Thus, it becomes Onan's duty as Tamar's brother-in-law to marry Tamar, his newly widowed sister-in-law. Onan, however, does not want to have a child that would not be his own, so he "spills his seed on the ground" (Gen. 38:8–10). Judah should then give Tamar to his youngest son, Shelah, but Judah disregards his duty (Gen. 38:11), a decision that leaves Tamar without a husband and without a child, particularly a male child, in a culture that is both patriarchal and patrilineal. As a result, Tamar, in trying to protect herself and survive, is left with no other choice than to trick her father-in-law Judah into having intercourse with her for the sake of bearing a child and, hopefully, a male child (Gen. 38:15–19).

Interestingly, Genesis 38:1–30 presents the obligation of the levirate marriage in a much more stringent fashion than the law was originally intended in Deuteronomy. A brother-in-law could decline his duty to his sister-in-law, in which case, the duty would then be passed on to all the surviving brothers (Matt. 22:24–27). Tamar's relations with Judah may have occurred during a time when it was understood that if a father-in-law did not have any other sons, then the duty to the widowed daughter-in-law would fall to the father-in-law. This practice was common among some people in ancient times. In the context of the story, however, Tamar's actions betray a woman desperate to care for herself and to ensure her future and the future of her household.

Prostitution

The second theme that emerges from Genesis 38 is prostitution. In the Ancient Near East, prostitution was common and, in fact, in many ancient pagan cultures prostitution received little or no censure. In Mesopotamia and Canaan, prostitution was associated with sacred ritual, and "sacred prostitutes" were part of the sacred ritual. These sacred prostitutes were associated with fertility rituals and fertility gods and goddesses, and those who engaged in prostitution were thought to be brought into communion with the gods and goddesses and the divine principle of fertility.

In Israel, however, prostitution was condemned, and those who engaged in it were in violation of Israel's moral codes. Israel was guided by the holiness codes described in Leviticus 17–26, which outlined exactly how the Israelites were to conduct their daily lives. The codes censured improper sexual conduct (Lev. 19:20–22). Israelite fathers were prohibited from giving their daughters to prostitution. Such a corrupt act was regarded as lewdness entering the land of Israel (Lev. 19:29). According to Israel's marriage customs, any woman who was a prostitute was considered unfit for marriage.

The Israelites in the land of Judah were also severely condemned for their participation in cult prostitution and idolatry (1 Kings 14:22–24). Prostitutes of both genders were present in Caananite sanctuaries, and Israel, influenced by its surrounding cultures, eventually followed this practice of ritual prostitution (see, for example, 1 Kings 14:24, 15:12, 22:47, and Hos. 4:14). Even though temple prostitution was condemned (see Deut. 23:18–19), the "sacred prostitutes" did find their way into the temple at Jerusalem (2 Kings 23:7). As a result, some kings tried to remove idols and temple prostitutes from the temple (1 Kings 15:12, 22:47). One such king was Josiah, whose reforms included the destruction of the apartments of the cult prostitutes (2 Kings 23:7). Israel's prophets condemned prostitution and harlotry as punishable by God, and they often used the symbol of prostitution to describe perversions of the covenant relationship between God and Israel (see Amos 2:7; Hos. 1–3; 4:12–14; Ezek. 16; and Jer. 3:1–8).

The prophets not only condemned prostitution but also considered it an act deserving of punishment (see, for example, Amos 2:7). The Wisdom literature considers adultery and prostitution to be equally despicable, and it characterizes the prostitute as one who is loud, defiant, brazen, unruly, and unintelligent (Prov. 6:26, 9:13). A man who becomes involved with prostitutes compromises his wealth, loses his strength (Prov. 29:3; 31:3), and violates the holiness codes. Finally, prostitution becomes a primary metaphor for Israel's idolatrous and apostate ways with respect to God. Israel stands indicted for having prostituted itself before other gods (Exod. 34:15, 16; Lev. 7:7, 20:6; Deut. 31:16; 2 Chron. 21:11, 13; see also Mic. 1:7).

Thus, the theme of prostitution that emerges in the story about Judah and Tamar in Genesis 38 is part of a long history and tradition. Interestingly, though, Judah is not condemned for taking pleasure in the one whom he thinks is a prostitute (Gen. 38:15–19). He is faulted, however, for not observing the levirate law with respect to his daughter-in-law Tamar (Gen. 38:26).

Power

The third theme that emerges from Genesis 38:1–30 is power. In the Ancient Near Eastern and Israelite worlds, power was viewed as something possessed and something exercised. Power was a quality of God and God's Spirit, and power was a quality given by God to others and, in particular, a gift given to the prophets (for example, see Mic 3:8). In the Hebrew Scriptures, God is viewed as having "power over" people, nature, and the course of history. God is the one who empowered the prophets. God is also the one whose power intervened in history and at other times let history run its course.

In human relations in the ancient world, power was associated with gender, specifically, the male gender, and culture. Gender, culture, and religion all influenced one another with respect to power. Power was also associated with status, the need for control, and the need to demonstrate authority, often at the expense of another's dignity. Finally, with regard to power resting in the male gender, the males in the ancient world were responsible for procreation, for providing for the women and children in their household, and for assuring that there were family heirs. Male power and authority were often reinforced by the image of a male deity — God — whose power was frequently used punitively.

For women, power rested in their own ability to protect themselves in the face of male dominance when power was asserted negatively instead of positively. Often women had to claim power by using their intelligence and knowledge of the law and also deception, trickery, subversion, or by "working the system" from within the system. In the story of Judah and Tamar in Genesis 38, Tamar has to wait on Judah to see whether or not the levirate marriage law made by men would be honored by Judah because he held Tamar's destiny in his hands. Through trickery and deception, Tamar lures Judah into prostitution and through their sexual encounter, she is able to secure protection and prosperity for herself by means of her two sons, the fruit of their union. Thus, the story of Judah and Tamar is about power and how one woman is able to secure justice for herself by holding responsible for his actions the one who held all the cards.

From a literary perspective, Genesis 38:1–30 consists of five units:

38:1–5	The Beginnings of Judah's family
38:6–12	The Expansion of Judah's family and unfolding hardships
38:13–19	An Encounter between Judah and Tamar
38:20–26	Judah's discovery
38:27–30	The Birth of Judah and Tamar's children

Of interest is the fact that while the story of Judah and Tamar interrupts the flow of the Joseph stories, it is nonetheless part of the ancestral stories of Jacob and Joseph, although its focus is directed at Judah, Joseph's brother.

The Beginnings of Judah's Family (Genesis 38:1–5)
The story opens as Judah departs from his brothers after encouraging them not to kill Joseph but to sell him to the Ishmaelites (Gen. 37:26–27). Judah

leaves to settle near Hirah, a person identified only as "a certain Adullamite" (v. 1).[1] In this new territory of Adullam, Judah meets an unnamed Canaanite woman whose father is named Shua.[2] Judah marries the woman. This is significant because he is an Israelite and she is a Canaanite. In ancient Israel, intermarriages were not acceptable, and thus this detail in verse 2 suggests that the story is very old, written long before "the preaching of the prophets and the injunctions of the Deuteronomist against intermarriage."[3] Abraham, Judah's great-grandfather, was concerned that Isaac not marry a Canaanite (Gen. 24:3), and this concern was shared by Isaac, Jacob's father (Gen. 28:1). By marrying a Canaanite, Judah breaks with the family tradition and expectation.

Verses 3–5 catalogue the birth of three sons to Judah and his wife. The firstborn son is Er, whose name means "watchful," "watcher." The second-born son is Onan, a name that means "strength," "vigor," "vigorous one," "healthy one." The third-born son is Shelah, a name of uncertain etymology. We read in verse 5 that Judah and his wife have migrated from Adullam to Chezib,[4] known also as Achzib, a city located in the central Shephelah. Thus, this first unit tells of Judah beginning his own family.

The Expansion of Judah's Family and Unfolding Hardships (Genesis 38:6–12)

This next set of verses features Judah's family in their adult lives; it describes the hardships that befall the family and sets in motion a series of incidents that will move the narrative forward. In verses 6–7, we learn that Judah has selected Tamar as a wife for Er, his firstborn. Er, however, acts wickedly, and the story's narrator tells us that the Lord put Er to death. What Er did is not revealed. In keeping with the tradition, it is Judah who selects a wife for his son, and Er appears to have no say in the matter. Little is known about Tamar but most likely she is a Canaanite woman, quite possibly from the regions of Adullam and Chezib. Tamar's name means "date palm."

Verses 8–10 focus on Judah's second son, Onan. After the death of Er, Judah commands Onan to take Tamar as his own wife, thus fulfilling the levirate law of marriage (v. 8). Onan bears the responsibility for providing for Tamar. Onan, however, does not accept his responsibility; instead of impregnating Tamar in hopes that she would have sons who would eventually look after her, Onan "spills his seed on the ground" (v. 9). The reason for Onan's failure to take responsibility is clear.

> [Onan] puts his own interests ahead of Tamar and Tamar's future child. Numbers 27:8–11 states that if a man dies without a son, then his inheritance is to pass to his daughter; if he has no daughter, then the inheritance is to pass to his brothers. Onan apparently does not want to father a son who will prevent him from receiving his deceased brother's inheritance.[5]

Increasingly sad for Tamar is the fact that while Onan acted as though he were going to take her as his own, he changed his mind. The consequence of his actions was death (v. 10). Judah then promised Tamar that when Shelah, the youngest brother, came of age, Judah would give him to her in marriage. Because of this promise, Tamar was considered betrothed and thus her intercourse with Judah later on in the story was adulterous.

Judah fears that the fate of Er and Onan will fall upon Shelah, and so he carefully plans the next events. While waiting for Shelah "to come of age," Tamar, now a widow, is sent back to her father's house. This is in keeping with the holiness codes of Leviticus as verse 22:13 states that a priest's daughter, a widow, or a divorcee without children may return to her father's house. In this case the purpose for Tamar's return is to establish economic security for herself until Shelah is able to take her as a wife. Tradition dictated few ways for a widow to secure financial security: marriage to a brother-in-law (Deut. 25:5–19), remarrying (1 Sam. 25:39–42; 2 Sam. 11:26ff; 1 Tim. 5:14), or remaining celibate and becoming self-supporting. Obviously this last option would be a very difficult path to set upon.

Tragedy pursues Judah and his family in verse 12, when Judah's wife dies. Now Tamar and Judah are widow and widower, respectively, and Judah's experiences of loss parallel those of his father, Jacob, who also lost not only a son, Joseph — supposedly — but also a beloved wife, Rachel. In customary fashion, Judah mourns the death of his wife and then reunites with Hirah the Adullamite. Together the two men travel north to Timnah to work with Judah's sheepshearers. Judah now moves forward with his life and his work.[6] Thus, for the family of Judah and for Judah himself, hardship, sorrow, and loss become their lot.

An Encounter between Judah and Tamar (Genesis 38:13–19)

The ingenuity of Tamar and her desire for rightful justice surface in verses 13 through 19. Tamar is informed that her father-in-law is going up to Timnah to shear his sheep, and immediately upon hearing the news, she alters her physical appearance. She takes off her widow's garments, puts on a veil, wraps herself up, and sits down at the entrance to Enaim, which is on the road to Timnah (vv. 13–14). Biblical scholar W. Sibley Towner points out:

> Veiling is not a usual practice by women in ancient Israel; both times it is mentioned in Genesis it is connected with a special moment in the erotic life of a woman (Rebecca's wedding veil in 24:65; Tamar's seduction veil here). It is most frequently mentioned in the Song of Songs. Yet if Assyrian law is any guide to early practice in Israel, for fear of corporeal punishment a prostitute would never have veiled herself.[7]

Tamar is about to seduce Judah because "she saw that Shelah was grown up, yet she had not been given to him in marriage" (v. 14). Victor P. Hamilton offers two possibilities as to why Judah did not fulfill his promise to Tamar:

On the one hand, it could have been an unconscionable oversight on Judah's part. On the other hand, it could well be that Judah never intended to bring Shelah and Tamar together, and therefore his earlier statement that she return to her father's house until Shelah comes of age was nothing but a ruse. If that is the case, then the trick Tamar played on Judah is a response to the trick Judah played against Tamar, rather than the initiative of trickery. What happens to Judah, then, parallels what happened earlier to his father, Jacob: the perpetrator of deceit is now the victim of deceit.[8]

Tamar is not content to remain in the keep of her father; she wants marriage to Shelah, which was promised to her by Judah, but she has no power or control over Judah, who has not fulfilled his promise. Thus she chooses an alternative way to secure her future independent of her father's household. Wrapped up, veiled, with her face covered, Tamar becomes unrecognizable to Judah, who thinks that she is a prostitute (v. 15) and thus makes an advance toward her: "Come, let me come in to you..." (v. 16a). He does not know that the veiled woman is, in fact, his daughter-in-law, the one betrothed to his son Shelah. Tamar is quick to respond to Judah: "What will you give me, that you may come in to me?" (v. 16b).

What follows next is a lively exchange between Judah and Tamar that results in Tamar receiving a pledge from Judah — his signet, cord, and staff, which she requests to be sure that he fulfills the promise made to her, namely, that he would send a kid from his flock in payment for her "services rendered" (v. 17).[9] With a pledge in hand, Tamar concedes to have relations with Judah and becomes pregnant (v. 18). With this accomplished, Tamar sheds her veil and dons her widow's garments once again (v. 19). At this juncture in the story, Judah has no idea that he has just fathered a child with his daughter-in-law.

Judah's Discovery (Genesis 38:20–26)

In verses 20 through 26 we learn that Tamar had posed as a temple prostitute and that when Hirah went looking for her on behalf of Judah, she could not be found in the town. Judah received Hirah's news, allowing Tamar to keep the items given to her in the pledge so that he would not become a laughingstock in the town.

The story about Judah and Tamar reaches its climax in verses 24 through 26. Judah learns of Tamar's pregnancy and the general assumption is that Tamar has "played the whore." At such news, an angry Judah orders that Tamar be burned. This punishment is harsh for such a transgression but this type of punishment was not uncommon in ancient Israel. In Proverbs 6:27–29 a connection between sexual indiscretions and burning is clearly established. In the law described in the Hebrew Scriptures, however, only two instances call for burning: (1) the crime of incest with one's mother-in-law (Lev. 20:14) and (2) prostitution by a priest's daughter (Lev. 21:9).

Judah's demand that Tamar be burned is the only place in the Hebrew Scriptures where one person has the power to order the execution of another for adultery. The specific punishment for adultery in Israel is usually stoning by the community (Lev. 20:10; Deut. 22:21). If a man is found guilty of sexual indiscretion with his daughter-in-law, then the Torah calls for the death penalty for both parties (Lev. 20:12), and that penalty is death by burning. Thus, Judah's demand that Tamar be burned seems to be an outburst of personal rage since the law does not call for burning in relation to harlotry (v. 24). What is evident, however, is the potential force of power that Judah has over Tamar, a force that is greater than that of her own father.

As Tamar is being brought out for punishment, she assertively sends word to her father-in-law. The note reveals the truth about her situation. The signet, staff, and cord provide the needed evidence to support her statement (v. 25). Judah acknowledges that the three items are his possessions, and at that moment he realizes what has happened. His response indicates that he has also considered his own decision not to give his son Shelah to Tamar as had been promised. Judah's confession is simple: "She is more in the right than I, since I did not give her to my son Shelah" (v. 26a). From that moment on, Judah did not have relations with Tamar again.

The Birth of Judah and Tamar's Children (Genesis 38:27–30)

With the truth revealed, the story's focus now shifts to Tamar's pregnancy. With the aid of a midwife, Tamar gives birth to twin boys named Perez and Zerah. Perez becomes the father of Hezron and Hamul (Gen. 46:18–22; 1 Chron. 2:5) and an ancestor of Boaz, Jesse, and David (Ruth 4:18–22), and according to Matthew's genealogy, Jesus as well (Matt. 1:2–26). Nehemiah 11:4–6 lists Perez's 468 descendants among the Judahite leaders in Jerusalem when it was restored in Nehemiah's day. Zerah eventually has five sons (1 Chron. 2:6). Tamar has now secured her own future. She has two sons who will care for her in her old age, and both sons now become heirs to the property of Er and Judah. Surprisingly though, Judah never takes Tamar as a wife nor do we hear that he gave Shelah to Judah in marriage. Furthermore, we do not hear that Jacob verbally acknowledges that the twins are his own sons. For a man of such stature, Judah pales in his ability to take *full* responsibility and, in the end, Tamar becomes a woman worthy of admiration because of her assertiveness in the face of unfairness and an unfulfilled promise.

Looking through the Communication Lens

Before turning to a discussion of the use of power in this story, it may be helpful to review the nature of the conflict between Tamar and Judah using a definition of conflict put forth by William W. Wilmot and Joyce L. Hocker: "Conflict is an expressed struggle between at least two interdependent parties who perceive incompatible goals, scarce resources, and interference from others in achieving their goals."[10] How did these incompatible goals contribute to conflict in this story, and how did each participant try to wield power to achieve their goals?

How Do Differing Goals Affect Our Understanding of Conflict?

In chapter 2 we saw that incompatible goals can exist at multiple levels. That means that identifying only one obvious point of conflict may leave deeper issues unexamined. In this account from Genesis, Tamar wanted to marry Shelah because she was without a husband, a precarious position for a woman at that time. On the other hand, Judah saw her as a threat: her two previous husbands, his sons, had already died. He feared for the life of his third son. The entire situation is a sufficient cause of conflict, but an analysis of the situation that ends here would miss additional levels of incompatible goals that are significant. In this case, each party's identity goals contributed a second, though less apparent, dimension to the conflict. Judah saw his family's honor at stake: if he rejected the opportunity to continue his oldest son's lineage, he brought disgrace upon himself and his family. This taps into the deepest kind of identity issues of that time: it was not only his identity at stake, but also that of his family and his descendants.

For Tamar, levirate law decreed that she could not marry outside the family unless her brother-in-law formally rejected her before the elders of the town. This jeopardized *her* identity: she was promised a husband, but she could not consider herself either wife or widow until Judah made good on his commitment.

Furthermore, emotional goals added to both the content and identity issues of this conflict. The fear that if Shelah married Tamar, Shelah would die as his brothers did had driven Jacob's behavior. We can conjecture that Tamar, abandoned by Judah at her father's house, felt angry and hurt and was fearful of her future. What was to become of her if Judah abandoned his responsibility? Clearly, goals involving content, identity, and emotion drove this conflict.

In any situation of conflict it is important to be aware that multiple goals may propel the conflict. For Tamar and Judah, norms of the culture, the physical distance between Tamar and Judah, as well as Judah's preferred strategy prevented direct confrontation about these issues. The choices we make about using power to resolve conflict are likely to be more effectively enhanced if we understand the multiple levels of our own goals as well as the goals of the other party.

How Does Power Influence Conflict?

Kenneth Boulding has defined power as "the ability to get what one wants,"[11] and Joseph Folger, Scott Poole, and Randall Stutman note that the power individuals can bring to a conflict depends on both their resources and their skills in using those resources.[12] When we read the story of Tamar and Judah, it is easy to see Judah as all-powerful in their relationship and to imagine Tamar being completely overwhelmed by her lack of power. Clearly, Tamar did not assess the situation in that way. Her behavior illustrates an important tenet of power. Power is not something one person "possesses," but rather power stems from the relationship between people.[13]

Can you identify the multiple goals in the following conflict?

Maria, a sophomore in college, wanted to change her major. Though she always thought she wanted to be a nurse and serve the poor, her first semester of volunteering in a hospital made it clear to her that she did not enjoy the work. She wanted to switch majors to communication studies and work with media. Her parents, however, were adamantly opposed. They were concerned with how quickly she abandoned her commitment, and they wanted to be sure she had a good job when she graduated. They wanted her to serve the needy. Moreover, they were paying her tuition.

If you were Maria, how would you structure your conversation with your parents to help them meet their goals without abandoning your own?

While Judah's multiple power bases gave him access to resources, those resources needed to be endorsed by Tamar in order for them to have power. In other words, simply because he had certain attributes that could give him dominance, she did not have to submit. By assessing her own power bases and strategizing, she was able to accomplish what she wanted. Many times in our own lives we may encounter work, family, or interpersonal situations in which the other party seems to hold all the power currencies, and we have few resources. The story of Tamar and Judah, however, illustrates for us how careful analysis of a situation may provide opportunities to level the playing field. Let's explore the power bases of both Tamar and Jacob.

As father-in-law, Judah had certain obligations to Tamar. He was supposed to betroth Tamar to his youngest son, Shelah. Tamar, as his older son's widow, was supposed to wait at her father's home until her father-in-law brought her back for the marriage. When Judah decided to ignore his obligation, what sources of power did each have?

John R. P. French and Bertram Raven have identified five sources of social power.[14] First, *legitimate power* derives from one's position of formal authority. Because of his status as male, older person, and father-in-law, Judah had legitimate power. The culture and its laws conferred that power on him. Legitimate power has the potential to exert an almost magical effect at times. For example, people may succumb to a move for dominance simply because of one's position as president, pope, or guru.[15]

Second, *coercive power* is the ability to punish another. From the story we know that Judah can coerce Tamar into not marrying Shelah simply by ignoring her. Later, having Tamar burned is clearly within Judah's purview.

While leaders of all types use coercive power, dictators use coercive power to the extreme.

A third source of power is *reward power.* An individual complies because he or she expects to benefit by doing so. Leaders exercise reward power as a means of securing loyalty. Judah could reward Tamar by marrying her to his youngest son.

Another source of influence is *referent power.* When one person accepts the orders or the direction of another out of respect or liking, referent power is at work. Perhaps Tamar waited as long as she did because of referent power, in other words, the respect she had for her father-in-law. When referent power coincides with legitimate power, leaders have an especially strong power base.

Finally, expertise, *information,* can be a source of power. Tamar's strongest source of power in this situation was probably her knowledge of the law. She was thus able to use her familiarity with the law to leverage her power.

In the example above, what kind of power base does the student Maria have? What type of power base do her parents have?

Though they come into play only indirectly in the relationship between Tamar and Judah, other power bases may be useful. William Wilmot and Joyce Hocker identify *interpersonal linkages* and *communication skills* as additional sources of power.[16] *Interpersonal linkages* refer to the power we derive from people we know who can help us achieve our goals and also from coalitions we can make. Friends, allies, and relatives can also be called on to put pressure on another party to help us get what we want. If Tamar had chosen to go directly to the elders of the community, she would have used interpersonal linkages as a power base. For us today communication skills, verbal and nonverbal, do offer a means of increasing our power base. Given the social milieu of the time, it is doubtful that better communication skills would have been useful to Tamar. Our ability to articulate a vision, however, to inspire others, to express empathy, and to clarify what others want and need can all contribute to helping us achieve our goals.

Clearly, Judah, the patriarch in a patriarchal society, had more power bases, and a significant imbalance of power existed. However, significant imbalances of power can have drawbacks for both the dominant and the weaker party. For example, the more powerful party may underestimate what the weaker person is willing to risk.[17] Indeed, Tamar's strategy — disguising herself as a prostitute, becoming pregnant, and risking being burned to death — is so fraught with danger that it's doubtful that Judah would ever imagine her executing such a plan. On the other hand, for the weaker party the primary danger of an extreme imbalance of power lies in feeling so overwhelmed by the power resources of the other person that the lack of power becomes self-fulfilling.

How imbalanced is the power relationship between Maria and her parents? What are the dangers of imbalanced power in that example?

The Usefulness of Social Exchange Theory

Another principle that affects the use of power, social exchange theory (SET), is described in the work of psychologists John W. Thibaut and Harold H. Kelley.[18] Understanding how social exchange theory works can open up opportunities to exercise power that might not otherwise occur to us. Basically, SET proposes that people are motivated to maximize their rewards and minimize their costs. People will accept a power move depending on how it will affect them personally. Using his power to keep Tamar away from Shelah initially came at no cost to Jacob. For Tamar, however, the cost of yielding to Judah's will was simply too great. In a relationship, when the costs exceed the potential rewards, we generally try to change the relationship in a way that will be more equitable and, if that does not work, we may end the relationship altogether. In this case, Judah underestimated Tamar's desperation, the cost she was willing to pay.

Another aspect of social exchange theory posits that we compare our situation to a hypothetical alternative. If no other alternatives offer better rewards, we may stay in a situation regardless of current drawbacks. From Tamar's behavior we can infer that death was preferable to banishment. To even the playing field, Tamar had to use an extreme measure. Many of us in our daily lives, however, want to exert power when we do not have legitimate power (we are not the boss, we are not the coach, we are not the head of the family), but we do not want to resort to extreme behavior. Whereas Tamar and Judah's interdependence was a win-lose structure, if it is possible to frame interdependence as win-win, we create more options for solving a situation of conflict.

Social psychologists Allan R. Cohen and David L. Bradford offer a schematic (on the following page) that demonstrates how individuals can influence each other whether or not they have the legitimate authority to do so.[19]

We can apply the model to the story of Tamar and Judah. Initially Tamar thought that she and Judah were allies, that they both subscribed to the same beliefs and values, and that their goals and priorities were aligned. According to Cohen and Bradford, assuming we are potential allies is generally a fruitful place to begin. Next, we need to be clear about our own content, identity, relationship, process, and emotional goals. Earlier in the chapter we showed how the identity goals of Tamar and Judah interfered with each

Cohen and Bradford's Model of Influence

other. Third, we should take time to analyze the "other's" goals and priorities. Judah underestimated Tamar in this regard, and Tamar surmised that Judah's goal was to ignore his responsibilities for her.

Fourth, we need to assess our power bases and our capabilities, as well as those of the other person. Tamar was fully aware of Judah's power resources, but Judah misjudged the intensity of Tamar's goals and her power resources. Fifth, we should then assess the best way to relate to the other person. After being exiled to her father's house and understanding the futility of her previous entreaties, Tamar devised a way to get Judah's attention. Finally, we need to assess what kind of "give and take" is possible. That is, we need to explore how we can help the other person meet his or her needs so that our own needs might also be met. Tamar, of course, did not do this.

In contemporary times, Cohen and Bradford point out that not only is this process useful for weaker parties to influence stronger parties, it is also a method for the stronger party to effectively influence the weaker party.

Power, the ability to get what one wants, depends on the nature of the other party, the power currencies or bases at play, and the context of the situation. As we have seen in the story of Tamar and Judah, cultural and religious norms and the historical period circumscribed the strategies available to Tamar.

How Do We Get Other People to Comply?

Contemporary research has explored a range of strategies we use to exert power and to gain compliance with our goals. As you read through this list, think about which of these tactics you use and with whom. Also, consider which tactics work best on you and under what circumstances.

1. *Direct requests:* one party directly asks the other to comply with a request: "Please clean last night's dishes." "I would like for us to spend Friday night together." "Please pick up the children from daycare."

2. *Exchange:* one party attempts to get the other to comply by offering an exchange of something of value, such as money or service: "I will cook tonight if you will clean." "I will continue my nursing courses and minor in communication studies."

3. *Coercive:* one party tries to get the other to comply by using pressure strategies such as punishment, making the other feel guilty or sad for not complying: "The last two Friday nights you hung out with your friends." "I'm not cooking dinner because you do not help clean up." "I will borrow money so I can study what I want."

4. *Rationality:* one party uses supporting evidence to convince the other to comply with a request: "We agreed on splitting housework 50/50. If I cook, you should clean." "Here are the jobs available with a major in communication studies."

5. *Face maintenance:* one party flatters or bolsters the self-image of the other to indirectly dispose the other person to comply: "You are an excellent cook. I would really enjoy dinner if you would make it." "You are wonderful parents who have raised me to serve others. I would like to do that but in a different setting than hands-on health care."

6. *Hidden request:* one party disguises a request as an observation: "There is a sink full of dirty dishes." The hidden request is a form of manipulation to get someone to do what we want without asking directly. In SET terms, we "owe" less if it appears that a person does something out of his or her own free will rather than because we have asked for it as a favor. "Supportive parents encourage children to follow their career passions."

7. *Ideal comparison:* one party tries to manipulate the other into yielding by comparing that person's behavior to what a good person would do. "If you were a good roommate, you would not pester me." "If you were supportive parents, you would allow me to study what I value."

8. *Negative comparison:* one party argues that the other person should yield because only a bad person would *not* yield: "Only a real slob would not want to help clean up." "Only self-centered parents would require their child to study a field he or she disliked."[20]

In this chapter, we have used the story of Tamar and Judah to explore concepts related to power. We identified the complex nature of the goals of both Tamar and Judah. Given their culture, goals, restricted communication, the win-lose nature of their relationship of interdependence, their power currencies, and the seeming imbalance of power between them, we have a better understanding of why the story unfolded as it did. The story illuminates for our own time the importance of understanding the many variables that influence the course of conflict and the wisdom of exploring our own power options. Power is neither good nor bad; it is a reality of human interaction and our choices determine whether it shall be used for good or evil.

Theological Reflection on Genesis 38:1–30

The story of Judah and Tamar is a complex one that involves cultural norms and expectations, human tragedy and unfulfilled promises, power, deception, and injustice. Tamar's act of deception is not ordinarily praiseworthy. Yet in her social context whereby a brother-in-law is not given to her in marriage, her deed becomes understandable as an act of self-preservation and security. Her future is dependent on marrying, and she has no power over Judah with respect to his decision not to give Shelah to her in marriage. Judah, for his part, acknowledges the wrong he has done to Tamar that precipitated her deception. Both Judah and Tamar show us the reality of the human condition in the midst of social constraints that involved both genders in an ancient world.

In Sum: Grace in the Wilderness

In the midst of power, cultural norms, and special pressure, grace abounds. With respect to Judah, grace enables him to admit that Tamar is more in the right than he is. Through his admission, he reclaims his integrity — at least partially. Judah does *not* blame Tamar, even though she did deceive him. Tamar, for her part, had the graced creativity and cleverness to care for herself in a culture that made her dependent on the male gender for survival. She does not point the finger at Judah, but simply lets the truth emerge. Both characters, in conflict with their social and religious culture, are graced in the midst of events that befall them. Grace works through the events: Tamar is blessed with not only one but two sons, Judah's third son Shelah remains alive and free to take a wife of his own choosing, and Judah through Tamar's and his two sons has built up his son Er's legacy and family.

From a communication perspective, a grace moment is present in Tamar's use of her power resource — her knowledge of the law. Despite the great imbalance of power, she used both her knowledge of the law and her intelligence to analyze the situation and leverage it, so that she was not defeated by the enormous resources that Judah had at his disposal. Though Tamar was not aware of the model of how to wield "influence without authority," she managed to influence the course of her own life and the life of future generations.

Reflection Questions:
Can You Now...?

1. Explain the religious and cultural norms pertaining to marriage in ancient Israel?

2. Describe prostitution as it was understood in ancient Israel?

3. Illustrate the difference between power as a possession and power as a relationship?

4. Identify power bases you personally possess with different people in your life? Give an example of how you have used them.

5. Explain a relationship within your family using the theory of social exchange?

6. Apply the "Model of Influence" to Maria's situation as she discusses changing her major with her parents?

7. Give two examples of how you have achieved a goal by using different types of compliance tactics.

Additional Resources

+ Watch the film *Invictus*, a drama that describes Nelson Mandela's efforts to influence the polarized South African society after his election (Warner Brothers, 2009). In what ways do "identity goals" contribute to the conflicts in the movie?

+ What sources of power does Mandela have, and how does he use them in various interactions?

+ What sources of power does François have, and how does he use them?

+ Can you apply the model of "influence without authority" to the movie?

+ Read the account in Exodus 1:15–2:10 in which Pharaoh decreed that all newborn Hebrew boys should be killed. Although Pharaoh possessed legitimate, reward, and coercive power resources, the women in this story — the Hebrew midwives and Miriam — recognized their own power resources. What elements of this chapter illustrate how these women exercised power resources and obtained their own goals even though they had no authority and a very uneven playing field?

+ The film *Erin Brockovich* tells the story of how the resourcefulness of a single mother led to the biggest settlement on record for a civil class action lawsuit. As you watch the film, list the various forces of power and how they are being used. You may want to read details about the actual court case online at *www.lawbuzz.com/famous_trials/erin_brockovich/erin_brockovich_ch1.htm#preface.*

Additional Reading

Boulding, Kenneth. *The Three Faces of Power.* Newbury Park, Calif.: Sage Publications, 1990.

Cohen, Allan R., and David L. Bradford. *Influence without Authority.* 2nd ed. New York: John Wiley & Sons, 1995.

Mayer, Bernard. "Power and Conflict." In *The Dynamics of Conflict Resolution: A Practitioner's Guide.* San Francisco, Calif.: Jossey-Bass, 2000, 50–70.

SUSANNA

Third-Party Intervention
(Daniel 13:1–64 / Susanna 1:1–64)

*Then Susanna cried out with a loud voice, and said, "O eternal God,
you know what is secret and are aware of all things before they come
to be; you know that these men have given false evidence against me.
And now I am to die, though I have done none of the wicked things
that they have charged against me!"*

*The Lord heard her cry. Just as she was being led off to execution,
God stirred up the holy spirit of a young lad named Daniel, and he
shouted with a loud voice, "I want no part in shedding this woman's
blood!"*

*All the people turned to him and asked, "What is this you are
saying?" Taking his stand among them he said, "Are you such fools,
O Israelites, as to condemn a daughter of Israel without examination
and without learning the facts? Return to court, for these men have
given false evidence against her." (Dan. 13:42–49)*

A Biblical Interpretation of the Book of Susanna
(Chapter 13 of the Greek Version of Daniel)

A righteous woman of exquisite beauty, married and faithful to her husband,
Susanna falls prey to two elders of the Israelite community whose lust for her
drives them to attempt to rape her.[1] Susanna refuses their advances, shouts
out to protect herself, but falls victim to the elders' malicious lies about
her. She is almost stoned to death by the community because the people
believe the elders' fictitious story instead of listening to Susanna's story and
gathering the appropriate information that would acquit her of the charge
of adultery.

Clearly the story of Susanna is about power, gender, and coalitions aimed
against an honest woman who refused to participate in a sexual act that
would "cool" the lust of two supposedly respectable men in the Israelite
community — two "elders" — but would cost her her life and bring shame
upon her entire household.[2] Only through the shrewdness of Daniel, another
male in the community who outsmarts the other two male elders, is the life

and reputation of Susanna and her entire household spared. Daniel separately interrogates the two elders with one simple, direct question, "Under what tree did you see them/catch them being intimate with each other?" (vv. 54, 58). Their varying answers brings truth to the fore, and he and Susanna prevail against human wickedness.

The story of Susanna in Daniel 13 appears in Greek but not in Hebrew manuscripts, and most modern editions of the Bible include the story among the apocryphal/Deuterocanonical books. Although the main focus of the story is on Susanna, at the end of the narrative Daniel emerges as a young wisdom figure. The setting of the story is Babylon, where the Israelites are living in exile. The story itself, however, was written during the Hellenistic period sometime after the death of Alexander the Great in 323 B.C.E. The text reflects these time periods, especially the time of the Israelite exile.

Daniel 13 shows particular concern for the Israelite people, namely, how they are going to maintain their integrity while living in diaspora among an alien people. Susanna's community appears to be fairly wealthy and politically stable; it gives no evidence of any kind of suffering endured while in exile. The wickedness of the elders, however, gives evidence of social corruption still existent within the community even after its exile. Typical of other Hellenistic narratives, the main female character — in this case, Susanna — represents the Israelite community threatened and/or under attack. In the case of Daniel 13, Susanna represents a community plagued by internal problems.

From a literary perspective, the narrative can be divided into nine units:

13:1–4	Description of Susanna and her family background
13:5–6	Description of the two elders
13:7–12	The elders' encounter with Susanna
13:13–14	The plot of the elders
13:15–27	The elders' attempt to rape Susanna
13:28–46	The elders' testimony against Susanna
13:47–51	Daniel's address to the community
13:52–59	Confrontation of the elders
13:60–64	The response of the community and family to Susanna's vindication

Description of Susanna and Her Family Background (Daniel 13:1–4)

The Babylonian setting for the story of Susanna is a beautiful garden adjoining the house of Joakim, a wealthy man (vv. 1, 4). In the opening verses of the narrative we are introduced to Susanna, the story's main character, and her family. Susanna, the daughter of a man named Hilkiah, is a very beautiful woman who is married to Joakim (v. 2). Susanna, whose name means "lily," is not only physically beautiful but also spiritually beautiful: she loves the Lord (v. 2)[3] and is trained in the law. Her parents are also righteous (v. 3). Furthermore, Joakim is very well respected among the Jews and is often sought out because "he was the most honored of them all" (v. 4). Pictured here is a well-to-do model family living an upright life in the midst of exiled Jews in Babylon. What is about to happen to Susanna will shock her and her family as well as the entire community.

Description of the Two Elders (Daniel 13:5–6)

In Israel, elders were respected for their wisdom, and so two elders within the community in exile have been appointed judges. They were part of the town's administration, they served as advisors on various issues (see Jer. 18:18; Ezek. 7:26), and they intervened in crisis situations (Lev. 4:15; Deut. 21:1–9).[4] As judges, these elders had authority within the community.[5] One would assume that these elder-judges would lead righteous lives, but much to the surprise of their community, they were seen as corrupt in the eyes of the Lord, who said of them, "Wickedness came forth from Babylon, from elders who were judges who were supposed to govern the people" (v. 6). Both of these men frequented Joakim's house, where they often tried their cases (v. 6), and thus they were familiar with Joakim's household and its daily routine.

The Elders' Encounter with Susanna (Daniel 13:7–12)

With all the main characters now introduced, the story's drama unfolds. Often at the noon hour, when the people with cases departed, Susanna would go for a walk in Joakim's garden (v. 7). At the mere sight of her, the two elders become lustful; however, they try to suppress their feelings since they are judges and she, of course, is a married woman (vv. 8–9). The elders' attempt to remain virtuous fails and their passion for Susanna intensifies. They lust after her to the point where they admit to each other that they desire to seduce her (v. 11). The narrator comments, "Day after day they watched eagerly for her" (v. 12), indicating how enthralled the two elders are with Susanna.

The Plot of the Elders (Daniel 13:13–14)

Passion, lust, and infatuation all lead to a premeditated plot on the elders' part to seduce Susanna when she is in the garden alone (vv. 13–14). Thus we see unbridled passion exert power over the sense of mission associated with the elders' office as judges.

The Elders' Attempt to Rape Susanna (Daniel 13:15–27)

The elders' plot takes shape in verses 15 through 27 when one hot day Susanna decides to bathe in the garden (v. 15). Sending her two maids off to fetch some olive oil and ointments, Susanna is now in the garden alone, so she thinks, with the gates closed (v. 17). The elders, who had been hiding in the garden, now approach Susanna, confess their burning desire for her, and attempt to rape her (vv. 18–21). Susanna finds herself "trapped" when the elders threaten to tell everyone that she was with a "young man" if she does not yield to them: "If I do this, it will mean death for me; if I do not, I cannot escape your hands" (v. 22).

With courage and virtue intact, Susanna refuses the elders' advances, deciding that the lesser of two evils would be to fall victim to their malicious story that they will spread about her to the entire community. For Susanna this choice is far better than committing adultery, a sin in the eyes of God (v. 23).

The story reaches its fever pitch in verses 24 through 27. Susanna cries out in a loud voice, the elders shout against her, and all the servants in the house rush to Susanna's aid only to find themselves feeling very much ashamed when they hear the story the elders relay about Susanna having had sexual relations with a young man. Thus, Susanna has supposedly brought shame upon herself and, more importantly, shame upon Joakim and his entire household, including the servants (vv. 26–27).

The Elders' Testimony against Susanna (Daniel 13:28–46)

Supposedly guilty of adultery, Susanna now goes "to trial." In Joakim's own house, the wicked elders bring their case against Susanna, and Susanna now has to appear before the community who will hear and try her case (vv. 28–30). Accompanied by her family, she arrives before the community, veiled. The two elders assert their power once again by ordering Susanna to be unveiled. Such an action is for their own selfish purposes: the two elders want to "feast their eyes on her beauty" (v. 32). Susanna's family weeps.

The unjust testimony of the two elders begins in verse 34. First, the elders lay hands on Susanna's head as Susanna gazes heavenward, trusting her God to come to her aid (v. 35).[6] Then the two scoundrels begin to relate their false story to the community members now assembled together at Joakim's house. Their story indicts Susanna, and no one dares to question them about the details of their story "because they were elders of the people and judges"; thus those assembled together believe the elders' story and condemn Susanna to death (v. 43).

Thus far, we see the virtuous Susanna standing in stark contrast to the villainous elders. We also see the shortsightedness of the people who defer to the testimony of the elders without making any attempt to gather any facts about the case. Clearly, Susanna appears before the community as a woman bereft of dignity and powerless in the face of false testimony. Sadly, no one speaks up on her behalf as a character witness nor does anyone press for further information or details about the case. In the community's eyes, Susanna has brought shame upon Joakim, his whole household, herself, and the community at large. For these reasons and a supposedly adulterous affair, she must be put to death (v. 41b).

Susanna's response to her accusers and the community is instructive. Instead of lashing out at the crowd gathered or speaking out in her own defense, she turns the entire situation over to God: "O eternal God, you know what is secret and are aware of all things before they come to be; you know that these men have given false evidence against me. And now I am to die, though I have done none of the wicked things that they have charged against me!" (vv. 42–43).

Susanna's address to God is prayer. Very simply and candidly, she tells God about the things that matter in her life and, in this case, her desperate situation, which is heading for a devastating outcome. In verse 44, the narrator makes a simple statement: "The Lord heard her cry." The God of Israel who heard the cry of the captive Israelites suffering unjustly and who raised up Moses to set them free from Egyptian bondage (Exod. 2:23–25; 3) has once again heard the cry of the poor and acts accordingly. As in the time of the Exodus when God raised up Moses, God now raises up Daniel to act on Susanna's behalf: "Just as she was being led off to execution God stirred up the holy spirit of a young lad named Daniel and he shouted with a loud voice, 'I want no part in shedding this woman's blood!' " (v. 46).

As in the case of Moses, God works through human beings to bring about justice. The reference to Daniel's "holy spirit" being stirred up indicates that he was a righteous person. The notion that he is a "young" lad is significant. Wisdom rests neither in the elders nor in the community; rather, wisdom rests with a "young lad," a change from the typical wisdom paradigm that associates age with wisdom.

Daniel's Address to the Community (Daniel 13:47–51)

Daniel's outburst triggers a response from the community, "What is this you are saying?" (v. 47), but Daniel puts everyone assembled on notice. He takes his stand among them, upbraids them with a rhetorical question, points out the fallacy of the elders' testimony, and in doing so, he defends Susanna: "Are you such fools, O Israelites, as to condemn a daughter of Israel without examination and without learning the facts? Return to court, for these men have given false evidence against her" (v. 48). Interestingly, Daniel refers to the elders as "these men." He does not use the title of their offices — elders, judges — when speaking about them. Perhaps he is indirectly indicating that they are not worthy of such titles.

In what may seem a somewhat surprising development, Daniel is recognized by the other elders in the community as having the "standing" of an elder, one whose wisdom is not age-related but has been divinely bestowed (v. 50). Daniel's plan is to examine the two scoundrels separately (v. 51).

Confrontation of the Elders (Daniel 13:52–59)

Daniel's confrontation with the two elders in verses 52 through 59 is astute and somewhat humorous. He begins his examination by addressing the first elder and disclosing the elder's past insidious crimes: "You old relic of wicked days, your sins have now come home, which you have committed in the past, pronouncing unjust judgments, condemning the innocent and acquitting the guilty, though the Lord said, 'You shall not put an innocent and righteous person to death'" (vv. 52–53). Daniel brings to the fore the fact that this "old relic" of an elder who has accused Susanna has an unsavory past himself. Daniel then separates the two elders and questions them one by one. When he asks the first elder under which tree he saw Susanna and the young man being intimate, the elder's response is "under a mastic tree" (v. 54).

Daniel then confronts the second elder, revealing his unsavory past actions as well, especially with other women with whom he has been intimate because they feared him! Daniel's comment— "but a daughter of Judah would not tolerate your wickedness," referring to Susanna — sheds light on the strength of character and courage Susanna possessed when she was approached by the two elders. Daniel then asks the same question of the second elder, and the elder responds "Under an evergreen oak." This response indicts both elders and acquits Susanna of her crime (vv. 55–59). Thus, the young lad Daniel has acted rightfully as an elder and judge appointed by God and not by the community.

The Response of the Community and Family to Susanna's Vindication (Daniel 13:60–64)

In response to Daniel's search for the truth, the first action of the community is to bless God, acknowledging that God saves those who maintain hope in the Divine (v. 60). The second act of the community is to mete out justice to the two elders who are put to death (vv. 61–62). The narrative draws to a close with Susanna's parents, husband, and relatives praising God for Susanna and for her acquittal (v. 63). Daniel, for his part, has gained a great reputation for righteousness among the people (v. 64). Justice has been served, truth has prevailed, and two citizens of the community remain models of integrity.

The entire situation would not have turned out as well as it did, however, if Daniel had not been able to break through the coalitions that had been formed between the elders and within the community, and if Susanna and Daniel had not been able to exercise such effective communication skills to counter the elders.

Looking through the Communication Lens

The story of Susanna reads like a melodrama. Susanna, a virtuous damsel, is trapped by two evil villains. When she cries out to God in her distress, God inspires a hero, Daniel, to rescue her, and the brave, skilled Daniel saves her life and restores her reputation. If we dismiss this familiar plot without further analysis, however, we lose the opportunity to further enrich our understanding of conflict.

As with the story of Tamar, and most narratives of conflict, power is a key player, but this story introduces a new dimension. The villains adopt the dynamic of building *coalitions,* which oil the wheels of their bullying. Next, Daniel's verbal panache opens the door for a discussion of some of the communication skills instrumental in the outcome of this and other conflict narratives. Finally, Daniel takes on the role of a third-party advocate, which provides an opportunity to explore the advantages and disadvantages of third-party interventions and to revisit the importance of interpersonal linkages.

The Use of Power Bases

The villains wanted Susanna to acquiesce to rape. They lusted for her, wanted her to let them "lie down with her," and wanted her to keep quiet. In an earlier chapter, we introduced the concept of *power bases.* Susanna faced two judges who had multiple power bases, with the most obvious being *coercive* power. If Susanna disobeyed, the assembly would try her as an adulteress and, based on the false testimony of the judges, stone her to death. As judges within the culture, the villains had both *legitimate* and *referent* power. People held them in respect and listened to them because of their appointed positions as judges and as elders. While these multiple power bases were strong power currencies, Susanna initially was not bereft of her own sources of power. At the story's onset, we learn she had referent power: "Her parents were righteous and had trained their daughter according to the law of Moses" (Dan. 13:3). Joakim, her husband, was very rich, and "Jews used to come to him because he was most honored of them all" (Dan. 13:4). The two judges, however, formed a coalition against her, which tilted the balance of power.

The law required two witnesses to convict a person of adultery. When the judges formed an alliance against Susanna, her only power base — referent power based on the respect or friendship of the community for her — was overwhelmed. However, she did not endorse their power: she did not submit to their attempted rape. At this point a closer look at alliances or coalitions may be helpful.

The Positive and Negative Use of Coalitions

A coalition is an alliance of two or more participants in a conflict against an opposing party or parties. Coalitions are common in many types of relationships, including those familiar family disputes where two family members "gang up" on a third. Examples would include two siblings uniting against a third, a parent forming a coalition with a child against the other parent, and a grandparent forming a coalition with a grandchild against a parent. Coalitions can also form in organizations wherein two departments ally themselves against a third department and on playgrounds when children take sides in disputes. When a family faces a serious conflict, such as an impending divorce, family members typically choose up sides.

People form coalitions for positive as well as negative reasons. Parties may want to "share conflict information, provide support and understanding for those involved in a conflict, give a sense of belonging to a larger cause, or gain power"[7] One only has to look to international conflicts to see an array of coalitions that can change in the face of newly emerging situations.

In our story, the most obvious reason for coalition formation was that it changed the balance of power. One elder's word against that of Susanna would not have held up in court. For such a case to go forward, the law required at least two witnesses. Together, the judges tried to bully Susanna into yielding.

> *Can you think of instances in your own life where coalitions have been established in a situation of conflict? In your own family, work setting, or current living situation, have you seen people forming bonds with each other in order to gain power?*

The Use of Communication Skills by Susanna and Daniel

Given the dynamics in play against Susanna, the outcome of this story is truly remarkable. How did she and Daniel manage to dominate the elders and win over the community?

Communication experts Judee Burgoon, Michelle Johnson, and Pamela Koch point out that aggression is one of the most consistent factors people use to dominate others, though not the only means.[8] Dominic Infante and Andrew Rancer identify several methods of communication used in attempts to dominate: verbal aggression, assertiveness, and argumentativeness.[9] *Verbal aggression* involves standing up for one's needs but in a way that violates the rights of others and includes attacks on the opponent's identity and self-esteem.[10] *Assertiveness* means standing up for one's own needs without violating the rights of others. Infante and Rancer view *verbal argumentativeness* as a subset of assertiveness that involves attacking issues, but not the character, identity, or self-esteem of the other person.[11]

Turning to each of the characters, we see the judges' use of verbal aggression with an added component of threat: "If you refuse, we will testify against you that a young man was with you, and this was why you sent your maids away" (Dan. 13:21). And they made good on their threat at the trial: "a young man, who was hiding there, came to her and lay with her" (Dan. 13:38). Verbal aggressiveness can be persuasive, especially when combined with credibility. The account gives evidence of their persuasiveness: "Because they were elders of the people and judges, the assembly believed them and condemned her to death" (13:41).

Susanna's assertive response at the time of the trial, however, is also noteworthy. She stood up for herself without attacking the character of the judges in her call to God:

O eternal God, you know what is secret and are aware of all things before that come to be; you know that these men have given false evidence against me. And now I am to die, though I have done none of the wicked things that they have charged against me. (13:43)

Susanna's appeal simply stated the facts; a more aggressive response would have reviled the judges. God then responded by "stirring the holy spirit of Daniel" (13:45).

Daniel's initial response was verbally aggressive and also argumentative, in that he presented facts supporting his case that the judges gave false evidence. He developed his argument by demonstrating inconsistency in the two different stories of the judges. Verbal aggressiveness emerged when he laced his words with personal attacks, "You old relic of wicked days" (Dan. 13:52) and "you offspring of Canaan" (Dan. 13:56).

Dominance also works through *nonverbal* communication. Burgoon has proposed at least eight nonverbal strategies to dominate, some of which we can observe in this story (see the list on the following page).[12]

In our own lives, we sometimes use these behaviors automatically, but we need to be aware that they can also be used strategically to negotiate through conflict. The story of Susanna clearly demonstrates the first nonverbal dominance strategy, that of threat, when the judges encroached on Susanna's primary territory of her garden. By enlarging their own space, they made themselves appear more threatening. "When the maids had gone out, the two elders got up and ran to her" (13:19). A physical invasion of territory is a classic expression of a desire to dominate.

The judges also demonstrated "expectancy violations" by entering into Susanna's private space. This violation demonstrated an unexpected cultural and social behavior and contributed to their dominance. And the judges made use of "activity," as shown in their dynamic, expressive, and fast-paced messages of confidence, "Look, the garden doors are shut, and no one can see us. We are burning with desire for you; so give your consent, and lie with us. If you refuse, we will testify against you that a young man was with you, and this was why you sent your maids away" (13:20–21). How fearful Susanna must have been to be confronted by both verbal and nonverbal attacks!

Daniel also incorporated nonverbal strategies of dominance. His harsh language — "and he shouted with a loud voice, 'I want no part in shedding this woman's blood' " — interrupted the court's routine and violated its expectations of proper behavior. Clearly, dynamic, expressive, and fast-paced messages helped his case as he accused the first judge:

You old relic of wicked days, your sins have now come home, which you have committed in the past, pronouncing untrue judgments, condemning the innocent and acquitting the guilty, though the Lord said, "You shall not put an innocent and righteous person to death." Now then, if you really saw this woman, tell me this: under what tree did you see them being intimate with each other? (Dan. 13:53–54)

Nonverbal Communication Strategies That Contribute to Dominance

1. *Threat, which consists of physical size or actions that enlarge one's total personage or territory, threat gestures, deep voices, erect postures, and the like that imply the ability to inflict physical harm*

2. *Elevation, which includes physical height, sitting or standing postures, and occupying locations that convey symbolic hierarchical cues and accrue advantages of surveillance and protection*

3. *Initiation and precedence, which include initiating conversation, initiating touch and interactional distance, determining topics of conversation, leading rather than following, and front rather than rear placements*

4. *Expectancy violations, which entail the prerogative to engage in all manner of nonnormative and unexpected behavior, such as adopting closer or farther distances than normal*

5. *Privileged access, which includes access to scarce resources, preferential treatment, possession of status symbols, ability to impose on others' time, ability to intrude on others' space, and the like*

6. *Activity, which combines dynamic, expressive, and fast-paced messages of confidence and authority*

7. *Relaxation, which connotes the privilege to be at rest while others must be attentive, to "drop one's guard," including postural and vocal relaxation that exceeds that of more subordinate individuals*

8. *Task performance cues, which encompass indicators of social status, rank, prestige, or task-related ability that enhance an individual's prestige and likely influence in a work group*

(Judee K. Burgoon, Michelle L. Johnson and Pamela T. Koch,
"Nature and Measurement of Interpersonal Dominance,"
Communication Monographs 65 [1998], 318)

What Role Did Credibility Play?

Thus far, we have looked at this conflict in terms of power currencies, coalitions, and dominance behaviors. Credibility is central to this conflict as well. In essence, the outcome depends on whether the people believe Daniel or the judges. Contemporary research views credibility as a judgment made by the receiver of a message about the sender of the message. It is composed of competence, trustworthiness, and goodwill.[13] Daniel generated more credibility than Susanna's accusers on all three dimensions.

Credibility is not a trait that an individual possesses, but rather a perception in the minds of message receivers. Initially, the judges' legitimate position as elders of the community worked in their favor: "because they were elders of the people and judges, the assembly believed them and condemned her to death" (13:41). When Daniel interrupted the proceedings to defend Susanna, he acquired a legitimate position as well: "The rest of the elders said to him, 'Come sit among us and inform us, for God has given you the standing of an elder'" (13:50–51). His credibility increased because his knowledge (of God) and expertise outweighed that of the judges.

Credibility also rests on two other primary dimensions: trustworthiness and goodwill.[14] When Daniel caught the judges in their lies, "because out of their own mouths Daniel had convicted them of bearing false witness" (13:61), he dispelled any misperceptions the people had about the judges' trustworthiness or honesty, thus enhancing his own trustworthiness. And Daniel's unselfish intervention on behalf of Susanna quickly and fully revealed his goodwill as opposed to the evil intentions of the judges.

The research of James McCroskey and Jason Teven identifies two secondary dimensions that contribute to perceptions of credibility: dynamism and sociability.[15] Dynamism encompasses how animated and energetic a person is, a quality that also contributes to dominance, as we have seen above. James Kouzes and Barry Posner point out, however, that dynamic presentation alone is not sufficient.[16] A leader must also inspire and energize followers, which Daniel does. Daniel's dynamism results in the assembly taking action against the two elders.

Sociability, another secondary dimension of conflict, relates to the sender's likeability. Psychologist Robert Cialdini identifies likeability as a means of social influence; people we like have an easier time persuading us than people we dislike or about whom we feel neutral.[17] While we do not know how Daniel might fare on a likeability scale, we can infer from the assembly's actions that the judges lost credibility as they were dubbed wicked, evil, and dishonest.

> *Political leaders face conflicts on many issues. Can you recall any newspaper accounts of recent conflicts that illustrate how political leaders use dynamism and sociability to prevail?*

The Role of Third Parties

The intervention of a third party occurs formally and informally in conflicts whenever someone outside the dispute takes a role in determining the outcome, and the types of interventions can vary according to the amount of control the differing parties have.[18] Three types of third-party intervention are possible: adjudication, mediation, and arbitration. In this story Daniel, an outsider, enters to change the course of the proceedings in an approach that is a form of adjudication. In *adjudication,* a judge or jury decides what the solution to the conflict will be. Daniel, for example, assumes a lawyer-like role and presents evidence before the assembly. Susanna has little control over the outcome.

Adjudication has the advantage of providing equal protection of the law, and to put adjudication into action, one does not need the prior agreement of the parties. One need only file a lawsuit. Rules for fairness are clearly laid down by the law, although the skill with which the rules are wielded depends on the characteristics of the third party. Typically, professionals help individuals prepare their case. One drawback is that adjudication is usually based on a win/lose assumption, which may lead to an escalation in the conflict. Moreover, decision making is taken out of the hands of the participants and put into the hands of the judge or jury, the third party.

Mediation, in contrast, typically gives a great deal of control to the participants. After the parties agree to mediation, a neutral third party helps facilitate a conversation between the parties to find areas of agreement. In mediation, the third party does not judge, make decisions, or give advice. Rather, the mediator helps the parties explore the broad range of issues (content, emotion, identity, relationship, and process) that may need addressing. Typically, when people participate in the process of making a decision through mediation, they are more willing to accept the decision than if it is imposed from outside.

Arbitration can also be used to work out areas of agreement between differing parties, but if the dispute cannot be resolved, participants agree to abide by the decision of the arbitrator. Sometimes these procedures are mixed, so that parties may try mediation, but if the dispute cannot be resolved through mediation, they may seek an arbitrator. Control leaves the hands of the parties if the arbitrator determines the outcome.

Daniel, a third party to the conflict between the judges and Susanna, entered the fray to change the balance of power. If the plot of the narrative has been dismissed as mere melodrama, we would have lost the opportunity to further enrich our understanding of conflict. Coalitions, Daniel's verbal and nonverbal communication skills, and the credibility he established were instrumental in the outcome of this narrative of conflict.

Theological Reflection on the Book of Susanna

The story of Susanna presents a portrait of two upright human beings whose courage and persistence save the life of one woman and bring justice to two men whose hidden corrupt ways shamed the Israelite community at large. Through the character of Susanna, we see the power of belief and prayer.

With her faith in God, she turns her entire situation over to God in prayer. God, in turn, acts through another human being to save her from death and to clear her of the crime of which she has been accused.

The story also shows us that the search for truth needs to be pursued courageously and persistently and that in searching for the truth all the information must be clearly presented and available, even if it involves confronting and challenging the word of those most revered and respected in a community. The story also provides us with an insightful glimpse into the human condition, specifically, how sordid people can be regardless of their holding a sacred office and how shortsighted a community can be about its own members who have been deemed "upright." Finally, the story of Susanna helps us to see that we are the keepers of one another, especially when injustice attempts to prevail over justice.

In Sum: Grace in the Wilderness

Grace is obviously at work in Daniel 13 in the character of Susanna. She is a woman of incredible integrity who is able to maintain her integrity under pressure and remain steadfast to the truth. Grace is also at work in Daniel, who, raised up by God, speaks out for the most vulnerable in the community — Susanna — a woman who has been condemned by an entire community. Only Daniel, with God's spirit, had the foresight, insight, skill, and courage to confront two revered members of the community — elders and judges — and by doing so, bring truth to light and justice to bear. Finally, through Susanna's and Daniel's choices and actions, integrity is restored to the community as a whole, which becomes a cause for blessing God and celebrating communally.

Through the communication lens, we focus on the courage and valor Daniel needed to speak truth to power. We also focus on his considerable verbal and nonverbal skills that helped him prevail over two people who seemed to have an "open and shut case." We admire his ability to change the perceptions of "truth" and to give credibility to Susanna's account, which in the end brought justice to bear on what really happened in the garden.

Reflection Questions: Can You Now...?

1. Define the various power dynamics at play in your own family? In your opinion does any single person have unexpected power? Why do you feel this way?

2. Explain what kind of power resources each of the main characters in the story — Susanna, the elders, and Daniel — possessed? How exactly did they use this power?

3. Describe a coalition you have formed recently with someone else. What was your goal? Did you use it positively or negatively?

4. With a partner, role play two employees objecting to an office-wide salary freeze with one person using verbal aggression and the other verbal argumentation?

5. Identify any nonverbal strategies of dominance used in the story of Susanna? Why were they employed?

6. Recall a time when you have been a third party to a conflict? Were you a mediator, an arbitrator, or an adjudicator? Were you effective in managing the conflict? Why or why not?

Additional Resources

+ Two Oscar-nominated movies illustrate many of the concepts in this chapter: *The Verdict* with Paul Newman and *To Kill a Mockingbird* starring Gregory Peck. In both films third-party advocates defend individuals with very limited power resources. Watch one of these films and then compare and contrast the verbal and nonverbal strategies used by the third party with those of Daniel.

+ In the account in John 8:7, Jesus intercedes as a third party on behalf of a woman accused of adultery. What nonverbal strategies, if any, of dominance does he use? What verbal strategies, if any, does he use?

Additional Reading

Cialdini, Robert. *Influence, Science and Practice.* 4th ed. Boston: Allyn and Bacon, 2001.

Rosenberg, Marshall B. *Nonviolent Communication: A Language of Life,* 2nd ed. Encenitas, Calif.: PuddleDancer Press, 2003.

7

JUDITH

Styles and Tactics

(*Judith 10–15*)

"See here, the head of Holofernes, the commander of the Assyrian army, and here is the canopy beneath which he lay in his drunken stupor. The Lord has struck him down by the hand of a woman. As the Lord lives, who has protected me in the way I went, I swear that it was my face that seduced him to his destruction, and that he committed no sin with me, to defile and shame me." (Judith 13:15–16)

A Biblical Interpretation of Judith 10–15

Because the tale of Judith is one of such high drama, it inspired the imaginations of painters like Caravaggio, Donatello, Botticelli, and Artemisia Gentileschi; composers such as Mozart and Scarlatti; and writers such as Chaucer and Dante. The vividly told story that appears in the Bible recounts how the pious and very beautiful widow, Judith, saved her people. The story opens as Nebuchadnezzar, king of the Assyrians, leaves his capital city of Nineveh to wage war against Arphaxad, King of the Medes (Jud. 1:1–6). Nebuchadnezzar sends messengers to all of his allies in the east and the west, petitioning them to join forces with him against Arphaxad (1:7–12). The allies in the east rally to his appeal, but the allies in the west refuse to join him in battle. These allies see Nebuchadnezzar as merely one man and they do not fear him (1:11). Nebuchadnezzar defeats Arphaxad (1:13–16) and then proceeds to avenge himself in the west, placing Holofernes, his best general, in command of the military operations. Any nation refusing to submit to Holofernes is destined for slaughter and looting (2:1–3).

Holofernes carries out Nebuchadnezzar's plans, destroying the other nations' sacred places and forcing the people to worship Nebuchadnezzar alone (2:14–3:10). These events send chills of fear down the spine of the people of Judea, causing the people to enter into prayer and penance as they petition their God to save them from the Assyrians (4:1–15). Holofernes, who decides to wage war against the Israelites, is warned by Achior, the leader of the Ammonites, not to pursue this plan. Achior maintains that the Assyrians would indeed be defeated by the Israelites, who have their

God on their side (5:1–24). Such news disturbs Holofernes, who rejects Achior's advice. Holofernes turns Achior over to the Israelites who, instead of putting him to death, praise him highly for his efforts at staving off the battle between the Assyrians and the Israelites (6:1–21).

Holofernes pursues his original plan and orders his entire army to move against Bethulia, where many Israelites are residing (7:1–18). The Israelites sink into great distress before such a formidable enemy (7:19–32) until the widow Judith rises up to their aid (8:1–9:14).

The focus of this chapter (Judith 10 through 15) describes how Judith triumphs over Holofernes and thus saves her people from the Assyrians. The account begins in the town of Bethulia, which is under siege by the Assyrian general Holofernes. Judith, having fervently prayed to God to deliver Israel, exchanges her widow's garb for her most beautiful clothes and jewelry. According to her plan, she leaves Bethulia and is seized by an Assyrian patrol that takes her into custody because she feigns to have information that would help Holofernes capture the Israelites without losing any men.

She begins by flattering Holofernes, "Not only do human beings serve him [Nebuchadnezzar] because of you, but also the animals of the field and the cattle and the birds of the air will live, because of your power" (11:7). Holofernes later sends for Judith so that he might seduce her. Judith arrives, but drinks only what her maid had prepared for her while Holofernes drinks "more than he had ever drunk in one day since he was born" (12:20). With Holofernes was "stretched out on his bed for he was dead drunk," Judith grabs his sword and with two strikes, she beheads him. The death of Holofernes becomes proof that God is on the side of the Israelites who go on to defeat the Assyrians.

Interestingly so, the events of the book of Judith seem to take place in the span of a couple of months. The general setting of the book, however, seems to cover several centuries from the time of the Assyrians (eighth century B.C.E.) to the time of the Persians (sixth to fourth centuries B.C.E.). Thus, the narrative as written does not reflect the actual historicity of the time period. Benedikt Otzen notes:

> A dominant problem, not least in earlier treatments of the book of Judith, is the description of historical and geographical conditions as a background to the events in Palestine. On the face of it this description is totally confused: the enemy of the Israelites is the Assyrians (eighth or seventh century B.C.E.), their king is the Babylonian Nebuchadnezzar (early sixth century B.C.E.), who resides in Nineveh, the Assyrian city that was devastated before his enthronement. His principal concern is a protracted war with Arphaxad, the king of the Medes, a war that is both unknown and unlikely.[1]

Otzen notes further that "all of the events of the book of Judith in later chapters are assigned to the time after the Babylonian exile (late sixth century

B.C.E.), and further details seem to take us far down into the Persian epoch (fourth century B.C.E.)."[2] Even the topography of the book is unclear. The geography of Palestine is obscure, and Holofernes's campaign in Palestine is not clearly defined.[3] Furthermore, Otzen points out that "we know nothing about the siege of a town called Bethulia, and the Assyrians drew near to Jerusalem only in 701 B.C.E. under the king Sennacherib (2 Kings 18–19)."[4] Thus, the story of Judith as it appears in the Bible today, like so many other biblical stories, reflects the creative imagination of its authors and editors who took some historical and geographical data and created a marvelous tale that spoke to the people and communities of its day and that continues to find a hearing today. Finally, like the story of Susanna (Daniel 13), the story of Judith appears in the apocryphal/deuterocanonical books in Greek but not in Hebrew manuscripts.

Chapters 10 through 15 of the book of Judith capture the essence of human courage and heroism in the midst of life-threatening conflicts. This account is composed of eleven units:

10:1–10	Judith's preparations to meet Holofernes
10:11–19	Judith's capture by the Assyrian patrol
10:20–23	Judith's encounter with Holofernes
11:1–23	Initial exchange between Judith and Holofernes
12:1–20	Further exchange between Holofernes and Judith
13:1–10a	Description of the beheading of Holofernes
13:10b–20	Judith's return to Bethulia
14:1–10	Judith's instructions to her people
14:11–19	Discovery of the death of Holofernes
15:1–7	The Flight of the Assyrians
15:8–13	Israelites' celebration of victory

Judith's Preparations to Meet Holofernes (Judith 10:1–10)

Earlier in the book of Judith we encountered Judith's people, the Israelites, living under the threat of the Assyrians. Judith, aware of her people's plight and well respected by her community, makes the decision to act on behalf of those whom she loves. Having prayed to God for guidance and strength (Jud. 9), Judith assumes a new image. Fresh from prayer and seemingly empowered with a renewed spirit and a new sense of self, Judith sheds her widow's garments, takes off her sackcloth, and beautifies herself in anticipation of meeting the Assyrian leaders, in particular, Holofernes. As a woman living in a time of international conflict, Judith uses the expression of power that she possesses as a woman — her beauty. Her appearance resembles a queen, complete with a tiara (vv. 2–4).

Judith's change of attire from mourning to celebration anticipates the glorious fate of her people: a victory over the Assyrians. In the midst of her plans to "entice" the men whom she will encounter, Judith remains mindful of her religious practices and commitment to them. Her maid carries a skin of wine, a bag full of roasted grain, dried fig cakes, fine bread, and some dishes so that Judith can continue to observe the Jewish dietary laws while living among the Assyrians in one of their camps (v. 5). In the face of impending danger, Judith remains faithful to her Jewish way of life, which is a testimony to her centeredness in God and the courage she draws from that experience.

Judith's piety and rootedness in God becomes even more evident in verses 6–8. Upon going out to the town gate, Judith and her maid encounter Uzziah, one of the town's magistrates, standing with two elders, Chabris and Charmis. The three men remark favorably about Judith's transformed presence and extend a blessing upon her: "May the God of our ancestors grant you favor and fulfill your plans, so that the people of Israel may glory and Jerusalem may be exalted" (v. 8a). Judith gives no response; instead, she simply bows down to God (v. 8b). This gesture expresses not only the homage being paid to God but, more importantly, her complete trust in God.

Judith wastes no time in setting out to do the task she intended on behalf of her people. A woman with a mission, she commands the king and the elders to open the gate of the town for her so that she can begin her work. The gates are opened, and as the men of the town watch, Judith and her maid leave the town, go down the mountain, pass through the valley, and fade into the distance (vv. 9–10). In the midst of a male-dominated, warring culture, the men of the town and we as readers have just watched in cinematographic fashion the birth of a heroine whose adventures have just begun.

Judith's Capture by the Assyrian Patrol (Judith 10:11–19)

Judith's first adventure of her mission begins in the valley where she and her maid encounter an Assyrian patrol, which takes them into custody and begins questioning Judith. In rapid succession, the Assyrians pose three questions aimed at establishing Judith's identity, her locale, and her destination. These questions are typical for an army patrol, but Judith's curious response sets the stage for her next ploy. Instead of saying that she is a daughter of the Jewish people or a daughter of Israel, she states that she is "a daughter of the Hebrews" (v. 12). Both in the book of Judith (see 2:11, 14:18) and elsewhere in the Hebrew text, "Hebrew" is often the term a foreigner uses for an Israelite. The Israelites preferred to be called "Hebrews," and for the Assyrians, the term "Hebrews" had positive connotations, recalling the time of Israel's enslavement (see Gen. 40:15; Exod. 1:15, 2:6, 3:18). Judith makes a series of deceptive statements to the patrol, the greatest of which involves Holofernes, the commander of the army. Supposedly she knows a way that he and his men can capture all the hill country without losing one person in battle (v. 13).

Verses 14 through 16 describe how Judith captures the thought and eye of the patrol soldiers, who comment on how her life-saving tactics will bode well for her when she meets Holofernes. The patrol encourages her to hurry down to Holofernes's tent. Carey Moore notes how the Assyrian patrol's response to Judith serves to foreshadow the fate of the Assyrians as a whole: "Judith's disarming beauty has just claimed its first victims among the enemy. Now the Assyrians are only captivated by Judith; later they will be killed by her."[5] Little does the Assyrian patrol realize what lies ahead for their leader and their people, and ironically, Judith — the one captured — has now, to some degree, not only ravished but also captured her captors.

Judith's journey to and arrival at Holofernes's tent occurs in verses 17 through 19. Having started out with only her maid, they are now accompanied by a hundred Assyrians, who lead the two women into Holofernes's camp, where they are greeted with much excitement. The Assyrian people at the camp marvel at Judith's beauty as she stands outside Holofernes's tent, waiting to be admitted to meet with the general. They also "admire" the Israelites for having women such as Judith (v. 19a). Their astonishment leads to a rhetorical question and a decisive decision: "Who can despise these people, who have women like this among them? It is not wise to leave one of their men alive, for if we let them go they will be able to beguile the whole world!" (v. 19b).

The irony here is that while the Assyrians fear that the whole world would be beguiled by the Israelites, especially through their women, the fact of the matter is that the Assyrians have already been beguiled by Judith, and indirectly by the Israelites, and the Assyrians do not even realize their sorry state. Her intelligence and her beauty have disguised her real mission.

Judith's Encounter with Holofernes (Judith 10:20–23)

The long-awaited encounter between Judith and Holofernes occurs in verses 20 through 23. Holofernes is depicted as a man living in regal splendor: he has servants and — unlike what we would expect of a general, namely, to be at a command post or out among his soldiers — he is "resting on his bed under a canopy that was woven with purple and gold, emeralds and other precious stones" (v. 21). He rises from his bed and goes out to the front of his tent to meet Judith, with "silver lamps carried before him" (v. 22).[6]

A man of wealth and power, Holofernes commands respect, and Judith responds in kind when she first meets him: she prostrates herself and does obeisance to him. Like the Assyrian patrol, Holofernes and his servants marvel at Judith's beauty (v. 23a), and as soon as Judith prostrates herself, the servants of Holofernes raise her up (v. 23b). We see that Judith has not only beauty but also grace and charm. Before someone who holds her life in the balance, Judith conducts herself with respect and deference. She appears to be impressed by Holofernes, and he seems to be captivated by her. Thus begins the seductive dance of conflict between these two characters.

Initial Exchange between Judith and Holofernes (Judith 11:1–23)

Following their initial encounter, Judith and Holofernes share an exchange. Holofernes begins the conversation with a word of reassurance for Judith, telling her that he has never hurt anyone who has chosen to serve Nebuchadnezzar (v. 1). Interestingly, Judith seems to have won the trust of Holofernes, and he thinks that Judith has defected from her own people (v. 3). Holofernes also informs Judith that her people are responsible for striking up animosity between themselves and the Assyrians because they have slighted him (v. 2). Before Judith can respond, Holofernes inquires as to why she has fled from her people and has "come over" to the Assyrians, and then he offers her another word of encouragement and consolation: "Take courage! You will live tonight and ever after. No one will hurt you. Rather, all will treat you well, as they do the servants of my lord King Nebuchadnezzar" (v. 4). No words could have been truer for Judith, spoken by a man who has no idea of his own gruesome fate soon to take place in his own tent!

To Holofernes's brief comment, Judith offers a long response (vv. 5–19). The first part of Judith's reply is filled with deception and tongue-in-cheek irony:

> Accept the words of your slave, and let your servant speak in your presence. I will say nothing false to my lord this night. If you follow out the words of your servant, God will accomplish something through you, and my lord will not fail to achieve his purposes. By the life of Nebuchadnezzar, king of the whole earth, and by the power of him who has sent you to direct every living being! Not only do human beings serve him because of you, but also the animals of the field and the cattle and the birds of the air will live, because of your power, under Nebuchadnezzar and all his house. For we have heard of your wisdom and skill, and it is reported throughout the whole world that you alone are the best in the whole kingdom, the most informed and the most astounding in military strategy. (vv. 5–8)

Judith does speak in truth to Holofernes. If he does follow out her words, God will indeed accomplish something through him: liberation of the Israelite people from the threat of the Assyrians — after Holofernes is dead and his head is displayed! Truly, when Judith says "My lord will not fail to achieve his purposes," she is not talking about Holofernes as her lord as Holofernes suspects; rather, she is talking about her "Lord" — her God. The word "lord," then, is a *double entendre*. In truth, like the Israelites, the creatures of the natural world will live in peace when Holofernes and the Assyrians are no longer a threat. Indeed, Judith's words are deceptive yet truthful, straightforward yet ironic.

In verses 9 through 20 Judith offers words of wisdom to Holofernes concerning Achior, the leader of the Ammonites, namely, that Holofernes should keep in mind Achior's truthful words delivered to Holofernes earlier in a report (Judith 5:5–21). The report indicated that the Israelites lived under both the promise and threat of their God. If the people did not sin, then they would prosper; if they did sin, then they would fall out of favor with their God, which would result in their being defeated in battle (Judith 5:17–18), among other tragedies.

In verses 11 through 15 Judith deceptively reveals what the Israelites plan to do that will allow Holofernes to overpower them. Supposedly the Israelites have been overtaken by a sin, and they are about to provoke their God to anger on account of their wrongdoing. Since the Israelites' food stock has run out and their water supply is exhausted, the people intend to violate their religious dietary laws (vv. 12–14). Guilty of transgression, the people will not be protected by their God, and they will be handed over to Holofernes to be destroyed (v. 15). Such news must have delighted Holofernes.

Judith continues her response in verses 16 through 19 where she states why she fled from the Israelites. She makes the claim that God has sent her to Holofernes to accomplish great things with him (v. 16). Again, this statement is truthful. What Judith will accomplish with Holofernes will, indeed, astonish the whole world. Little does Holofernes know that Judith's accomplishments will include his death and the assured security of her people. In verses 17 through 19 Judith then discusses her continued plan with Holofernes and leads him to believe that he will, together with Judith, defeat the Israelites.

Verses 20 through 23 describe his response to Judith. He and all his servants are pleased with the information and plans Judith has disclosed. They also marvel at her wisdom (v. 20), which, again, is ironic. Judith is indeed wise. She has gained the trust of Holofernes and his servants and the people in the camp. Little do any of them realize that her "wise" scheme is a deception aimed at serving her own people and not the Assyrians. Surprisingly Holofernes pledges that if Judith does as she has said then her God would be his God (v. 23b). Thus, his trust will rest not only in Judith but in her God as well (see Ruth 1:16). Holofernes, for his part, promises Judith residence in the royal palace of Nebuchadnezzar and predicts that her deeds among the Assyrians will make her world famous. Holofernes has become completely beguiled by Judith to the point that he invites her to dine with him (v. 23b).

Further Exchange between Holofernes and Judith (Judith 12:1–20)

Totally enamored with Judith, Holofernes orders his servants to bring her into his dining area, where they are to spread a feast before her (v. 1). Upon her arrival into Holofernes's dining area, Judith refuses his offering in order to maintain her customary dietary laws. She chooses to dine on the food that she has brought with her (v. 2), and Holofernes wishes to accommodate her in every way (vv. 3–4). Judith then takes her rest and spends the next three days in the camp, praying to God to direct her efforts (vv. 5–9).

The plot of the storyline begins to thicken on day four in the camp, when Holofernes decides to host a banquet and seduce Judith. The banquet will be for Holofernes, his personal attendants, and Judith; Holofernes invites none of his officers (vv. 10–12). Judith accepts his invitation to the banquet and adorns herself accordingly, vowing to Holofernes's eunuch, Bagoas, who had charge of the general's personal affairs, that she would comply with Holofernes's wishes (v. 14). To Holofernes invitation, she replies: "Who am I to refuse my lord?" Once again, her statement is ironic. Bagoas understands "my lord" to refer to Holofernes, but Judith is simply affirming her obedience to God and not making any commitment whatsoever to Holofernes.

The use of irony throughout these chapters thus far highlights Judith's cleverness and also underscores the use of humor by the biblical author. Judith appears to be a compliant, self-effacing woman, but in reality she knows exactly what she is doing and is quite artful in her choice of words. Her word choice with all the double meanings implied keeps Judith from telling a bold-faced lie to Holofernes and his men, which, in turn, maintains her good standing with them and with her God.

Shortly after the invitation is extended, Judith arrives in Holofernes's tent and lies down (v. 16a). Holofernes is ravished and passionate because he had been waiting to seduce her ever since he laid eyes on her (v. 16b). He and Judith then enjoy some fine wine after Judith proclaims, ironically, that this present day will be the greatest in her whole life (v. 18). Holofernes, filled with lust, drinks much too much wine (v. 20), which seals his fate at Judith's hand. Indeed, Judith's wisdom is a marvel, and her deceit is most successful.

Description of the Beheading of Holofernes (Judith 13:1–10a)

As the feast begins to wind down, the commander's servants depart, leaving Holofernes and Judith alone in the tent, but Holofernes, dead drunk and stretched out on his bed, is no company to Judith (vv. 1–2). Holofernes had hoped to overtake Judith, but now the wine has overtaken him. Instead of Judith surrendering to him, he has surrendered to Judith. His drunken stupor provides Judith with the opportunity she needs to complete her mission.

Verses 3 through 5 anticipate Judith's mission. Judith dismisses her maid as well as Bagoas from the bedchamber (v. 3). At last she is completely alone with a drunken Holofernes, and before her next move, she prays to God from her heart, imploring God to be with her as she completes her task: "O Lord God of all might, look in this hour on the work of my hands for the exaltation of Jerusalem. Now indeed is the time to help your heritage and to carry out my design to destroy the enemies who have risen up against us" (v. 5). Judith does nothing apart from her God, who is not only her strength but also her source of wisdom and power.

Verses 6 through 10 are the high point of this unit of Judith and the book as a whole. Judith performs the task that she had set out to do. With a prayer on her lips uttered to her God of all strength and wisdom, she takes Holofernes's sword from above his bedpost, strikes his neck twice, and cuts off his head (vv. 6–8).[7] She then rolls his body off the bed,[8] pulls down the bed canopy from its posts, and gives the head to her maid, who places it in a food bag (vv. 9–10). Interestingly, we hear no comment from Judith's maid after she receives the leader's bloody, gruesome head, nor does the maid comment on Judith's deed. The mission has been accomplished.

Judith's Return to Bethulia (Judith 13:10b–20)

With her mission accomplished on behalf of her people, Judith continues on her set course as she had done each day while in the Assyrian camp: she and her maid go out "to pray," which serves as a foil for their escape from the camp. She had won the trust of the people and officials, so why should this day and gesture be any different from all the other times? This move to go to prayer, however, is different. This time Judith and her maid leave the Assyrian campgrounds, circle around the valley from whence they had originally set out, ascend the mountain of Bethulia, and arrive at the town's gate, where Judith calls out to the sentinels, petitioning them to open the gate (v. 10b) as she proclaims her praise to God and the success of her mission: "Open, open the gate! God, our God is with us, still showing his power in Israel and his strength against our enemies as he has done today!" (v. 11).

Upon hearing the sound of Judith's voice, all the townspeople, including the elders, hurry to the town's gate. Judith's return stirs enthusiasm, and once again Judith attributes her success to the power and fidelity of Israel's God as she proclaims: "Praise God, O praise him! Praise God, who has not withdrawn his mercy from the house of Israel, but has destroyed our enemies by my hand this very night!" (v. 14). As a testimony to the success of her mission, all performed with the power, wisdom, and grace of God, Judith then pulls out the head of Holofernes from her bag and again attributes the success of the deed to God:

> See here, the head of Holofernes, the commander of the Assyrian army, and here is the canopy beneath which he lay in his drunken stupor. The Lord has struck him down by the hand of a woman. As the Lord lives, who has protected me in the way I went, I swear that it was my face that seduced him to his destruction, and that he committed no sin with me, to defile and shame me. (vv. 15–16)

The astonished people in turn bow down and worship God themselves and proclaim: "Blessed are you our God, who have this day humiliated the enemies of your people" (v. 17). The last person to congratulate Judith is the magistrate of her people, Uzziah, who with words of praise elevates her to the realm of incomparable and unsurpassable holiness and indirectly dubs her a "heroine." He also offers a word of gratitude to his God:

> O daughter, you are blessed by the Most High God above all other women on earth; and blessed be the Lord God, who created the heavens and the earth, who has guided you to cut off the head of the leader of our enemies. Your praise will never depart from the heart of those who remember the power of God. May God grant this to be a perpetual honor to you, and may he reward you with blessings, because you risked your own life when our nation was brought low, and you averted our ruin, walking in the straight path before our God. (vv. 18–20a)[9]

The people respond with a double expression of affirmation: "Amen. Amen" (v. 20b). Judith, a woman of profound piety and love not only for her God but also for her people, has freed her people from the fear of their enemies and has deepened their faith in the God of Israel. As in the days of Egyptian bondage before the Exodus (see Exod. 1–15), God has heard the cry of the people, has seen their plight, and has set them free through Judith, one whom God raised up from within the community. Judith does not bask for long in the praise of Uzziah and the people but immediately turns to give them a set of wise instructions that they need to follow to save their lives fully (Judith 14).

Judith's Instructions to Her People (Judith 14:1–10)

With the death of the Assyrians' main commanding officer in the background, Judith now mobilizes her own people for the final defeat of the Assyrians. She provides them with wise instructions and has them set up the head of Holofernes upon the parapet of their wall like a trophy to remind them that the central commander has already been destroyed and that the task now at hand is for the people to complete the mission. Judith artfully teaches her people's warriors how to deceive the Assyrian warriors (vv. 1–10).

One interesting sidebar in this section of the story is Judith's relationship with Achior the Ammonite, whom the people summon from Uzziah's house (vv. 5–6a). Achior arrives and stands in Judith's presence. When he sees Holofernes's head, he pays homage to Judith. After hearing her remarkable and adventurous story, Achior recognizes the power of Israel's God, has himself circumcised, and joins the house of Israel (vv. 6b–10).[10] Thus, for Achior, Judith's experience becomes a transformative moment that leads to his conversion. Through Judith, Achior is evangelized in the midst of times filled with dreadful and life-threatening conflict. The scene is a welcome interlude before chaos breaks out as the Assyrians discover what has occurred in their camp (vv. 11–19).

Discovery of the Death of Holofernes (Judith 14:11–19)

The Israelite warriors heed Judith's advice and set out in companies to the mountain passes (v. 11). As the Assyrians spot their approach, they send word to Holofernes, only to have Bagoas discover his dead, decapitated body in his bedchamber (vv. 12–17). At once, Bagoas informs all the people that have been tricked by a single Hebrew woman (v. 18). Such an experience causes mourning, dismay, and outcry among the Assyrian leaders (v. 19).

The Flight of the Assyrians (Judith 15:1–7)

With the execution of Holofernes and the wise instructions directed to her people, Judith has successfully set the stage for the Israelites to make their move against the Assyrians and defeat this bullish enemy. Verses 1 through 7 describe the Assyrians' state of affairs and the Israelites' victory over and plunder of the enemy that was long the cause of their fear and trembling. The news of the death of Holofernes sends sheer panic among the Assyrians, who begin to flee for their lives (vv. 1–3a). The Israelites take advantage of their weakened, panicked, chaotic state and rush upon the Assyrians, cutting them down in battle, plundering their camp, and acquiring great riches for their community (vv. 3b–7). Thus, the Israelites defeat their fearsome enemy, a cause of great celebration.

Israelites' Celebration of Victory (Judith 15:8–13)

The victorious celebration begins when the high priest Joakim and the elders leave Jerusalem to travel to Bethulia "to witness the good things the Lord had done for Israel, and to see Judith and to wish her well" (vv. 8–10). For thirty days the Israelites loot the Assyrian camp, and the victors also share some of the wealth with Judith, who acquires the tent of Holofernes, along with his silverware, beds, bowls, and all his furniture. She has enough goods now to refurnish her own home as a memory of her victory (v. 11).

What follows next in the story is the sheer jubilation of the people. Judith receives the blessing of all the women of Bethulia and, together with Judith in the lead, they all dance and wear olive crowns on their heads. The male soldiers, bearing their arms, wearing garlands, and singing hymns, follow behind the women (vv. 12–13). The enemy has been defeated and the Israelites can now live without fear. Their faithful God has been acknowledged and praised for divine work among a forlorn, faithful people. Judith's life is forever changed, and once more the hearts of God's people rejoice and make merry in the midst of relentless battles and moments of conflict that leave us wondering about how we should handle conflict today in a world that is growing increasingly violent.

Looking through the Communication Lens

To contemporary students of conflict, the story of Judith is disturbing. She addresses the conflict by cutting the throat of her enemy. Is there anything positive to glean from this story? Using the communication lens, we will approach the story in three ways. First, we will compare Judith with other female characters studied thus far; second, we will look at the tactics Judith chose from a range of tactics and styles available; and finally we will look at how the context of war affects the story.

The Role of Power Resources

Like Tamar and Susanna, Judith appears to be limited in her power resources. As the story begins, compared to the resources of Holofernes and his army, Judith lacks both the power to reward and the power to coerce. Holofernes, in contrast, can use reward power by sharing the bounty with his supporters, and the coercive power of his dominant and mighty army can destroy his opponents.

Similarly, Judith, although a wealthy and highly respected widow, has no legitimate power: she is not a leader of Bethulia, and she does not command an army. Like Tamar and Susanna, her opponent has far greater power resources. Her great beauty might give her some referent power — and perhaps even reward power — but Holofernes can choose to rape her without her assent. While her piety might give her referent power among her own people, it will not influence her relationship with Holofernes. Instead, like Tamar, Judith turned to her intelligence, a form of information power, in her choice of tactics. And like Tamar she prevailed.

The context of war greatly influenced Judith's choices. In studying conflict management, the hope is never to go to war, literally or figuratively, with the significant others in our lives. When we use the metaphor of war in thinking about or describing our own conflicts, it affects in a negative manner how we approach and conduct a situation of conflict.[11] In order to avoid such an approach, this chapter examines different styles of engaging in conflict and their usefulness in various situations. It also introduces other mental models, or metaphors, for how to conduct conflict.

Styles of Conflict

A conflict style is the orientation that governs the behavior people adopt in a conflict. Some scholars believe that individuals have a primary style with which they typically respond to conflict, similar to a permanent trait. Others scholars emphasize that conflict style can be a choice, a strategic response to a given situation. Given this perspective, the overall context, the situation, and the behavior of the person we are dealing with all set the stage for the style of conflict a person chooses. All styles have advantages and disadvantages. While a variety of approaches to conflict style have been studied, the most common one offers five different categories or models: competition, avoidance, accommodation (or obliging), compromise, and collaboration.[12]

A *competitive* conflict style is characterized as win-lose. What matters is satisfying one's own concerns. Parties influence others using their superior, coercive power. Clearly, Nebuchadnezzar demonstrated this approach when he said, "I am coming against them in my anger, and will cover the whole face of the earth with the feet of my troops, to whom I will hand them over to be plundered" (1:4–8). Indeed, Holofernes modeled his behavior after his king: "He [Holofernes] ravaged Put and Lud, and plundered all the Rassisites and Ishmaelites on the border of the desert. . . . He . . . destroyed all fortified towns . . . and killed everyone who resisted him" (2:23–25). Clearly, Judith's style reciprocated that of Holofernes. Instead of military strength, she used deception and physical aggression to prevail. Both employed a competitive conflict style with the goal of victory rather than compromise.

In everyday life, conflict is usually not this dramatic, although conflicts can escalate and get out of control. For example, Harry and Sam are elderly neighbors. Over time, their relationship has deteriorated. When Sam put a chemical barrier around his trees to dissuade aphids, Harry snuck over to Sam's property and attached a popsicle stick to the substance, a little bridge, so the ants could get to the tree. This so enraged Sam that when he saw Harry get out of his car, he went over and began hitting him with his fists. Eventually, their highly competitive tactics forced neighbors to call the police. Competitive tactics include threats, shouting, aggressively pursuing personal goals, avoiding sacrificing any goals at all, denying others' power, and whatever else might compel others to comply.[13]

The second style, *avoidance,* is characterized by withdrawal. If Judith's style had been avoidance, she probably would have remained in seclusion and not involved herself in the conflict. In everyday life, many of us prefer avoidance as a basic conflict style. Avoidance includes such behaviors as not engaging an issue, changing the subject, joking about it, leaving the room, or finding an excuse to break off the conversation or "get off the phone."

Accommodation, or *obliging,* means yielding to the other's preferences. We communicate our point of view but will give in to the other. Sometimes we yield because an issue really is not very important to us, because we just want peace, or because we feel we have no choice. Sacrificing one's needs and goals can be useful in some situations, but habitual use of this tactic may create the role of a martyr, complainer, or saboteur.[14] When Nebuchadnezzar summoned all who lived in the region to join him in war (7–11), he wrongly anticipated that all would oblige him and simply yield to his demands. He expected accommodation.

Compromise calls for each party to give up a little so that no one completely wins, but no one completely loses. Sometimes, "splitting the difference" is the most effective way to resolve a conflict. Compromise depends, however, on the two parties dealing with each other in good faith and with trust. Clearly, Judith had no partner interested in compromise.

The tactic of *collaboration* uses problem solving to create a win-win situation in which both parties attempt to meet the needs and most important interests of each other. Collaboration relies on a variety of skills. Participants need to be able to identify the underlying concerns for themselves and for others, and they need to be willing and able to confront vital issues without threatening the other party and without having the conflict escalate. Brainstorming and creativity are helpful for generating ideas that can lead to a win-win solution. Like working for a compromise, the parties must be able to trust each other.

The Advantages and Disadvantages of Each Style

Knowing the benefits and costs of each style positions us to choose how we wish to respond to a provocation rather than merely relying on our habitual way of reacting.

Competing can be useful in standing up for one's interests and ideas to make sure they are taken seriously, particularly when dealing with someone who is already using a competitive style. If one has enough power, one can press for a quick decision. The downside is that strained relationships usually result on the part of the losing side. And if the initial tactics fail, the likelihood of escalation is great.

Avoiding a conflict may temporarily reduce stress and in that way this tactic may offer an advantage. If an issue has a low priority or a relationship is not very important, avoidance can be advantageous. Avoidance can also be a constructive strategy if better timing will aid in resolving the conflict, and avoidance can be a helpful delaying tactic while a party plans another approach. When compromise and collaboration are not likely to work and avoidance is possible, avoidance may be the most advantageous choice.

The downside of avoidance is that if an issue is important, feelings can escalate and when the conflict finally is addressed, it explodes. Avoiding a discussion may also ignore the needs of the other party who wishes to problem solve or seek redress. And at times avoidance may not be possible. While Judith as an individual could have avoided a conflict with Holofernes, her people as a whole could not. If no action was taken, total destruction was inevitable.

Accommodation can be advantageous when it helps other people meet their needs and one's sacrifice is not too great. Indeed, an act of generosity can help restore harmony, and doing favors usually builds social capital. Accommodation can also be useful in cutting one's losses and moving on.

Accommodation, however, has serious disadvantages when one concedes on an issue about which one cares deeply and resentment festers. Furthermore, a person who always gives in may lose the respect of others and even self-respect. If the issues are complex, quick accommodation may limit exploring the complexities of the issue and arriving at a more satisfying solution.

Compromising allows all parties to achieve some of the goals that are important. Compromise, however, also leaves some residual frustration because each party has to give up some goals that matter.

Collaboration shows concern for the others' goals as well as for one's own goals. Collaboration, at its best, results in high quality decisions that creatively weave together the interests of both parties. Because both parties work to achieve desirable ends to meet all needs, the parties are more likely to be committed to the decision. Moreover, concern for the needs of the other party is more likely to forge a good working relationship that will allow the parties to work together in the future.

Collaboration has the disadvantage of being time-consuming. Collaboration also requires the commitment of all parties. While one individual might prefer collaboration, if the other party in the dispute prefers to avoid talking about the conflict, collaboration is not an option. And if one party is dealing with a competitive opponent, collaboration may leave one vulnerable because collaboration entails a good deal of information sharing.

War as a Metaphor for Conflict

It was noted above that the context of conflict in the story of Judith was that of war. It would be comforting if we could reassure ourselves that the world has moved beyond such extreme behavior in dealing with conflict. Current events, however, have put beheading into the news as a means of influencing opponents. On February 9, 2009, the Associated Press reported that the Taliban broadcast the beheading of a Polish engineer, Piotr Stanczak.[15] To amplify the effect of the beheadings, the Taliban regularly broadcasted decapitations and punished any villager who did not listen.[16] Then in this country, on February 19, 2009, in New York City, the founder of a television station was accused of beheading his wife.[17]

Too often war is the only operating metaphor for people involved in conflict. It has been pointed out in a compelling way that metaphors not only reflect our thinking, but also strongly influence how we behave.[18] War implies the tactics of competition, coalitions, winners and losers, and all or nothing thinking and behavior. A more transformative metaphor for conflict is that of a journey.[19] Such a metaphor minimizes competitive behavior and emphasizes cooperation and problem solving. A journey implies movement, hills and valleys, and perhaps arrival at a destination. William Wilmot and Joyce Hocker offer other transformative ways of thinking about conflict,[20] including thinking of conflict as a dance. To dance well, partners need to know the steps, determine how close or distant they must be to their partner, and develop some skill. Conflict can also be like a garden. Human relationships need careful planting and fertilization; while some need to be in the sun and some in the shade, they all take time to develop. Then the fruits of careful labor can be harvested. Judith was an actor in a time of war, but we have no need to be warriors in our daily lives. Important to remember, however, is that *how* we conceptualize conflict will undoubtedly contribute to how effective we are in *transforming* conflict into right relationships.

Theological Reflection on Judith 10–15

As alluded to earlier in this chapter, the story of Judith and how she handled conflict is disturbing. It could be because what we have experienced in this tale is the use of violence to deal with violence, which, as history has shown us, has short-term but not enduring effects. Today nations and people continue to struggle with all sorts of conflicts: battles are fought and won, and yet bloody conflicts and raging wars continue to mar the face of the earth, tear at the web of life, harm and annihilate innocent victims, and take the lives of people. Without their armor, allegiances, military weapons of power and protection, these people are really brothers and sisters of one another within the human community, the human family.

In the case of Judith, with a powerful enemy raging against the Israelites and threatening their lives, Judith and her people had no other recourse but to defend themselves using the means available to them in their time and their day — deception and military weaponry. Judith and her people lived in a violent culture, and they responded to attacks and threats accordingly. Thus, Judith's choices and the choices of her people do need to be understood in the context of war. The hope is that today we do not go to war, literally or figuratively, with the significant others in our lives.

Additionally, Judith's God is portrayed as one to whom Judith looked for strength and power in her decision to destroy Holofernes. In a culture of war, the metaphor warrior God looms large on the horizon precisely because the Sacred Presence, we call God will be with the people however, whenever, and in whatever circumstances they find themselves. In these circumstances God will be forever trying to sustain, grace, and "be with" the people in the midst of all. This understanding of God as a warrior God, however, is a human construct, a human metaphor ascribed to the Sacred Presence who ultimately is the one who has created and who continues to sustain, nurture, grace, and love all unconditionally down through the ages. This Sacred Presence we call "God" works through people to try to bring about peace, even though the human way of trying to bring about peace is often sordid and deeply reflective of a culture and a world in need of healing and transformation.

Judith's competitive style of conflict and the other styles and tactics she employs do defeat the enemy, but we are left with a win-lose situation that involves the loss of life for one group of people so that another group of people can live. Sadly, we as a global human community have not moved too far beyond this way of dealing with conflict, and because we have not, the story of Judith becomes prophetic in its own way: violence only begets violence, and if we are to break this downward spiral that leads to a moment of peace but certainly not an enduring peace, then we as a global human community have no other choice than to reconceptualize conflict and how we handle it. The dance in the garden awaits us all.

In Sum: Grace in the Wilderness

In spite of the story of Judith being one that should disturb us, grace does exist in the story. First, Judith embraces her own personal courage to confront conflict when she could have stayed in her widow's clothes, doing nothing but continuing to mourn her dead husband. Second, Judith not only listens to but also follows the deep love in her heart that she possesses for her people. She rises to the threat of the Assyrians, and with deference to her God, she acts on her people's behalf for their common good. Third, Judith exhibits "grace under fire"; she does not pale from her decision, her mission, and her duty even in the face of life-threatening circumstances. Instead, she acts with grace and wisdom, defeating the main commander of Israel's enemy, thereby paving the way for her people to finish the task. Finally, a woman of "world renown," Judith exercises profound humility. She attributes her success to God who, for Judith, is the source of her power, strength, and wisdom. A woman of great faith and deep piety, Judith walks with God, and God walks with Judith.

Reflection Questions:
Can You Now ... ?

1. Define piety as expressed by Judith?

2. Understand how culture affects how we view God and our images of God?

3. Understand how Judith's actions represent her cultural and historical time?

4. Understand how wisdom plays an important role in conflict and conflict management?

5. Identify situations in your own life where conflict has been competitive? If a roommate tried to dominate, what were the consequences for the relationship? Or if you had siblings, what were the consequences when one sibling tried to force his or her will on the other?

6. Recall dealing with someone who avoided conflict? Have you had a friend or romantic relationship in which you wanted to raise an issue and the person either changed the subject, left the room, or went silent? What were the consequences?

7. Do you think that texting, instant messaging, e-mailing, and social networking sites make it easier to avoid or confront conflict?

8. Recall a friend or acquaintance you have had who always "folded" in an argument? What image did you have of that person?

9. Identify what style of conflict Tamar used? Susanna? Daniel?

10. Recall the use of collaboration to solve a conflict? If so, what challenges did you observe?

11. Would any of the conflicts we have studied so far meet the minimum conditions for collaboration?

Additional Resources

• The triumph of Judith over Holofernes has been captured by many artists over time. Research some of these images online. How do they make you feel?

• Cokie Roberts's book, *Founding Mothers: The Women Who Raised Our Nation,* recounts the stories of many women, none of whom had legitimate power but all of whom exercised influence in war. Analyze the conflict styles used by these women at the birth of this nation.

MOSES AND GOD

The Art of Negotiation

(*Exodus 32*)

The LORD said to Moses, "Go down at once! Your people, whom you brought up out of the land of Egypt, have acted perversely; they have been quick to turn aside from the way that I commanded them; they have cast for themselves an image of a calf, and have worshiped it and sacrificed to it, and said, 'These are your gods, O Israel, who brought you up out of the land of Egypt!'" The LORD said to Moses, "I have seen this people, how stiff-necked they are. Now let me alone, so that my wrath may burn hot against them and I may consume them; and of you I will make a great nation."

But Moses implored the LORD his God, and said, "O LORD, why does your wrath burn hot against your people, whom you brought out of the land of Egypt with great power and with a mighty hand? Why should the Egyptians say, 'It was with evil intent that he brought them out to kill them in the mountains, and to consume them from the face of the earth'? Turn from your fierce wrath; change your mind and do not bring disaster on your people. Remember Abraham, Isaac, and Israel, your servants, how you wrote to them by your own self, saying to them, 'I will multiply your descendants like the stars of heaven, and all this land that I have promised I will give to your descendants, and they shall inherit it forever.'" And the LORD changed his mind about the disaster that he planned to bring on his people. (Exod. 32:7–14)

A Biblical Interpretation of Exodus 32:1–35

Among the best-known stories in the book of Exodus is the narrative about the golden calf. There are many levels and types of conflict between its main characters — Moses, God, Aaron, and the Israelites. Set in the context of Exodus 31:18 through 34:35, which deals with the violation and renewal of covenants, Exodus 32 juxtaposes two dramatic scenes. First, in Exodus 31:18, when God finishes speaking with Moses on Mount Sinai, God then gives Moses the two tablets of the covenant "written with the finger of God."

This event is momentous, and we can scarcely imagine the feelings of Moses as he holds those tablets.

Following this event, however, we are immediately transported to the foot of the mountain. In sharp contrast to the reverent atmosphere of the previous scene, rebellion is fermenting among the people. The Israelites clamor for an idol, a god to worship, and so Aaron crafts for them a golden calf. God, who is furious, wants to be left alone so that "my wrath may burn hot against them and I may consume them" (Exod. 32:10). Moses's responsibility as a leader is to deal with the immediate crisis of God's anger, the people's disobedience, the misstep in Aaron's leadership, as well as his own disappointment and anger, and to negotiate with God for the future of the Israelites. This story of the golden calf, then, can be seen as a biblical example of "conflict and negotiation."

The drama of the construction of the golden calf and its repercussions unfolds in six episodes:

32:1–6	The construction of the golden calf
32:7–14	The exchange between Moses and God
32:15–20	The descent of Moses from the mountain
32:21–24	The exchange between Moses and Aaron
32:25–34	The address of Moses to the Israelites
32:35	The consequences of idolatry

The Construction of the Golden Calf (Exodus 32:1–6)

The narrative of the golden calf opens with the Israelites unsettled when Moses, accompanied by Joshua, has gone up on Mt. Sinai to converse with God and is slow to return. Moses has entrusted his brother, Aaron, with the care of the Israelites while he, Moses, was up on Mt. Sinai. Fearing that they have been left without a real leader, the people petition Aaron: "Come, make gods for us, who shall go before us; as for this Moses, the man who brought us up out of the land of Egypt, we do not know what has become of him" (32:1).

Aaron complies with the Israelites' wishes instead of encouraging them to be patient, to trust, and to continue to wait for the return of Moses. Instead of exercising the leadership entrusted to him by Moses, Aaron yields to the wayward spirit of the people. With a simple command, he bends to idolatry and crafts the golden calf, severing the right relationship between the Israelites and their God and the right relationship between the Israelites and Moses:

> Aaron said to them, "Take off the gold rings that are on the ears of your wives, your sons, and your daughters, and bring them to me." So all the people took off the gold rings from their ears, and brought them to Aaron. He took the gold from them, formed them in a mold, and

cast an image of a calf; and they said, "These are your gods, O Israel, who brought you up out of the land of Egypt!" (32:2–4)[1]

Within biblical circles, the interpretation of the actions of the Israelites and Aaron is unclear and has evoked much discussion. Carol Meyers lays out the various possibilities:

> Were the people asking literally for a god? Note that the NRSV translation of "make gods for us" in 32:1 (and v. 23) is misleading, for the Hebrew just as readily allows for the rendering "make a god for us." Or, rather, did they seek something to indicate divine presence? Are they asking for a representation of Yahweh? Or do they seek an image of any god who would do what Yahweh has promised? Or, is it possible that they simply want an image of the absent Moses, God's messenger and the one who is credited in 32:1, 7–8 for bringing the Israelites out of Egypt? . . . Is the calf itself a theriomorphism (representation of a deity having the form of an animal)? Or, like the cherubim, is it a throne or pedestal on which the invisible presence of a god rests? . . . Can it be that God is condemning the golden calf not because it signifies the worship of other gods but because it violates the prohibition against bowing down to and serving images of living beings?[2]

The questions that Meyers outlines are important not only for interpretation purposes but also because they remind us that the biblical stories and, in this case the story about the golden calf, are multilayered. Meyers concludes that none of the questions "can be resolved with certainty."[3]

Aaron's response to the people's exclamation about the golden calf is curious. He builds an altar before it and then makes a proclamation: "Tomorrow shall be a festival to the Lord" (v. 5). Is the calf, then, a symbol of the divine presence, a representation of Yahweh, as two of Meyers's questions suggest?[4] The text remains obscure. The sacrifices of the people are burnt offerings and sacrifices of "well-being" (referring to animals without blemish), two types of acceptable sacrifices common to ancient Israelite worship (see Lev. 22:17–30).

Quite possibly the people's reveling in verses 17–18 could have involved a sexual orgy since the cow/bull is an ancient symbol of fertility.[5] Another suggestion is that the reveling is associated with the celebration of a military victory. Moses's comment in verse 18, however, disputes this possibility (see also v. 17). At any rate, the Israelites have worked themselves into a highly excited state.[6]

The Exchange between Moses and God (Exodus 32:7–14)

This next section is the heart of the story of the golden calf. The narrator portrays God as burning with fiery rage and wrath at the action of the Israelites to the point that God wants to consume this wayward people

(vv. 7–10). Moses, caring deeply about the Israelites and faithful to his God and God's ways, begins to negotiate with God on behalf of the Israelites (vv. 11–14), which results in God changing God's mind (v. 14). Divine disaster does not befall the Israelites. In his negotiations with God, Moses uses great skill, beginning with a rhetorical question that begins with the vocative, "O Lord": "O Lord, why does your wrath burn hot against your people, whom you brought out of the land of Egypt with great power and with a mighty hand? (v. 11). He then raises a second question: "Why should the Egyptians say, 'It was with evil intent that he brought them out to kill them in the mountains, and to consume them from the face of the earth?' " (v. 12a). Then in verse 13 Moses gives a direct command to God that is spoken without any apprehensiveness: "Turn from your fierce wrath; change your mind and do not bring disaster on your people." These rhetorical skills demonstrate some of the different types of negotiations that we will discuss further on when we turn to the lens of communications.

Moses is successful in his efforts. God changes God's mind and disaster for the Israelites is abated (v. 14). Lastly, this act of interceding for the people situates Moses in the prophetic tradition. Classically, Israel's prophets always intercede to God on behalf of the people, especially when the people have turned from their God (see, e.g., Mic. 6:6–8; Hab. 1:1–17).

The Descent of Moses from the Mountain (Exodus 32:15–20)

Having successfully pleaded with God for the people, Moses now descends the mountain with Joshua. Moses carries with him the two tablets of the covenant written by God.[7] Although he has heard about the Israelites' deeds through God (vv. 7–14) and through Joshua (vv. 17–18), he has yet to see for himself what exactly is going on among the people. When Moses finally sees for himself the state of the people and the calf that had been crafted, he, like God, responds out of anger. The fact that Moses sees the extent of the people's depravity *after* he interceded for them and not *before* is, perhaps, better for the people. While they are not all destroyed by divine wrath, they do experience the consequence of their actions. After smashing the tablets (v. 19), Moses destroys the calf by burning it with fire. He then grinds the calf to powder, scatters it on the water, and makes the Israelites drink the putrid water (v. 20). Biblical scholar J. Gerald Janzen notes that the breaking of the tablets symbolizes the breaking of the covenant between God and the Israelites.[8]

The Exchange between Moses and Aaron (Exodus 32:21–24)

The time has come for Moses to confront Aaron. Moses does so with one simple question: "What did this people do to you that you have brought so great a sin upon them?" (v. 21). Aaron's evades his own culpability. First, he tries to quell the burning anger of Moses (v. 22a), and then he deflects Moses's question away from himself and refocuses Moses on the Israelites and indirectly on Moses himself: "You know the people, that they are bent on evil. They said to me, 'Make us gods, who shall go before us; as for this Moses, the man who brought us up out of the land of Egypt, we do not know what has come of him' " (vv. 22–23).

Aaron takes no responsibility for the people's actions. He exonerates himself from any wrongdoing, informing Moses that the people did what they did first because they are "bent on evil" and second because Moses took too long to come down from the mountain.

Aaron thus attributes blame for the chaos in the camp to the people and indirectly to Moses, letting Moses know that his delay in returning from the mountain is what incited the people to want a god. Aaron fashioned the golden calf only in response to the people's request (v. 24).

Aaron faced a potential mob in a state of rebellion. How do you evaluate his leadership? What other options might he have chosen to handle this conflict?

The Address of Moses to the Israelites (Exodus 32:25–34)

Having addressed Aaron, Moses now turns to address the Israelites themselves. It is interesting to note that the story's narrator holds Aaron responsible (v. 25: "for Aaron had let them run wild"). Moses confronts the people with one question and a command: "Who is on the Lord's side? Come to me!" (v. 26a).

A group of the Israelites, the Levites, respond positively (v. 26b). Using a formula of a prophet, "Thus says the LORD, the God of Israel,"[9] to lend authority to his words, he commands the Levites to act decisively against those who are not on the Lord's side (v. 27), and the narrator reports that "three thousand fell on that day." The Levites receive Moses' praise for having acted in the service of the Lord (v. 28).

Following this act of "purification," Moses confronts the remainder of the people. He indicts them but then promises to make atonement on their behalf (v. 30). Moses returns to the Lord, asking God to forgive the sins of the people, and offers himself as a sacrifice for them. Although Moses is willing to be blotted out of God's book,[10] God does not allow Moses to become a scapegoat or sacrificial lamb for the faithless people (v. 33). God wants Moses to continue, to lead the people into Canaan to fulfill the divine promise; God, in due course, will chastise the people: "Whoever has sinned against me I will blot out of my book.... Nevertheless, when the day comes for punishment, I will punish them for their sin" (v. 34).

Israel's God does not bring about intended divine disaster upon the people (v. 14) but is relentless in making the people realize that sin has consequences. In this account in Exodus, Israel's God is an unforgiving God, not yet ready to take back the people. The people, however, will not be denied the divine presence even though they have sinned; but because they have sinned, they will be made to suffer at the hand of God.

The Consequences of Idolatry (Exodus 32:35)

Following God's avowal that the people be punished for their sin, God sends a plague on the people "because they made the calf — the one that Aaron made." Despite Aaron's lengthy attempt to justify his actions (vv. 22–24), the narrator does not allow him to be acquitted. Both the people and Aaron stand guilty of sin, and Aaron even more so, according to the biblical author who closes the narrative with a reference to Aaron's actions. Aaron, who failed to exercise responsible leadership, is ultimately responsible for the people's waywardness. If Aaron had been a stronger and more skillful leader, then Moses would not have had to negotiate with God

Looking through the Communication Lens

The story of Moses negotiating with God over the building and worshiping of the golden calf illustrates a phenomenon common in our everyday lives. Sometimes we are thrown into a situation that unexpectedly demands negotiations. The interaction between Moses and God highlights some important elements that have a role in negotiating.

Choosing a Perspective

To begin with, we can consider the interactions in this story from multiple viewpoints. Describing this story as a religious failing of the Israelites is quite easy. From God's viewpoint, creating an idol was about the most egregious affront the Israelites could have chosen. While the narrator doesn't clearly describe the motives of the group who wanted to build a god in the form of a golden calf, in fact their actions grew out of their "common sense" knowledge, in other words, their experiences in Egypt. Given that the people had only recently left slavery, that the social structure familiar to them no longer existed, and that their new leader, Moses, disappeared for forty days, the clamoring for a calf perhaps becomes comprehensible. In a sense, the people were experiencing social change as much as religious change. They simply reverted to the way of being that they knew in Egypt. Laws were not yet in place, and consequences for breaking those laws had not yet been spelled out. Nonetheless, their behavior created a conflict between themselves and God.

Because Moses had little time before ascending Mount Sinai to advocate among the Israelites for social change, much needed to be done to *educate* the Israelites in how to create a civil society and how to remain observant of God's commandments. Much of what follows after the incident of the golden calf consists of Moses *advocating* for God's laws and the consequences of breaking them. At the juncture of the golden calf Moses acted as a *mediator* between God and the Israelites. Clearly, Moses needed to persuade the Israelites as well as God to view the situation in a different perspective.

In his book *Making Peace,* Adam Curle describes education, advocacy, and mediation as the three key elements in peacemaking.[11] Education is aimed at erasing ignorance and raising awareness, and part of transforming any conflict involves education on both sides about the various issues. Advocacy involves increasing awareness of issues, needs, and interests, along with working to pursue change and a balance in power. The third element, mediation, was a primary tool of Moses as he negotiated with God over the fate of the Israelites.

The challenges Moses faced in his negotiation with God can serve as a guide for our discussion of negotiation. First we will lay out the characteristics of most negotiations, next we will identify key features of collaborative negotiation, then we will review the basic rules of collaborative negotiation, and finally we will focus on specific communication skills that can be helpful.

The Nature of Negotiation

Roy Lewicki, Bruce Barry, and David Saunders identify the basic structure of any negotiation, which includes opening offers, counteroffer, concession process, and the closing of agreement.[12] We can see the skeleton of the negotiation process in our story:

+ The *opening offer* from God: "Now let me alone, so that my wrath may burn hot against them and I many consume them; and of you I will make a great nation." (Exod. 32:10)

+ The *counteroffer* from Moses: "Turn from your fierce wrath; change your mind, and do not bring disaster on your people" (32:12).

+ The *concession process*: Rather than annihilating *all* the people, the story says, "And the Lord changed his mind about the disaster that he planned to bring on his people." (32:13)

+ The *closing agreement*: Implicitly, Moses and God reach an agreement that not all the people would be annihilated, although they would be punished.

There are two main types of negotiation: competitive and collaborative. In chapter 6, we discussed the advantages and disadvantages of various conflict styles. Competitive negotiation results from a win-lose conflict and shares the advantages and disadvantages of a win-lose orientation. Our focus in this chapter will be on collaborative negotiation.

William Wilmot and Joyce Hocker identify four features of collaborative negotiation: (1) participants engage in conflict rather than avoid it, (2) they resist using domination, (3) they use persuasive tactics, and (4) they reach the stage of problem solving.[13] Let's examine the extent to which the conversation between Moses and God included these features.

An interesting examination for us would be to try to determine to what extent the conversation between Moses and God included these features. To begin, once aware of the idolatrous actions of the people, God might have avoided conversation with Moses altogether, simply not engaged with him, and annihilated the people. Instead God directed Moses,

> Go down at once! Your people, whom you brought up out of the land of Egypt, have acted perversely; they have been quick to turn aside from the way that I commanded them; they have cast for themselves an image of a calf, and have worshiped it and sacrificed to it.... " The LORD said to Moses, "I have seen this people, how stiff necked they are. Now let me alone, so that my wrath may burn hot against them and I many consume them; and of you I will make a great nation." (32:7–10)

God, however, did not immediately resort to domination. Instead, God was open to persuasion by Moses, and Moses used a variety of persuasive tactics: facework, cognitive dissonance theory, and referent power.

Recall from chapter 3 that facework involves maintaining one's self-image. As a persuasive tactic, Moses suggests that God might lose face with the Egyptians if he destroys them:

> O Lord, why does your wrath burn hot against your people, whom you brought out of the land of Egypt with great power and with a mighty hand? Why should the Egyptians say, "It was with evil intent that he brought them out to kill them in the mountains, and to consume them from the face of the earth?" (32:11–12)

Suggesting that God would *lose face* with the Egyptians, Moses implored, "Turn from your fierce wrath; change your mind and do not bring disaster on your people" (32:12).

A second strategy involves *cognitive dissonance*. Cognitive dissonance theory describes our need to maintain a consistency among our beliefs, feelings, and actions.[14] Basically, when we experience a discrepancy between our beliefs and actions, one or the other must change. Moses created such a discrepancy by reminding God of God's promise to Abraham and his children, "Remember Abraham, Isaac, and Israel, your servants, how you swore to them by your own self, saying to them, 'I will multiply your descendants like the stars of heaven, and all this land that I have promised I will give to your descendants, and they shall inherit it forever'" (32:13). Moses highlighted that annihilating the people would renege on the promise that God had made, using persuasive tactics to try to change the outcome.

In chapter 4 we discussed various types of power, one of which was referent power. Recall that referent power allows us to influence others because they like us. Notice how Moses persuasively leverages his referent power when he asks God to go among the people. The narrator points out that God spoke to Moses "face to face," as one speaks to a friend (33:11). As the following passage indicates, Moses has marshaled most of the influence tactics described in chapter 4 in his negotiation with God.

> Now if I have found favor in your sight, show me your ways, so that I may know you and find favor in your sight. Consider too that this nation is your people.... For how shall it be known that I have found favor in your sight, I and your people, unless you go with us? In this way, we shall be distinct, I and your people, from every people on the face of the earth.
>
> The LORD said to Moses, "I will do the very thing that you have asked; for you have found favor in my sight, and I know you by name." Moses said, "Show me your glory, I pray." And he said, "I will make all my goodness pass before you.... But," he said, "you cannot see my face, for no one shall see me and live." (Exod. 33:13–20)

Clearly, God and Moses shared an interest in having a good relationship with each other, although they differed on how the relationship would be expressed.

Basic Rules for Collaborative Negotiation

Moses's interaction with God demonstrates some of the give and take that is the goal of negotiating, albeit at a very elementary level. Experts Roger Fisher, William Ury, and Bruce Patton have developed some basic rules for principled negotiation:[15]

1. *Seek common ground.* Focus on interests rather than positions and look for common concerns that both parties share.

2. *Separate the people from the problem.* It is tempting to blame the other party as the source of the problem rather than recognizing differences exist. It is easy to impute intentions to the other side. When anger arises, it is easy to attribute character faults to the other person.[16] It is more effective to look at the situation as a problem in which perceptions are bound to differ, in which emotions are bound to run high, and in which face-saving is an important dynamic.

3. *Invent options.*

   - Brainstorm: Generate as many solutions as possible without evaluating them at the onset.

   - Expand the pie: Add resources so that both parties can meet their needs.

   - Logrolling: Trade off among issues so that one party gets its desired outcome on one issue, and the other party gets its desired outcome on a different issue.

   - Consider the best alternative to a negotiated agreement (BATNA): In any negotiation it is useful to consider the best-case scenario if the negotiation does not yield an acceptable outcome. A BATNA is a standard that asks, "Is this negotiated agreement better than my alternatives if I turn it down?" A BATNA helps us think about what our interests are and how a proposed agreement measures up against the alternative of no agreement. It is also worthwhile to consider the worst alternative to a negotiated agreement (WATNA). Both skills encourage thinking about options.

> *Chris likes a clean house all the time. Pat likes to clean up one in a while and is especially motivated when company comes over. Brainstorm some options that can help them with their conflict.*

4. *Develop objective standards.* Criteria should be fair to both sides.[17] A variety of standards can be used: moral standards, equal treatment, reciprocity, costs, and so forth.

> *Using the standards above, how might each be applied to the conflict between Chris and Pat?*

Important Communication Skills for Collaborative Negotiation

Collaborative negotiation requires a number of communication skills. Below we identify some of the other skills that are valuable for collaborative negotiation:

- *Use of open-ended questions.* Open-ended questions allow participants to express whatever information they deem important. They often provide clues to the feelings and the interests of each party and can gain useful information about the nature of the conflict. Here are some examples of open-ended questions that can be helpful: Please tell me how *you* view the situation. What is your perspective on this? Can you give me an example? Could you tell me more about how you view...? Can you help me understand why...? Could you describe what happened when...?

- *Active listening.* When feelings run high, reflecting them back to the other person lets him or her know they have been heard. When people are angry, they often repeat their point of view over and over again. Sometimes this happens because their feelings have not been acknowledged. Active listening lets each party know their feelings have been understood.

If the involved participants do not demonstrate active listening, a mediator can fulfill this role and help clarify the feelings of each party. A useful question to ask after both parties have talked about the emotional impact of a transgression is, "Was there any new information here?" Quite often we are not aware of the emotional impact of one party's behavior on the other.

**Role Play Activity
(Mediator and Two Neighbors)**

The two parties are neighbors. One neighbor, who has lived in the neighborhood for only one year, would like to build a fence and wants the other neighbor, who has lived in the adjacent property for ten years, to contribute to the cost. They disagree on the height of the fence, how the work is to be done, and the sharing of costs. The mediator must make use of active listening skills because both parties are entrenched in their own perspective.

+ *Analysis* of the other party's needs. The other party may not distinguish between positions and interests. Collaborative negotiation may mean that the more experienced negotiator needs to help the less experienced party discover its underlying needs and interests.[18]

Role Play: Three People

Housemates are in dispute about cleanliness in the kitchen and common living area. It has gotten to the point that instead of talking to each other, one just leaves notes. They used to be good friends. The mediator should help the parties move from their positions (level of cleanliness) to their underlying needs in the situation (how clean the areas need to be and their relationship with each other). Then move to problem solving.

+ *Description rather than evaluation.* When we provide feedback, we should focus on describing behavior rather using evaluative language. Evaluative language labels people, such as "You are stubborn" or "You are bent on evil." The natural response to such a label is defensiveness. The use of "I" statements can be helpful in such situations. Instead of "You are stubborn," describe the behavior and your response to it. For example, "When three ideas are presented and you reject all of them, I feel frustrated."

- *Assertiveness.* Stand up for your own needs without violating the rights of others. Avoid imputing motive and intent to the other person.

- *Reframing* means recasting a situation using a different perspective. A frame names a situation and provides an interpretation that helps us and others understand how we see a situation.[19] Frames put some aspects of a situation in the foreground and other aspects in the background.

Change these evaluative comments to descriptive comments. Compare your changes with a partner.

- *You have been sloppy in the work you've sent out to customers.*

- *You are self-centered and never remember my birthday.*

- *You always want your own way.*

- *You always have excuses when your work is late.*

The Importance of Reframing

Reframing is extremely important in handling conflict. It requires that we understand the cognitive and emotional perspective of ourselves and the other, and it requires that we can offer a different way to conceptualize a situation of conflict. There are different types of frames that can be useful.

Identity frames relate to how we see ourselves, our beliefs, and our values. Conflicts that threaten identity are often difficult to resolve because they challenge our sense of self and they generate defensiveness.[20] In a way, the Israelites experienced a conflict of identity. Moses and God expected that the Israelites would have abandoned their identity as Egyptian, idol-worshiping slaves. From the Israelites' behavior, however, we can infer that such a change had not yet taken place.

Many ethnic conflicts revolve around identity. In American history, we often focus on the conquest of land. Conflicts, however, were also about identity. For example, the identity of some Native American tribes depended on warrior status, hunting rights, and ownership of horses. Frontier settlers' identities depended on farming and peace.[21] The settling of the United States was as much a conflict about identity as it was about land use. Contemporary international conflicts are also rife with identity issues. In the conflict between the Palestinians and Israel, the identity of one group negates the identity of the other group because both parties view their identities as bound up in the land.[22] Awareness of an identity frame can help a mediator understand the dynamics of a conflict when negotiating in a polarized conversation.[23]

A contemporary example might have involve neighbors trying to work with a mediator on noise issues. When the mediator began to talk to each party, however, one of the parties said they didn't think that noise was the real issue. That party thought racism was really at the heart of the dispute. As a result, if the mediator did not address the frame of race, which seemed central to the identity of one of the parties, moving forward might be difficult. Attacks on identity can easily derail discussion from the main issue.

Characterization frames consist of positive or negative labels for people. Often negative characterizations lead to reducing communication with the other party. If we do communicate, we often interpret the communication through a negative characterization frame. Without positive direct interaction, characterizations cannot be diffused.

In another contemporary example, a father and his eighteen-year-old son appeared in a small claims court. The father was divorced from the boy's mother, and the separation had been contentious. The boy, who spent most of his time with his mother, had adopted many of her negative views toward his father. The son was suing his father because the son felt the father had "cheated" him by withholding an inheritance from the son's grandfather. The father felt the son was not sufficiently mature to handle the funds. The son had characterized the father as a cheat; the father had characterized the son as immature. The actual issue of whether or not the father, by law, was supposed to give the money to the son could be settled by a judge. The conflict, however, could not be transformed unless these mutual characterizations were transformed.

When we are in situations of conflict, we commonly paint a picture of the other party that strengthens our side and denigrates the other. These characterizations provide justification for negative interactions or for ceasing interaction altogether. As we see in the father-son example, a conflict can be resolved but not transformed unless the mutual negative characterizations of the other evolve. A mediator can provide an opportunity for positive direct interaction that can dispel the negative characterization and help the parties become less polarized.

Power frames relate to how participants in a conflict conceptualize their power relationships and resources. They help people decide what forms of power are likely to help them accomplish their goals. Disputes settled by coercive power usually have clear winners and losers, but conditions often exist for the conflict to pop up again.[24] If one party feels completely dominated by the other party, it will make a difference in what communication strategies he or she chooses. If a participant believes he or she has legitimate power, it will make a difference in how communication strategies are enacted. If participants have expert power or referent power, their expertise or prestige will give them choices about how to accomplish their goals.

Power frames can blind opponents to opportunities for transforming conflict. In a dispute between a renter and a landlord, for example, the landlord believed he had legitimate, reward, and coercive power to demand the rent due. The renter, however, thought legitimate power was on her side because the landlord had violated city safety ordinances. While a judge could easily decide the merits of the case and "resolve" the conflict, the embittered relationship between tenant and landlord might lead to further clashes. Working with a mediator, however, participants broadened the frames through which they perceived the conflict. Indeed in this particular example, both parties came to see that their dispute was fueled not only by power frames, but also by identity frames (what it meant to be a good tenant or a good landlord) and by characterization frames (sleazy landlord and lousy tenant). Helping participants to reframe the conflict offered more than "resolution." Reframing the conflict transformed the relationship.

For Role Play and Discussion

You are mediating a case between a customer and a dry cleaner. The owner of the dry cleaner is a Chinese American woman. The customer is an African American man. The man was irate because although he was a longstanding customer of the cleaners, three of his sweaters had come back shrunken, and he wanted monetary compensation for the ruined sweaters. The owner of the cleaners quietly said that no other items in the batch had shrunk. She could not be sure that the sweaters had not been cleaned elsewhere and were already shrunken when he brought them into the store.

- *Which frames (identity/characterization) might be operating in this example?*
- *How might a mediator work with these frames?*

Interest frames can be used to help people shift their focus from power or rights to underlying interests. What are the underlying needs of the parties? In one case a towing company brought an errant driver into court to collect towing fees. Before going in front of the judge, the parties had an opportunity to mediate their dispute. The party who had been towed felt the towing company had been unfair. He had come back to the parking spot just as the car was being winched up. He thought the judge would certainly see things his way. The towing company argued that by law it had the right and legitimate power to tow the car.

At this impasse, the mediator asked to speak with the parties separately. The mediator asked the driver to think about his best and worst case scenario (BATNA and WATNA). The mediator helped the driver to see that if the judge did not see things his way, he would have to pay not only the towing charge, but also any court costs, a "prevailing party fee," and have a judgment on his record. By asking an open-ended question, the mediator helped shift the frame to what was in the best interest of the driver. The driver then negotiated a payment plan with the towing company.

Loss and gain frames. Most solutions can be framed in terms of benefits or harms. If we know that people are more sensitive to losses, we can reframe the issue in terms of the benefits it offers.

A *rights frame* is also illustrated by the above example. When the party who had been towed said that the act was "unfair," he was using a rights-based frame. Ury and his colleagues point out that when we appeal to fairness, standards, or a legal code, we are framing the dispute in terms of rights.

In a negotiation, a mediator needs to listen to the frame that each party uses and determine whether participants are using similar or different frames. If they are using different frames, a mediator can intervene in three ways: (1) a mediator can support a particular framing pattern if it appears more productive; (2) the mediator can explore the conflict from each of the participants' frames; or (3) the mediator can point out that the participants are using different frames for the same issue and thus making it more difficult to resolve the issue.[25]

Suppose you are the mediator and are called in to negotiate the following conflicts. How would you mediate the conflict using an "interests" frame? How about using a "power" frame?

1. *The board of a religious organization has just received a donation of $30,000. The youth director would like the money to be put toward a van for youth programs. The choir director would like the money to be used to repair the organ, to buy new music, and to supply new robes. The building director would like the money used for a "reader board" so potential new members and current members would know about programming and maintain membership.*

2. *A father and his twenty-one-year-old son are in conflict about the use of the family's second car. The father wants to withhold use of the car if the son brings it back without filling the tank, if he brings it home after midnight, or if the son gets a "C" average at school.*

John Paul Lederach has noted that "In essence, negotiation means that various people or groups involved recognize they cannot simply impose their will or eliminate the other side, but rather must work with each other to achieve their goals."[26] In our discussion, we have seen that God did not simply impose God's will but rather engaged in negotiation with Moses. Moses, making use of a variety of perspectives and strategies needed for successful mediation, was able to stake out a middle ground between the two parties and save most of the Israelites from God's anger, at least until the next time they succumbed to human weakness.

Theological Reflection on Exodus 32

The story of Moses negotiating with God over the building of the golden calf and the fate of the Israelites is theologically complex. First there is Moses, a man chosen by God to lead God's people out of bondage, through the wilderness, and to the promised land Canaan (Exod. 3:1–12). Moses enjoys a wonderful relationship with God, and Exodus 32 opens with Moses on Mount Sinai with God, who has written the Law of the Covenant on two tablets of stone (Exod. 31:18–32:1). God is willing to listen to Moses and to be persuaded by him as well. When God is ready to bring disaster upon the Israelites, Moses intercedes for them and God has a change of mind, averting disaster (vv. 11–14).

Yet despite God's change of mind, God maintains the upper hand as Lord of creation and Lord of history. Even though Moses begs God to forgive the people for their wrongdoing (vv. 30–35), God informs Moses that the guilty people will suffer consequences. Moses appears as a righteous man who, because of his righteousness, has influence over God. Moses is also a strong leader who does not shrink from his responsibilities to the people. He does not hesitate to confront Aaron and the people about their wrongdoing (vv. 21–20), and he takes action to restore order to the camp (vv. 27–29).

Aaron, the brother of Moses, seems easily persuaded by a crowd. Lacking moral and religious stamina, he blames others for the bad behavior of the Israelites. Aaron gives in to the people's lack of trust in Moses and God and, indirectly, is responsible for the people falling out of right relationship with their God. As characters in the account, the people themselves are weak and, like Aaron, lack religious stamina. They quickly lose trust in their leader Moses and, in doing so, in God as well. The construction of the golden calf attests to their need for some sort of physical assurance of a divine presence.

The Exodus account presents a mixed portrait of God. On the one hand, there is a God who hears and listens to the voice of Moses (vv. 11–15); on the other hand, the reader encounters a God who ignores the request of Moses (vv. 30–35). Instead of receiving divine forgiveness, the people receive divine consequences — a plague — for their transgression and they are blotted out of God's book (vv. 33–35).

According to the text, the God of Israel can be persuaded to act on behalf of the people while at the same time remaining in control of the people's lives and destiny. We also encounter a God of righteous anger who becomes infuriated with the people when they doubt that God's abiding presence remains with them even when they think God is absent. The people's lack of trust fills Israel's God with rage to the point of God wanting to devastate this faithless people. This multilayered portrait of God shows us that Israel's God is a jealous God — jealous for the people with whom this God shares a covenant — and that breaking the covenant with God and violating the Torah will bring punishment.

At this point in Israel's history and religious tradition, forgiveness is not automatic. Tension exists with the God of the prophets who pardons iniquity, passes over transgression, does not retain anger, delights in showing clemency, has compassion, treads iniquities underfoot, and casts all sins to the depths of the sea (Mic. 7:18–19).

Important to remember is the fact that the portrait of God throughout the Bible is historically, culturally, and theologically conditioned, and that God is portrayed anthropocentrically and anthropomorphically throughout much of the biblical text. Additionally, underlying any portrait of God in the Hebrew Scriptures is either the influence of a God's of retribution or a God of love or both.[27]

When looking at the Hebrew and Christian Scriptures as a whole, however, we see how the portrait of God evolves in relationship to human consciousness. New metaphors for God emerge from the people's lived experience of God and not from their theologizing about God. The Spirit of God in Genesis 1, in the end, becomes light and love. Thus, when viewing God in Exodus 32, we need to remember that while the text presents a metaphorical portrait of God, the Sacred Presence is beyond metaphor and beyond human articulation.

Finally, Exodus 32 makes the claim that even though the people fall out of right relationship with God, the divine promise is not revoked. Life does become more difficult, and the people have learned that any violation of right relationship with God is not without consequences.

In Sum: Grace in the Wilderness

In Exodus 32 as a whole, three instances of grace are at work in the human condition, particularly through the character of Moses. First, Moses has the courage to stand up for his people in the face of the all-powerful God of Israel. Second, Moses is willing to confront and deal with those who have transgressed. And, third, Moses is persistent in addressing God. Moses is a person of great stature who loves his God and his people deeply, and also a person of great rhetorical skill who knows how to present himself and his case before God. Finally, grace is active in God who, open to the pleas of Moses, has a change of mind and remains present to the people despite their waywardness.

The communication lens reminds us that laying blame is not helpful in resolving a conflict, although it comes quite naturally to us. Rather than laying blame, it is more helpful to ask, "How has each party contributed to the conflict?" Given the historical and cultural context of Exodus 32, Moses did the best he could for the times. Moses offers us a rudimentary introduction to the art and skill of collaborative negotiation, which is the essence of grace in the wilderness. Now our task is to develop our own knowledge and abilities to facilitate transformation of conflict.

Reflection Questions:
Can You Now...?

1. Explain the negotiating skills Aaron might have used to confront the situation in which he found himself?

2. Identify the communication skills Moses used in his interaction with God?

3. Pair up with a partner to rewrite the dialogue between God and Moses on the building of the golden calf, using the steps of principled negotiation (seek common ground, separate the people from the problem, invent options, develop objective standards)?

4. Describe a situation in which you have had to negotiate. Which communication skills did you find useful or effective?

5. Explain how you might use conflict and reframing skills in this situation?

6. Explain the difference between BATNA and WATNA? Can you identify what they would be in the following situation?

   Pat's family lived next door to Chris. Chris had a dog that was kept outside in a fenced area. Whenever Pat's family walked past the fence, the dog barked ferociously. Pat said that Chris had no right to keep the dog loose and that the entire family was afraid that the dog would get out and hurt them. Chris said that the dog was fenced and that he wasn't breaking any rules.

Additional Resources

+ The scene between Moses and God is not the only negotiation with God in the Bible. See, for example, Genesis 18:23–19:33 in which Abraham negotiates with God over the fate of Sodom. To what extent does Abraham's negotiation contain the basic elements of negotiation identified by Lewicki, Barry, and Saunders (offer, counteroffer, concession, closing)? To what extent did their negotiation contain the features described by Wilmot and Hocker (engaging in conflict, resisting domination, using persuasion, doing problem solving)?

+ The film documentary *Save the Last Dance: Mediation through Understanding* produced by the Harvard Negotiation Research Project provides an example of negotiation within a mediation context.

◆ The following websites present useful information about negotiating:

http://library.findlaw.com/2001/Jan/1/130785.html
   (fundamental elements of a negotiation)

www.mindtools.com/stress/cwt/TeamNegotiationSkills.htm
   (negotiating skills)

http://jobsearch.about.com/od/salaryinformation/a/salarynegotiat.htm
   (negotiating skills to salary improvement)

Additional Reading

Fisher, Roger, William Ury, and Bruce Pattton. *Getting to Yes: Negotiating Agreement without Giving In.* 2nd ed. New York: Penguin Books, 1991.
Lewicki, Roy, Bruce Barry, and David M. Saunders. *Essentials of Negotiation.* 4th ed. Burr Ridge, Ill.: McGraw-Hill, 2007.

JEREMIAH

Defensiveness and Conflict
(*Jeremiah 37–39*)

King Zedekiah sent for the prophet Jeremiah and received him at the third entrance of the temple of the LORD. The king said to Jeremiah, "I have something to ask you; do not hide anything from me." Jeremiah said to Zedekiah, "If I tell you, you will put me to death, will you not? And if I give you advice, you will not listen to me." (Jer. 38:14–15)

A Biblical Interpretation of Jeremiah 37–39

One of the most poignant characters of the Hebrew Scriptures is Jeremiah, God's prophet par excellence.[1] Throughout the book of Jeremiah, this marvelous preacher is forever calling his people back to right relationship with God. He discloses the transgressions of the Israelites with the hope that they will change their ways and once again embrace Torah. Forever performing symbolic actions that warn the people of weal and woe and also of good fortune that lies on the horizon, Jeremiah has an intimate relationship with God. Surprisingly, he is also a trusted advisor to some of the leaders of his day, even if they do not heed his words or advice.

One king who seeks out Jeremiah is Zedekiah, the king of Judah. (Recall that at this time the Israelites inhabit two kingdoms: Israel in the north and Judah in the south.) These chapters of Jeremiah recount the difficult and conflict-laden encounters Jeremiah has with Zedekiah, who, in the end, does not heed the prophet's advice and thus pays a grim price for his poor choice. These chapters can be divided into seven units:

37:1–10	Jeremiah's first word to Zedekiah
37:11–21	Jeremiah's first encounter with Zedekiah
38:1–6	Jeremiah's experience in the cistern
38:7–13	Jeremiah's rescue by Ebed-melech
38:14–28	Jeremiah's second encounter with Zedekiah
39:1–10	The fall of Jerusalem and the end of the monarchy
39:11–18	Jeremiah's fate

Jeremiah's First Word to Zedekiah (Jeremiah 37:1–10)

Verses 1 and 2 set the stage for the conflict between Jeremiah and Zedekiah. The account presents Zedekiah as a new character although, in fact, Jeremiah prophesied to Zedekiah earlier in Jeremiah 34 (see also 21:1–10); even then, Zedekiah paid little attention to Jeremiah. Once again Jeremiah addresses Zedekiah, the son of Josiah, the king of Judah, who reigned from around 640 to 609 B.C.E. Zedekiah is "appointed" king of Judah by King Nebuchadnezzar.[2] Zedekiah succeeded Coniah, son of Jehoiakim (v. 1).[3] Verse 2 explains that "Neither he [Zedekiah] nor his servants nor the people of the land listened to the words of the LORD that he spoke through the prophet Jeremiah." This statement seems not only to recapitulate the situation presented in Jeremiah 34 but also to foreshadow what follows in Jeremiah 37 through 39. Jeremiah receives the reward typical of a prophet: his words are not welcomed.

In verses 3 through 5, King Zedekiah sends two of his men to petition Jeremiah to pray to God for the sake of all the people in Judah. Jack Lundbom offers this observation:

> Troop movement out of Egypt has forced a Babylonian withdrawal from Jerusalem (v. 5), and the new king now wants intercession to the end that the siege be abandoned for good. Will Yahweh respond favorably? When Zedekiah sent his earlier embassy (21:2), the word coming back was unfavorable. Zedekiah also received an unfavorable word at some other point during the siege (34:1–7).
>
> Zedekiah may also be testing the prophet and the word he is delivering. The first embassy was sent in the hope of securing a withdrawal, and although Yahweh's answer promised nothing of the kind, the Babylonians now have withdrawn, and Zedekiah might think his earlier instincts right and Jeremiah's prophetic word wrong. But the beleaguered king may also fear the worst.[4]

As the conflict among the nations begins to heat up, Zedekiah gains hope from the northward movement of the Egyptian troops (37:5). This movement seems to be why the Babylonians are withdrawing from Jerusalem.[5]

When Zedekiah sends for Jeremiah to ask him to pray for the people of Judah, Jeremiah sends back a twofold divine message. In verse 6 the narrator states, "Then the word of the LORD came to the prophet Jeremiah." This prophetic word is not something Jeremiah can grasp or attain himself; rather, the word is something that "comes to Jeremiah." Preceding the actual divine word proclaimed by the character Jeremiah is the formula announcing a prophetic messenger: "Thus says the LORD, God of Israel" (v. 7).[6] Jeremiah first tells Jehucal and Shelemiah, the emissaries of Zedekiah, exactly what they are to say to the king. The first part of the message is that the Egyptians who were helping the Judahites stave off the Babylonians in Jerusalem are now going to retreat back to Egypt, and then the Babylonians are going to return and take over Jerusalem with force, eventually destroying it (vv. 7–8).

In the second part of the message (vv. 9–10), Jeremiah tells the men to put Zedekiah and the Judahites on notice. They are not to deceive themselves with the thought that the Babylonians will retreat from them as they will not, and no show of strength on the part of the Judahites will save Jerusalem; the city is destined to be burned. Nothing is said at this point about the two men's responses. Jeremiah then travels from Jerusalem to the land of Benjamin.

Jeremiah's First Encounter with Zedekiah (Jeremiah 37:11–21)

As the siege of Jerusalem is being lifted and Jeremiah heads out of the city on family business to complete a land transaction (v. 11),[7] ill fortune befalls him at the Benjamin Gate.[8] He is arrested by Irijah, apparently a well-known person in the community, and charged with deserting to the Babylonians. Jeremiah denies the accusation but Irijah, who refuses to listen to Jeremiah, takes him to the officials who, enraged at Jeremiah, beat him and imprison him (vv. 13–15).[9] John Bracke notes that "Jeremiah's effort to leave Jerusalem during the Babylonian siege will have easily been interpreted by persons loyal to Judah's leadership as another sign of Jeremiah's treasonous behavior."[10]

This section of the narrative closes with an editorial comment: "Thus Jeremiah was put in the cistern house, in the cells, and remained there many days" (v. 16). The cistern house — the "pit" into which Jeremiah is placed — is a near-empty water cistern, a fate he will again encounter in Jeremiah 38:6. This is the suffering of a prophet of God whose mission is to be faithful to the word, the message that must be proclaimed no matter what the cost.

Verses 17 through 21 provide an account of a meeting between Zedekiah and Jeremiah, after Zedekiah has had the prophet brought to him. The two meet in secret in Zedekiah's house. Lundbom points out that "the summons is done secretly, because if the king makes it known he will inflame all the more the princes who imprisoned Jeremiah. Here we begin to see a weak king at the mercy of his princes, unable to deal effectively with a crisis."[11]

After paying no attention to Jeremiah's word in the past (see vv. 1–2), Zedekiah now asks Jeremiah if the Lord has a message for him. Jeremiah assures the king that indeed, the Lord does have a message for him, but not one that Zedekiah will want to hear: "You shall be handed over to the king of Babylon" (v. 17b). Jeremiah rebukes Zedekiah for having imprisoned him (v. 18) and then confronts Zedekiah with other prophets (whom Zedekiah has apparently listened to) who have assured Zedekiah that no harm would come to him or Judah: "Where are your prophets who prophesied to you saying, 'The king of Babylon will not come against you and against the land?' " (v. 19). Jeremiah convinces Zedekiah not to send him back to prison (v. 20) and thus he is committed to the "court of the guard" but given food (v. 21). Although a helpless king has conceded to a helpless prophet, Jeremiah's woes are not yet over.

Jeremiah's Experience in the Cistern (Jeremiah 38:1–6)

Unfortunately, more trouble is brewing within the community. Four officials — Shephatiah, Gedaliah, Jucal, and Pashhur — hear Jeremiah's prophecy to the people of Judah and take opposition to Jeremiah's foreboding message:

> These who stay in this city shall die by the sword, by famine, and by pestilence; but those who go out to the Chaldeans [the Babylonians] shall live; they shall have their lives as a prize of war, and live.... This city shall surely be handed over to the army of the king of Babylon and be taken. (38:2–3)

While Jeremiah's message is a dire warning to the people, he is also offering them a way out: surrender to the Babylonians, allow yourselves to be exiled, and you will save your own lives.

The officials urge Zedekiah to have Jeremiah put to death (v. 4), and Zedekiah's response is distressing. Instead of ruling in Jeremiah's favor, he turns Jeremiah over to the officials, making them responsible for his fate: "Here he is; he is in your hands; for the king is powerless against you" (v. 5). Once again, Zedekiah appears to be an ineffective leader, and once again Jeremiah is thrown into a muddy cistern.[12] In the end, however, his life is spared because of the divine promise he received when he was raised up by God to be God's prophet (see Jer. 1:4–19, especially v. 19).

Jeremiah's Rescue by Ebed-melech (Jeremiah 38:7–13)

Fortunately Jeremiah is not without anyone to intercede for him. Ebed-melech, an Ethiopian eunuch in Zedekiah's house, speaks out on Jeremiah's behalf (vv. 7–9) and persuades the king to order Jeremiah's rescue (vv. 10–13).[13] With three other men,[14] Ebed-melech fashions a rope to hoist up Jeremiah. It is significant that Zedekiah is now exercising his power as king in the face of a group of officials who usurped his power earlier. The section closes with a simple statement: "And Jeremiah remained in the court of the guard" (v. 13b). The officials who once had power over Jeremiah are temporarily defeated.

Jeremiah's Second Encounter with Zedekiah (Jeremiah 38:14–28)

Zedekiah once again seeks Jeremiah's counsel. This time, however, the two men have an honest exchange. When Zedekiah approaches Jeremiah, Jeremiah immediately poses a rhetorical question to him, followed by a brief statement, both of which indicate a no-win situation for Jeremiah (v. 15). The rhetorical question presses Zedekiah into pledging an oath to God that assures Jeremiah his life and freedom, but Zedekiah does *not* pledge that he will heed Jeremiah's advice. Zedekiah and Jeremiah remain in conflict with one another.

Verses 17–26 capture the lively exchange between Jeremiah and Zedekiah. Once again Jeremiah advocates that Zedekiah surrender to the officials of the king of Babylon. By surrendering, Zedekiah would secure his life and those of his house, and Jerusalem would not be burned. If Zedekiah does not surrender, however, then Zedekiah and the city will be destroyed. Finally, we hear Zedekiah's true feelings, and we experience his own sense of powerlessness. He is paralyzed by fear and seems unable to hear or heed Jeremiah's words. Zedekiah admits: "I am afraid of the Judeans who have deserted to the Chaldeans, for I might be handed over to them and they would abuse me" (v. 19). Zedekiah fears his own traitorous people!

Jeremiah offers Zedekiah words of reassurance (v. 20) but also warns him again of what will happen if he does not surrender (v. 21). Zedekiah makes no decision but creates an alibi for himself, asking Jeremiah to pass it on to the officials if they should question him (vv. 25–26). As this section ends, Jeremiah returns to the court of the guard until Jerusalem is taken (v. 28). Its destruction is described in Jeremiah 39.

The Fall of Jerusalem and the End of the Monarchy (Jeremiah 39:1–10)

Zedekiah's inaction leads to the destruction of Jerusalem, the king, and his household. When Jerusalem is captured, Zedekiah and his army attempt to flee but to no avail. Zedekiah is captured by the enemy and brought before King Nebuchadnezzar of Babylon. King Nebuchadnezzar slaughters the nobles of Judah and puts out the eyes of Zedekiah himself before binding him and exiling him to Babylon (vv. 5–7).[15] Following the capture of Zedekiah and the death of his sons, Zedekiah's house and the houses of the people of Judah are burned and the walls of Jerusalem are breached. The Judeans who had deserted to the Babylonians and those who remain in Judah are then exiled to Babylon, leaving behind only some poor people who now received vineyards and fields from the Babylonians (vv. 8–10).[16] Although the kingdom of Judah is not completely emptied out by the Babylonians, Zedekiah, if he had heeded Jeremiah, could have saved it, along with his eyesight, his sons, and many people of the land. Zedekiah's decision had tragic consequences. Although Jeremiah did his best to convince Zedekiah to change his course, the prophet's words did not move Zedekiah.

Jeremiah's Fate (Jeremiah 39:11–18)

Surprisingly, Jeremiah does not suffer the fate of the Judean community. King Nebuchadnezzar issues a command that Jeremiah is to be treated well by the Babylonian officials (v. 12). He is released from the court of the guard (v. 14a) and allowed to return home to his own people (v. 14b). Perhaps King Nebuchadnezzar favors Jeremiah for having advised Zedekiah to surrender peacefully to the Babylonians. Jeremiah, for his part, is trying to save Jerusalem, Zedekiah, and the Judean community.

Verses 15 through 18 return to Ebed-melech, the Ethiopian who helped free Jeremiah from the cistern. Jeremiah tells Ebed-melech that his life will be spared on the day of doom. He will *not* be handed over to the dreaded enemy because he trusted in God (vv. 17–18), as evidenced by his rescue of Jeremiah (38:7–13).

In the end, the narration presents the Babylonian invasion of Jerusalem and all the events surrounding its eventual destruction, including the suffering of Zedekiah, his family, and the Judean community, as part of God's "plan" (Jer. 39:16) to chastise a people and a land that are guilty of apostasy, idolatry, and the breaking of covenant and Torah.

Looking through the Communication Lens

As we have seen, King Zedekiah and the people ignored the warning of Jeremiah, yet the king asked Jeremiah to "please pray to the Lord our God for us" (Jer. 37:3). The king obviously held Jeremiah in esteem as a prophet of God. What could be the reasons that Zedekiah refused Jeremiah's counsel? Was it due to Zedekiah's character? Was it the way Jeremiah's message was delivered? Was it due to Jeremiah's character or skill? And, what, if anything, can we learn for our own lives with respect to conflict?

The context indicates that Jeremiah was not the only prophet of the time. Other prophets, including Hananiah (Jer. 28:11), prophesied that God would break the yoke of Nebuchadnezzar. Diviners, soothsayers, and sorcerers preached that Zedekiah should not surrender to the king of Babylon (Jer. 27:10).

When someone tries to tell you "the truth" and others tell you what you want to hear, which voice are you likely to listen to and under what circumstances?

Who Are the Heroes, Victims, and/or Villains in This Narrative?

Conflicts are generally described by a story or narrative that lays out the events of the dispute. One characteristic of a conflict narrative — and a characteristic usually determined by the teller or writer — is whether the people involved see themselves as victim, villain, or hero.[17] Usually, the narrator will characterize himself or herself as *victim,* someone who is innocent and powerless and hurt by the other party. Often both parties will see themselves as victims of harmful intentions and experience the other party's story as an attack on their values, self-esteem, or face. Conflict usually results in feelings of powerlessness, alienation from the other person, and self-absorption.[18]

No matter how strong a person is, feelings of diminishment and victimization also result, often accompanied by hostility, suspicion, and anger toward the other party.[19] More concretely, both parties fear the other party will deprive them of something desired or needed.

> *To what extent might King Zedekiah have seen himself as victim? How about Jeremiah?*

Another role we sometimes assign to ourselves is *hero*, someone who risks discomfort in order to correct a wrong or injustice.[20] In casting ourselves in the role of hero, we rationalize that there is a good reason and good intentions behind our actions. If we have done anything wrong, we find ways to justify it.

> *Can you find any evidence in the story that King Zedekiah might have seen himself as a hero? How about Jeremiah?*

If we cast ourselves as victim or hero, the other participant in the conflict most often is cast as *villain*. The villain represents the other, an "aggressive" side that is unjust and has evil intentions. We tend to see all the evil and underhanded things the *other* does, while being completely blind to any action on our part that might be hurtful. Conflict specialist Gary Harper maintains that when we see ourselves as victims and/or heroes in our narrative about conflict we automatically create villains.[21] This is a primary reason, in any conflict, to listen carefully to how participants construct *their* narratives. Acknowledging the other's narrative can benefit the outcome; ignoring the other's narrative limits our ability to interact most effectively. Careful listening helps to prevent further characterizations of villains and polarized thinking.

> *Think of a conflict with someone close to you over an incident when each of you thought you were right and each of you tried to get the other person to change his or her mind. What prevented the other person from seeing things your way? What prevented you from seeing the other person's side? What prevented King Zedekiah from seeing things Jeremiah's way?*

Zedekiah is not alone in his inability to take in negative messages. Receiving negative messages is hard for most of us. Yet messages with which we do not agree, that make us feel defensive, that make us feel like the other person is antagonistic to us are common in conflict. This wall of defensiveness, of our refusal to hear what we don't want to acknowledge must be broken down.

The Nature of Defensiveness

Communication scholar Ronald Gordon sees defensiveness as an event that is physiological, cognitive, emotional, and behavioral.[22] Defensiveness is aroused by a perceived threat in which "the communicator tends to become tensed, gripped by the situation, estranged, and feels like moving against the other."[23] It is *physiological* because it is generated by the fight or flight reflex in the body. Survival of early human beings depended on their ability to either fight a marauding tiger or flee from it. Thus both our brain and endocrine system are primed to respond to perceived threats. Those physiological processes may be set in motion when we are faced with a perceived threat. Defensiveness is also a *cognitive* event in that when we perceive a threat, we typically engage in a flood of self-justifying thought. The thinking can escalate or deescalate the enormity of the situation. Defensiveness is *emotional* in that the thinking is generally colored by anger, fear, or hurt. Defensiveness is *behavioral* when we respond through speech or other physical action to defend ourselves.

The account in Jeremiah reveals how fearful Zedekiah was: "I am afraid of the Judeans who have deserted to the Chaldeans, for I might be handed over to them and they would abuse me" (38:19). And so Zedekiah ignores Jeremiah's warning.

In our own lives defensiveness can

- lead us to react without really thinking,
- prevent us from hearing information that may be useful to do our job,
- result in quid pro quo: equally defensive behavior from our opponent,
- cause or intensify conflict,
- wreck relationships,
- limit learning,
- embarrass us by our loss of control.

Given that defensiveness does not usually contribute to a good outcome, it is important to understand how the sender of the message, the message itself, and the receiver of the message can each contribute to or help negotiate the conflict.

Defensive Behavior

Some people are simply more defensive than others, although most of us demonstrate these characteristics at various times. Characteristics of defensive individuals include:

- They ignore their feelings as long as possible, denying their feelings to themselves and others.
- They concentrate on rebutting arguments.
- They blame others for their reactions.
- They dwell on the perceived injustice long after the argument is over.

Highly defensive individuals, however, incorporate most of these characteristics most of the time. Regardless, of how carefully a negative message is crafted, the fight or flight reflex of a highly defensive individual receiving a negative messages kicks in quickly and strongly. Researchers Glen Stamp, Anita Vangelisti, and John Daly found that in addition to the personality traits of an individual, a self-perceived flaw, sensitivity to that flaw, a perceived attack by another person, and a feeling that the attack is focused on the flaw generated defensive behavior.[24]

What flaw of Zedekiah did Jeremiah attack? To what extent does the interaction between Zedekiah and Jeremiah fit this description of defensive behavior?

While the receiver of a message may become defensive, the sender may make others defensive by the way the message is communicated, and the message itself may inadvertently trigger defensiveness. Jack Gibb identified six categories of verbal or nonverbal behavior that contribute to defensiveness or supportiveness:[25]

Defensiveness	*Supportiveness*
Evaluation	Description
Control	Problem orientation
Strategy	Spontaneity
Neutrality	Empathy
Superiority	Equality
Certainty	Provisionalism

An *evaluative* message passes judgment on another person's character:[26] "You are uninformed/careless/stupid to say/think/do that." When a message tries to change or influence someone or something, it is categorized as *controlling*.[27] Jeremiah clearly says, "Do as I say or else!" A *strategic* message, on the other hand, tries to maneuver or manipulate a person into doing what is wanted.

Neutrality communicates indifference to the other person as a human being, saying, basically, "You are unimportant to me — I don't care about you." One researcher found that conveying indifference to the interests of the other party was one of the hallmarks of an antagonistic climate.[28] *Superiority* is communicated by emphasizing one's position of power, greater ability, or higher status.[29] Though Jeremiah was Zedekiah's prisoner, he possessed the word of the Lord and communicated that superiority. Finally, a message of *certainty* says, "I'm right; you're wrong," which does nothing to encourage compromise. And it is very important to note that tone of voice and facial expression may contribute to perception of these elements in any message.

How to Minimize Defensiveness

There are also categories of communication that can minimize defensiveness. An important category is the use of *description,* which can present feelings and describe events or perceptions without directly requesting any change of behavior from the listener.[30] Rather than globally evaluating a person, the sender describes a specific behavior and his or her reaction to that behavior. For example, rather than charge someone with being careless, a descriptive alternative might be, "When you leave the lights on, I worry that our electricity bill will be unnecessarily high." This statement does not ring of control but it implies that a joint effort be used to work together to find a solution.

Spontaneity means that we remain open, listening to the other person with a willingness to set goals together instead of trying to force another person into our preferred solution. *Empathy* provides reassurance that we identify with the other's problems.[31] Research has indicated that ignoring a romantic partner's feelings strongly contributed to the defensiveness of the other person.[32] In conflict, most of us want to know that the other person understands us and the feelings that contribute to our point of view.

Equality means not putting one's own interests above those of the other person; any effective negotiation must be based on fairness. Finally, Jack Gibb suggests *provisionalism* over a message of certainty. A message that allows for alternative interpretations is less likely to elicit a defensive response.[33]

Important to remember is that in conflict people may connect the dots differently. Sometimes one party has information the other doesn't have, which affects the interpretation of data. Sometimes people will choose to ignore some information because it does not fit the picture they have created or assumed. Defensiveness can occur when one party imputes motivation and intention to another person. Most of us get defensive when our intentions are misunderstood or misstated. Questioning why someone has acted a certain way — expressing curiosity — is less likely to generate defensiveness than conveying that we know why the other party behaved in a particular way.[34]

In the discussion of attribution theory in the introduction of this book we noted how most of us tend to attribute shortcomings of another person to their character rather than to a given situation. This form of "blame frame" can also feed into the other's defensiveness. Rather than accuse the *other* person of "causing" an interpersonal conflict, we do better by jointly considering how *both* have contributed to the current situation.[35]

Clearly, Jeremiah and Zedekiah were not in a position to benefit from present-day research. Jeremiah, a prophet who received messages directly from God, merely conveyed what he heard, regardless of the consequences for himself. Zedekiah, on the other hand, behaved defensively, blocking information that might have contributed to a better outcome for him and his family. A willingness to avoid certain behaviors and engage in certain others can certainly minimize defensiveness and aid in conflict resolution.

Theological Reflection on Jeremiah 37–39

The story of the encounter between Jeremiah and Zedekiah provides a clear example of the nature of a prophet, and also of how one person's defensiveness and stubbornness bring dreadful consequences to an entire city and people. It is the prophetic word of Jeremiah that generates conflict. Functioning as God's prophet, he delivers a harsh message to Zedekiah, who refuses to listen to it or heed it. In the course of his experience with Zedekiah, Jeremiah suffers imprisonment because of his prophetic vocation: a prophet is called not to be successful but to be faithful. Despite all odds, Jeremiah continues to proclaim his message and, in turn, his life is spared, as promised by God (see Jer. 1:19). Ebed-melech's life is also spared because he too trusted in God. King Zedekiah, the king's servants and officials, and the people who rejected Jeremiah's message and counsel are destroyed or led into exile as the dreaded enemy, the Babylonians, invade the land. Zedekiah's defensiveness and his inability to receive Jeremiah's message has sealed the fate of a family, a people, and a city.

One point in need of ongoing theological reflection is the indication that God had "planned" the outcome of events all along, as we read in Jeremiah 39:16. What kind of a God would plot and plan such a tragedy even while sending an emissary to try to change the people's ways? Readers of the text are reminded that undergirding the proclamations and writings of the prophets, as well as their later editors and redactors, is belief in a God of retribution (see Deut. 28) that not only influenced the theology of the people during the writing but also colored their theological imagination. The theological agenda underlying the prophetic texts in general is that Israel's God is the Sovereign One who is Lord over creation and history. As the Sovereign One, God is a God of justice who metes out justice to all peoples and nations according to their actions. Thus, as we have seen earlier, the biblical text is historically, culturally, and theologically conditioned and demands that we continually discern who God is, then and now.

In Sum: Grace in the Wilderness

One cannot help but admire Jeremiah for his steadfastness, his courage, and his selflessness in the face of opposition. Despite the many trials he endures, Jeremiah continues to preach the prophetic word, continues to offer a beleaguered, stubborn, defensive, and frightened king a word of hope and a way out of impending danger. For Zedekiah, Jeremiah and his divine word is grace in the wilderness. For Jeremiah, Ebed-melech is also grace in the wilderness. Had Ebed-melech not approached Zedekiah and spoken out on Jeremiah's behalf, which led to Jeremiah's rescue, the prophet would surely have died.

This story helps us to see that even in the most dire of circumstances grace abides, but that grace can effect change ony if human beings remain receptive to it and work within it. Sadly, Zedekiah misses the opportunity to respond to the grace in the wilderness that came to him through the prophet Jeremiah and, sadly, his inability to respond leads to a sequence of tragic events.

From a communication perspective, we acknowledge the challenge of delivering a message that brings truth to power. The courage needed to speak out at risk to one's own life cannot be minimized even in our own times. Confronting powerful leaders is of inestimable value to a society, and multiple communication skills can be employed to make a positive outcome more likely.

Reflection Questions:
Can You Now...?

1. Explain Jeremiah's vocation as a prophet?

2. Think of instances where you have taken on the role of victim, hero, or villain in a conflict? Why did you choose that role?

3. Recall a conflict you were involved in? Can you determine if you became defensive? Recalling that defensiveness involves physiological, cognitive, emotional, and behavioral components, can you recognize those components? What contributed to your defensiveness: a "self-perceived flaw," evaluative language, loss of face in front of others?

4. Understand how, if at all, did defensiveness in the situation affected the way the conflict unfolded?

5. Consider what remedies to your own defensiveness seem viable for you to work on?

6. Explain how, if King Zedekiah had not been so defensive, he might have responded to Jeremiah? Would the outcome have been different?

7. Explain if Jeremiah, as God's prophet, could have been supportive in speaking with Zedekiah?

Additional Resources

♦ Can you apply the concepts from this chapter to the biblical story of Jonah?

♦ In the film *Lean on Me,* principal Joe Clark sets out to turn around a troubled school. The movie provides stark examples of both defensive and supportive communication. If you have a chance to watch the film, how would you compare Joe Clark's behavior to that of Jeremiah?

♦ In the film *Inception* the protagonist's specialty is conquering others' defenses that block their receptivity to new ideas. The movie cinematically visualizes how fierce our defenses can be.

Additional Reading

Dempsey, Carol. *Jeremiah: Preacher of Grace, Poet of Truth.* Collegeville, Minn.: Liturgical Press, 2008.

Harper, Gary. *Joy of Conflict Resolution: Transforming Victims, Villains and Heroes in the Workplace and at Home.* Gabriola Island, B.C.: New Society Publishers, 2004.

Stone, Douglas, Bruce Patton, and Sheila Steen. *Difficult Conversations: How to Discuss What Matters Most.* New York: Viking, 1999.

10

MICHAL AND DAVID

Conflict in Romantic Relationships

(1 Samuel 18:17–30, 19:11–17, 25:43–44;
2 Samuel 3:14–16, 6:15–23)

Michal, daughter of Saul, had fallen in love with David.
(1 Sam. 18:20)

As the ark of the LORD came into the city of David, Michal daughter of Saul looked out of the window, and saw King David leaping and dancing before the LORD; and she despised him in her heart.
(2 Sam. 6:16)

A Biblical Interpretation
of 1 Samuel 18:17–30, 19:11–17, 25:43–44
and 2 Samuel 3:14–16 and 6:15–23

Family relationships can at times become complicated, causing tension and conflict. These situations are not novel to our present-day world; they existed even as far back as the days of ancient Israel. In the biblical story, Michal, the daughter of King Saul, loves David, one of Saul's friends and warriors. Saul gives Michal as a wife to David. Saul also plots to have David killed in a battle with the Philistines because he feels threatened by David. Saul knows that God favors David and also that Michal loves David very much. By deceiving her father through trickery, Michal tries to keep David from being killed. Saul, in turn, causes tension between David and Michal. In the end, Michal's love for David turns cold, and David turns against her. She suffers the loss of marital intimacy, never to conceive and bear a child with David.

We find ourselves *in medias res* with respect to the story of Michal and David. We're unsure of whom to support. Who is Saul? Who is David? What is their relationship prior to the arrival of Michal? Who is Michal? The background of the story about Michal and David needs to be explored before engaging in a detailed study of the narrative.

Saul

Saul, the son of Kish, is a member of the Benjaminite clan of Matri (1 Sam. 10:21). Anointed by Samuel, Saul is the first king of Israel (see 1 Sam. 8–2 Sam. 1). A valiant warrior, he defeats enemies on every side, including the Moabites, Ammonites, Edomites, the kings of Zobah, the Philistines, and the Amalekites (1 Sam. 11, 13–14, 15, 17, 28–31). Saul's tragic flaw, however, is his arrogance.

Saul and David

One of Saul's friends is David, who is also befriended by Saul's son Jonathan. The beginning of the relationship between Saul and David is pleasant. David is willing to take on Goliath, a mighty Philistine and an enemy of the Israelites who terrifies Saul and his army. When, with a sling and stones David defeats the mighty Goliath, Saul and Jonathan marvel at David's great strength. Saul, in turn, makes David a part of his household and promises him a wife, and Jonathan clothes David in royal robes.

The friendship between Jonathan and David is solid, but the friendship between Saul and David begins to deteriorate as Saul grows jealous of David. Eventually the Spirit of the Lord leaves Saul to rest on David (1 Sam. 18:12, 15). Saul, increasingly estranged from David, acts with duplicity against him three different times. First, Saul offers him his older daughter, Merob, but just as the two were about to marry, Saul gives Merob to another man (1 Sam. 18:17, 19). Saul then sends David into battle, hoping he will be killed by the Philistines (1 Sam. 18:17). Third, Saul offers David the status of son-in-law if he will deliver one hundred Philistine foreskins, a task exhibiting great military might. Saul secretly hopes that this task will end David's life, but Saul is sadly proven wrong (1 Sam. 18:25). It seems unusual that throughout his relationship with Saul, David seems unaware of Saul's mounting animosity (1 Sam. 18:26). In the end, Saul gives his younger daughter. Michal, to David in marriage. Saul eventually dies in the battle of Gilboa, and David succeeds to the throne.

David

David is regarded as the best loved king by the Israelites, a king of heart-felt fidelity to God. David also possessed great military and political genius and had the gift of winning people over to his side. He defeated the Philistines, extending Israel's borders, and captured the Canaanite city of Jerusalem from the Jebusites, making it the capital of Israel. David then moved the Ark of the Covenant to Jerusalem, establishing a divine covenant with God (2 Sam. 7:1–17). Considered God's "anointed one," he was continually blessed by God.

Michal

Michal, the younger daughter of Saul, was first the wife of David (1 Sam. 18:27), then the wife of Pali/Paltiel (1 Sam. 25:44; 2 Sam. 3:15–17), and finally the wife of David again (2 Sam. 3:15–17).

Michal's relationship with David was unsettled, moving from love to hate. She was a woman under the power of strong men: her father, Saul; her husband, David; and King Ishbosheth, who was a son of Saul and Michal's brother. Her conflict with David was both a royal conflict and a personal conflict, and it left her childless by David. The story of David and Michal unfolds in five episodes:

1 Sam. 18:17–30   Saul's promises to David

1 Sam. 19:11–17   David and Michal's plot

1 Sam. 25:43–44   Interlude

2 Sam. 3:14–16   David's message to Ishbaal

2 Sam. 6:15–23   David's encounter and exchange with Michal

Saul's Promises to David (1 Samuel 18:17–30)

Right at the beginning of the story involving Saul, David, and Michal, we experience conflict. Saul offers Merab, his elder daughter, to David for a wife. David is quite humbled by such a gesture, but when the time comes for her to be given to David, she is given instead to Adriel, the Meholathite, as a wife (18:17–19). David Toshio Tsumura notes that "Saul keeps raising the bar for David's marriage. Now the victory over Goliath is not enough; David must continue fighting."[1] Now David must fight the Philistines and prove himself in battle yet again. At this juncture in the story, it is not clear that Saul really intends to confer the title of "son-in-law" on David.

The conflict between David and Saul continues in verses 20–29, and we learn that another of Saul's daughters, Michal, has set her heart upon David (18:20). Michal's desire for David greatly pleases Saul, who decides to use Michal as a way of putting an end to David: "Let me give her to him that she may be a snare for him and that the hand of the Philistines may be against him" (v. 21a). To sweeten the offer even more and to persuade David to respond affirmatively to the prospects of becoming Saul's son-in-law, Saul sends messengers to David to inform him that indeed the king is delighted with him, that all the king's servants love David, and that David should respond affirmatively to Saul (v. 22).

The plot and plan intensify in verses 23 through 26. The servants deliver Saul's message to David only to have David humbly respond: "Does it seem to you a little thing to become the king's son-in-law, seeing that I am a poor man and of no repute?" (v. 23). The servants return to Saul and deliver David's reluctant response to the king. Saul, in turn, sends the servants to tell David that Saul does not desire a marriage present. In ancient biblical times, the "groom-to-be" had to provide to the father of a future bride a stipulated sum of money that would indicate the seriousness of his intention. In the case of Michal, Saul asks for no money but, instead, a hundred foreskins of the Philistines, Saul's enemies of longstanding (v. 25a; Gen. 34:11–17; Exod. 22:16). This request pressures David to immediately wage war against the Philistines.

David delights in the prospect of being Saul's son-in-law and immediately sets out to fulfill the preposterous task that, for David, seemed somewhat effortless. Together with his men, David kills one hundred Philistines and brings their foreskins to Saul (v. 27a). Saul, in turn, gives Michal to David (v. 28b). The accomplishment of such a great feat, however, leaves Saul uneasy because he becomes aware that indeed the Lord is with David, that David is a powerful warrior, and that his daughter Michal does, in fact, love him.

The mounting animosity within Saul reaches a crescendo, resulting in an unfortunate fractured relationship between himself and David. After Saul gives Michal to David as a wife, Saul declares David his enemy; ironically, David is unaware of Saul's intentions and his growing hostility (vv. 28–29). David's defeat of the Philistines is a step in his rise to power, and Saul's fearful reaction to David betrays his character flaws and a growing wickedness of heart. Just as Saul uses Michal for ill purposes, so also God uses Saul in David's ascent to greatness. David's success in battle against the Philistines continues in verse 30 and, surprisingly, he is more successful than Saul's own servants in battle (v. 30).

David and Michal's Plot (1 Samuel 19:11–17)

Saul's plan to have David die in battle at the hand of the Philistines has backfired, so "Saul sent messengers to David's house to keep watch over him, planning to kill him in the morning" (v. 11a). Michal, aware that David's life is now endangered, plots with David to save his life. After she warns him of the imminent danger, she lets him down at night through a window (v. 11). After he escapes, she ingeniously places a dummy with goat's hair on its head on their bed (v. 13). Michal takes Saul's messengers by surprise when they go to put David to death and are told that he is sick (v. 14). Saul, however, has no compassion. He orders the messengers to observe David themselves and to bring him to Saul so that Saul himself can kill him (v. 15). Saul's insecurity and fear have turned into vicious hatred.

Although Michal's trickery is soon discovered, once again she schemes on David's behalf. She lies to her father when he confronts her about David's escape (v. 17) to save the life of her husband and future king, and David flees to Ramah, the home of Samuel.

Interlude (1 Samuel 25:43–44)

Verses 43 through 44 interrupt the flow of the narrative and provide us with additional information pertaining to the story's main characters: David marries Ahinoam of Jezreel, and Michal is given in marriage to Palti (later Paltiel), son of Laish. She also remains married to David.

David's Message to Ishbaal (2 Samuel 3:14–16)

The next section of the story is also filled with tension and conflict. After David left Michal to save his own life, Michal was given in marriage to someone else. Now David sees the benefit in having her back. David's relationships with his wives are rooted more in politics than in love. Eugene H. Peterson notes that "the political implications, at least, of [David's] demand are obvious: Saul's daughter returned to him as his wife would be a signal to Israel that Saul's kingdom is being handed over to him as well."[2]

David makes a bold demand of Ishbaal, Saul's son: "Give me my wife Michal, to whom I have been engaged at the price of one hundred foreskins of the Philistines" (v. 14). Since David has never divorced Michal, he has the right to reclaim her. Michal's return to David is part of a negotiated deal between Abner, the commander of Saul's army, and David. Ishbaal follows David's orders and takes Michal from her husband Paltiel. What follows next is poignant. Unlike David, Paltiel loves Michal simply for who she is and not for political interests. Weeping, Paltiel follows her all the way to Bahurim. Patiel, acting as a foil for David, sheds light on David's paltry character. Lillian R. Klein notes that "Palti's devotion and helplessness provide a marked contrast to David, who has become decisive and aggressive since his wordless escape from Michal's window. The reader is pulled in two directions: by Palti's love for Michal and by recollections of Michal's love for David."[3]

Michal is now caught in the middle, and she is passive as she is transferred "from male to male as an object."[4] As for David, by the time he and Michal come in contact again, David has taken six additional wives, and with each wife he has fathered a son. Danna Nolan Fewell and David M. Gunn note that "David's policy is to dissipate all power but his own. He will not have one wife but several. And no wife will be first in his house."[5] Thus, Michal indirectly becomes David's pawn, his ticket to the throne.

David's Encounter with Michal (2 Samuel 6:15–23)

This next group of verses reflects a new set of circumstances. Saul has been killed in the battle at Gilboa, and David has ascended to the throne. One of his first tasks is to bring the Ark of the Covenant to the City of David — to Jerusalem (v. 15). He completes this task amid much festive celebration, leaping and dancing before the Lord as the ark enters the city (v. 16). From her window, Michal watches, despising David in her heart (v. 16). Klein's reading of this portion of the text sharpens the contrasts and conflicts in this story thus far. Klein observes:

> The contrast of this scene at the window with the earlier window scene is notable. In the earlier scene, Michal represents the royal family as

the daughter of Saul, and David is the powerless son-in-law. In the later scene, David *is* royalty — the king — and Michal is merely one of several wives. The window which provided David freedom and saved his life becomes a window which confines Michal, evidenced by the bitter tones of her words.[6]

Verses 17 through 19 describe the arrival of the ark into the City of David and into the tent that David has pitched for it. As a sign of welcome and gratitude to God, David offers various sacrifices, blesses the people assembled for this festive occasion, and then shares with them some food as a gesture of celebration. With the ark now in place, the people return to their homes and David returns to his household to bless it (v. 20a). To his surprise, however, he meets a hostile Michal, who boldly upbraids him: "How the king of Israel honored himself today, uncovering himself today before the eyes of his servants' maids, as any vulgar fellow might shamelessly uncover himself!" (v. 20b). David is dressed only in a linen Ephod, a garment usually worn by priests.

Klein notes:

These words reveal an image of Michal entirely different from the one we encountered when Michal last spoke — the young woman resource-fully saving her husband's life even as she sends him away from her side. Interim events have apparently made Michal angry and sharp-tongued. Michal may regret her separation from Palti; she may feel that David is "beneath her," as demonstrated by his exhibitionist behavior; she may resent the fact that she, who enjoyed the prestige of being the king's daughter, is merely one of several wives of this boorish king — and childless to boot. Michal's angry words to David suggest that she is displacing the shame she experiences in her situation on to David.[7]

Although we can only presume reasons for Michal's outburst, one thing is certain: she has found her own voice. A woman matured and no longer controlled by her father Saul, Michal emerges as a strong female figure who uses her own power to confront David, and in doing so she claims her place in the text and in the life of David. She becomes her own person rather than a passive, silent object under the thumbs of the men in her life.

David's response to Michal is blunt and straightforward: "It was before the LORD, who chose me in place of your father and all his household, to appoint me as prince over Israel, the people of the LORD, that I have danced before the LORD. I will make myself yet more contemptible than this, and I will be abased in my own eyes; but by the maids of whom you have spoken, by them I shall be held in honor" (vv. 21–22).

In dancing before the Lord, David establishes worship as a priority in the community and celebrates the fact that he is chosen by God to lead the people. David's primary commitment is to his God, whom he understands to be sovereign, and worship, over and above his great political and militaristic gifts, is David's main contribution to Judaism. Michal, however, is not pleased with David's ritual performance.

The story closes on a somber note: "And Michal the daughter of Saul had no child to the day of her death" (v. 23). Throughout the biblical texts, God remembers various barren women, such as Sarah, Rebecca, and Hannah, and opens up their wombs. To be able to give birth is not only a sign of fertility but also a sign of God's blessing. Michal seems not to be remembered or blessed by God. One possible reason for her inability to bear children is because as a young woman she may have worshiped idols, a violation of covenant and Torah. Another possibility is that David refused to have relations with her because of her change in attitude toward him. Whatever the reason, Michal is left childless, without a son to inherit and care for her in her old age.

Michal, a symbol of the rivalry that existed between her father and husband, has dared to confront male authority and in doing so reaps the disfavor of her husband and ultimately that of Israel's God. She is a woman who has expressed her feelings honestly throughout the story, and in the end such honesty has cost her the joy of motherhood and descendants. She is a figure to be praised and respected for following her own senses and for being courageous and clever. Yet such praise has come with a great personal cost to her, a cost that leaves us — the readers — with a sense of sadness at how such a romantic relationship with all its political and "distance" complexities can evaporate into a "marriage of convenience" that brings neither David nor Michal the fullness of joy associated with the exchange of true love.

Looking through the Communication Lens

The story of Michal and David is a sad tale of a relationship. The narrator tells us, "Michal, daughter of Saul, had fallen in love with David" (1 Sam. 18:20). Robert Alter observes, "This love... is the only instance in all biblical narrative in which we are explicitly told that a woman loves a man."[8] Yet by the end of Michal's narrative, the text tells us that Michal's love turned into hate. As the biblical analysis showed, some aspects of this story are unique to them, their times, and the political relationships surrounding them. Other aspects of their story, however, can apply to many long-term romantic relationships.

The Influence of Context on the Relationship

Why did Michal move from loving David to despising him? Part of the answer comes from the changing situations surrounding their relationship. Joseph Folger, Scott Poole, and Randall Stutman identify three important elements in a context of conflict: the history of the parties, the climate of the social situation, and the nature of the surrounding organization.[9] Given the historical period in which marriages were used primarily to build alliances, King Saul, both as king and father, decided whom Michal would marry and to whom she would stay married. Michal had little or no say in the matter.

Although readers are not told much about the "climate," or the generalized atmosphere of their relationship, we can assemble some facts. We know that David was brought to Saul because he played the lyre well, and the music was soothing to Saul (1 Sam. 16:23). We can speculate that Michal might have first encountered David during this period. David was described as a youth who was "ruddy, and had beautiful eyes, and was handsome" (1 Sam. 16:12). We also know that while David was delivering provisions to his brothers who were fighting the Philistines, David heard of Saul's reward for destroying Goliath: "the king will greatly enrich the man who kills him [Goliath], and will give him his daughter" (1 Sam. 17:25). After killing Goliath David was a hero. We read next that "Saul's daughter Michal loved David" (1 Sam. 18:20).

From Michal's perspective, David was a star: a handsome skilled musician who was also a brave warrior. At this stage of the story, from Michal's perspective, the climate for their relationship was full of positive and hopeful expectations. At this point in the history of their relationship, she had no reason not to trust David.

Then the plot thickens. While love motivated Michal, Saul promoted the relationship for his own purposes: "Let me give her to him [David] that she may be a snare for him and that the hand of the Philistines may be against him" (1 Sam. 18:20–21). Michal got the husband she loved, and though David brought "one hundred foreskins" of the Philistines (thus, the death of one hundred Philistine warriors) as payment for her, the narrative does not mention his feelings for Michal. Although he had already been anointed by the prophet Samuel to replace Saul as king (1 Sam. 16:13), he still had to earn the people's support. Not mentioning David's reciprocal love for Michal is likely no mere oversight because the text *does* include David's feelings of love for her brother Jonathan (2 Sam. 1:26). While Michal may not have been aware of her father's motivations, David might have been, and, hence, trust may not have been mutual.

As Saul's jealously of David grew, David had the trust and support of Michal. She warned David of her father's plots against him and helped him escape (1 Sam. 19:11–15). The climate of their early relationship was certainly charged with emotion, but Michal was clearly dedicated to David.

The Role of Power

Since Saul was set on doing away with David, David's mere survival likely preoccupied both Michal and David. The evidence in the text, however, suggests only that Michal was devoted to David; there's no evidence that her devotion was reciprocated. While David feared for his life, it appears that Michal had more emotional involvement in the relationship than did David.

As noted before, while some aspects of the relationship between David and Michal were historically set, this imbalance in emotional involvement is one aspect of their relationship that can be generalized. A classic study of power in relationships points out that *power in a relationship goes to the person who is least interested.*[10] This held true for Michal and David, and it is also supported by contemporary research.

> *Have you ever been in a relationship or witnessed a relationship in which one person was more emotionally committed than the other? What were some of the consequences of that imbalance? To what extent did the less interested person wield more influence? If the relationship ended, what led to the breakup?*

Susan Sprecher, Maria Schmeeckle, and Diane Felmlee describe some of the consequences of an emotional imbalance between couples. They found that the person who is less interested in the relationship perceives his or her partner as having more control over whether the relationship continues.[11] Moreover, unequally involved couples had lower levels of satisfaction than those who reported equal emotional involvement.[12] Couples who perceived themselves as unequally involved reported higher levels of negative emotions.[13] Particularly relevant to the story of Michal and David is their finding that perceptions of unequal emotional involvement contributed to a change in perceptions of the *quality of relationship* over time for female participants.[14] These findings hold true for Michal and David, and also in many of our own relationships.

As the account tells of the continuing struggle between Saul and David, no mention is made of Michal until much later when the text reveals that "Saul had given his daughter Michal, David's wife, to Palti son of Laish, who was from Gallim" (1 Sam. 25:44).

After the deaths of Saul and Jonathan and the anointing of David as king, the text notes that David had married two other women, a widow named Abigail and Ahinoam of Jezreel. And a struggle ensued between David and Abner, the commander of Saul's army, who supported another of Saul's sons. At some point, David and Abner appear ready to strike a truce with Michal becoming, once again, part of the arrangement: "bring Saul's daughter Michal when you come to see me" (2 Sam. 3:13). On David's command, Michal's brother Ishbaal retrieves her from her husband Palti and delivers her to Abner.

No wonder that the climate of David and Michal's relationship changed markedly from the early verses to the later ones! In 1 Samuel, communication was driven by David's immediate survival, and Michal submerged her identity as Saul's daughter into her relationship with David, acting as his helpmate. By the time of 2 Samuel, their relationship had gone through a number of different stages. Various factors contributed: poor communication, tension, an imbalance of power, and the absence of any effort to maintain a good relationship.

How Relationships Change

Early in the story, Michal is immersed in saving David's life. Infatuation often accompanies the first stages of forming a romantic relationship. Excitement and novelty, suppression of negative emotion, and putting one's best face forward are common occurrences in new relationships. Mark Knapp describes five stages accompanying the formation of a relationship: initiating, experimenting, intensifying, integrating, and bonding.[15] *Initiating* describes the first encounter with the other person. *Experimenting* is a bit like an audition. Each person learns a little more about the other and whether or not he or she would like the relationship to continue. *Intensifying* involves sharing more information about each other and becoming closer. *Integration* occurs when couples make increased commitments to each other and the relationship takes on its own identity. *Bonding* means the couple publicly announces their connection.

Clearly, the biblical text does not provide details of how David and Michal's relationship progressed. Indeed, in those times, formal relationships occurred by the will of the king. The narrative in 1 Samuel, however, does suggest that Michal's identity shifted from being "daughter of Saul" to "wife of David." Generally, during the early stages of relationship formation, conflict is at a minimum, as seems to be the case with Michal and David, and excessive conflict during the early stages typically dooms the relationship from the beginning.

Generally, the deterioration of a relationship also includes five stages: differentiating, circumscribing, stagnating, avoiding, and terminating.[16] By knowing the warning signs of deterioration, we can take steps to reverse the process. In *differentiating,* couples note differences in personality, values, or behavior and see these differences in a negative light. Claiming one's identity also occurs during differentiation, and increased conflict is common. *Circumscribing* begins when couples tiptoe around each other in order to avoid conflict. When couples reach the *stagnating* stage, they go through the motions of the relationship, but have mentally "checked-out," perhaps anticipating negative dialogue that comes from repetitious conflicts. *Avoiding* involves increasing physical and emotional distance and, finally, *terminating* means officially ending the relationship. The biblical text does not yield enough details about Michal and David's interactions to know if they went through these steps.

From what we do know in the text, after Michal saved David's life, her father the king sent her off to be the wife of Palti. When David asked for her back, she was returned to him as her second husband, Palti, weeping, followed her. Can we infer that David could have gotten Michal back at any time? Such thoughts could have easily shifted Michal from a stage of "bonding" to a stage of "deterioration." After saving David's life, Michal might have expected that David would come for her. The Bible makes no mention of this so perhaps Michal was left to mull over David's avoidance. We might well imagine the cascade of negative feelings on the part of Michal.

Denise Cloven and Michael Roloff have established that "mulling" increases the perceived severity of a dispute.[17] Prolonged thought about a conflict increases the likelihood of hostile interactions. And as earlier discussions of attribution maintained, when looking for the reason for another's behavior, we are more likely to ascribe cause to defects in character rather than any external circumstances.

Of course, Michal's role as a king's daughter at her time in history made her very much a pawn without the power to engage in any analysis of her relationship with David. We should not suffer from this disadvantage but benefit from the knowledge that if we can understand the dynamics of a relationship, we can also move to change course.

Marital Conflict

The most frequently identified issues that negatively affect marriages are money, sex, communication, household chores, raising children, relationships with in-laws, and jealousy.[18] Researcher Larry Erbert adds personal criticism as a primary cause of conflict,[19] and John Gottman identifies four behaviors that predict marital distress: criticism, contempt, defensiveness, and stonewalling, calling these the "Four Horsemen of the Apocalypse."[20] *Criticism* involves attacking someone's personality or character rather than stating a specific behavior or problem to be addressed and includes blame. *Contempt* adds the dimension of an intent to insult, mock, or degrade. *Defensiveness* implies reduced listening and excuses, denial, cross-complaining, and angry disagreement. Finally, *stonewalling* entails hostile withdrawal and silence that shuts out the other person.

The narrator relates the last scene between Michal and David: "As the ark of the LORD came into the city of David, Michal daughter of Saul looked out of the window, and saw King David leaping and dancing before the LORD, and she despised him in her heart" (2 Sam. 6:16).

When David returned to bless his household, Michal went out to meet him and said, "How the king of Israel honored himself today, uncovering himself today before the eyes of his servants' maids, as any vulgar fellow might shamelessly uncover himself" (2 Sam. 6:20). Contempt and sarcasm rippled through her speech. David reacted in kind and derided Michal, "It was before the LORD, who chose me in place of your father and all his household, to appoint me as prince over Israel, the people of the LORD, that I have danced before the LORD. I will make myself yet more contemptible than this, and I will be abased in my own eyes; but by the maids of whom you have spoken, but by them I shall be held in honor.' And Michal the daughter of Saul had no child to the day of her death" (2 Sam. 6:21–23).

Michal's criticism of David stands out starkly. Both Michal and David demonstrate all of Gottman's "Four Horsemen." Three times the narrator labeled Michal as "daughter of Saul." Readers already know the familial connection of Michal, so this identifier serves another purpose. Just as Saul resented David, so too does Michal resent David. She is "her father's daughter" not only by blood, but also by attitude. Contempt and criticism spew forth from Michal. David replies defensively, escalating the conflict.

We cannot be sure whether Michal's hostile communication is genuinely a reaction to David's dancing, or whether it erupts from her anger at David's withdrawing from their relationship and then removing her from the home she had established. Researchers have identified three types of withdrawal in marital functioning: angry withdrawal, conflict avoidance, and intimacy avoidance.[21] Negative emotion can produce *angry withdrawal,* communication about anger, hostility, rejection, or a combination of these behaviors. Stonewalling, slamming doors, and hanging up the phone on someone are common examples. *Conflict avoidance* can occur without negative feelings and does not imply rejection of the partner; rather, the person simply tries to evade a conflict. *Intimacy avoidance* means not meeting the other's needs for closeness and contact.

Research also demonstrates that certain behaviors contribute significantly to the failure or success of relationships, and that many attempts at communication are bids for emotional connection.[22] One party may communicate a gesture to end hostilities. Whether the other party shows interest, validating the outreach, or rejects it by expressing anger, disgust, or belligerence, will regulate the conflict.[23] In this biblical narrative, David arrives home "to bless his household." Michal, presumably consumed by layers of anger, cannot respond to his bid for connection and rejects it with derision and hostility.

We have no direct information about why David did not reclaim Michal after Saul "reassigned" her to another husband. David's ongoing struggle with Saul undoubtedly was an obstacle. He might have wanted to spare Michal from further conflict with her father. By not communicating with her, however, she was left to mull over her situation. It is likely that she was pessimistic about her future, blamed David, and felt deep anger. Indeed, Michal's greeting to David was filled with all of these, and his response was "intimacy avoidance," so that "she had no child to the day of her death."

Without evidence to the contrary, we must assume that David did nothing to sustain his relationship with Michal once Saul intervened. The story, however, raises two important topics: What behaviors help maintain relationships? What special challenges accompany distance relationships?

What Behaviors Help Maintain Good Relationships?

Communication experts Daniel Canary and Laura Stafford identified five types of behavior that contribute to healthy relationships: positivity, openness, assurances, network interaction, and sharing tasks.[24] *Positivity* means trying to make interactions pleasant.[25] Acting cheerful, being optimistic and uncritical, and doing favors for others characterize positivity. In the early stages of a relationship, positivity is easy. During the stage of differentiating, positivity may disappear. Knowing that such behavior is important for sustaining good relationships, we can seek opportunities to make interactions, even though they may have deteriorated, deliberately more positive.

Openness refers to messages that directly discuss the nature of the relationship and convey that one is listening well to one's partner. In the intermediate stages of relationship development, openness comes easily. In the middle stages of relationship deterioration, the opposite is generally true and listening may be at its most superficial. Being alert to one's partner's attempts to improve the situation, however, and validating that bid can contribute to maintaining the relationship.[26] Important to note is that mature relationships may have fewer opportunities for openness, so validating those opportunities that do come along is important.

Assurances include messages that reassure one's partner that he or she is valued and that the relationship has a future. Once David plucked Michal from her life with Palti, reassuring communications from David might perhaps have helped put their relationship on a healthier footing.

Network implies interaction with friends and family, and such interactions are often accompanied by perceptions of love and satisfaction.[27] Clearly, this avenue of relationship maintenance was closed to Michal and David; indeed friendships and family ties seem to have contributed to the conflict.

Sharing tasks, doing household chores together, is a fifth way of maintaining relationships. Given the period in which Michal and David lived and their distinct roles in their society, sharing tasks was another missed opportunity for them.

> While Michal and David's relationship was doomed from many vantage points, our own relationships do not have to be negatively circumscribed. Have you ever deliberately tried to reverse a deteriorating relationship? What are the advantages and disadvantages of using maintenance behaviors?

Managing Dialectical Tensions

Oppositions naturally occur in most relationships because they are based on fundamental human needs.[28] We long for inclusion and *connection* to other people, but we also long for *autonomy* with time for ourselves apart from our significant other. Because both autonomy and connection are desirable, these oppositions can be termed dialectical tensions.[29] Three tensions, or contradictions, that occur in most relationships are autonomy/connection, openness/closedness, and predictability/novelty.[30]

Openness refers to the extent to which we want our partner to be expressive and share thoughts; *closedness* refers to our need for privacy. We want our lives to have some *predictability* and stability, but we also enjoy *novelty* and spontaneity. While these contradictions may produce tension, it is possible to manage them without conflict. How couples manage these everyday tensions may determine whether conflict is antagonistic or nonantagonistic.[31] Michal wanted more connection and disclosure than David could or would provide. Just as she apparently achieved stability in her life with Palti (who followed her, weeping), David shifted her into unpredictability. The dialectical tensions in Michal's life contributed to conflict rather than to building a healthy relationship.

Distance Relationships

Michal and David's "long distance" relationship, imposed on the couple by Saul, may seem unique today. Other external forces, however, can also impose long-distance relationships. Serving in the armed forces, taking a new job assignment, or going to a different school may require partners to negotiate their relationships at a distance. Not surprising is the fact that long-distance dating relationships are less likely to endure than same-city relationships.[32] Contemporary research, however, also shows that communication processes in long-distance relationships are not qualitatively different. In some instances, idealization of the other person may actually enhance the sense of closeness.

Research does suggest that distance may increase the risk to these relationships. A major factor appears to be the sense of stability couples experience and also the amount of their negative affect, a personality characteristic that involves "pessimism about the future, low self-esteem, and the tendency to experience negative emotions such as anxiety and depression."[33] While there is not enough information about Michal and David to describe them in these terms, the lack of communication between them surely affected the security of their relationship.

Contemporary couples separated geographically, on the other hand, can benefit from using the maintenance behaviors described above to improve the quality of their relationships. The technology available today provides opportunities for relationship maintenance that were inconceivable in Michal and David's time.

Dangers in Communication by Media

Communication at a distance can involve phone, e-mail, instant messaging (IM), texting, and videoconferencing, and each of these media can impact conflict. A primary pitfall is that all but videoconferencing reduce the nonverbal cues that others can use to appropriately interpret messages. Opportunities for misunderstanding by inferring incorrect meaning or intent abound. E-mail, which generally does not occur in real time, allows for increased mulling. As noted earlier, mulling generally heightens conflict. Instant messaging does allow the quick correction of misunderstandings if the parties recognize that more information is needed. On the other hand,

IM has such quick turnaround that conflict can also escalate very quickly. So while we have modern conveniences to improve communication, we must also be cognizant of their pitfalls and work around them.

Michal and David are both unique and archetypal. Clearly, the period, culture, and mores under which they lived circumscribed their relationship. At the same time, communication processes that undermined their relationship can and do undermine many relationships today. Understanding how couples create their own relationship culture through communication is an important beginning to understanding conflict in romantic relationships. Understanding that relationships go through predictable stages of formation and deterioration and knowing how to reverse deterioration can bring about healthier relationships.

Theological Reflection on 1 Samuel and 2 Samuel

The story of Michal and David offers us a window into the complexity of romance and marriage, especially when romance and marriage involve the high stakes of politics, and show how power can distort relationships. Saul is not fair with David when offering him a wife, and he is unjust in his insidious planning for David's death, supposedly at the hands of the Philistines. Such inordinate use of power on Saul's part corrupts even his role as a father: he uses his daughter and her affection for David to plot David's death.

In trying to save David from death, Michal uses the only power afforded to her in her situation within a patriarchal world: her courage, ingenuity, and cleverness. In the end, however, Michal suffers at the hands of a male-dominated society. She is given in marriage to another man while she is still married to David and then taken away from her second husband and returned to David, who has acquired several other wives by then. When Michal does express her honest feelings to David, she is given a price to pay: she will bear no children.[34]

Even the men in this story are victimized by the inordinate use of power. David is given an outlandish task by his king, Saul, that must be accomplished if he is to have Michal as a wife. Paltiel is given Michal as a wife and then Michal is taken away from him. Paltiel, who genuinely loved Michal, had this love dashed to pieces. Finally, the story of Michal and David portrays the fragility of human relationships, especially when competing forces and politics exist.

In Sum: Grace in the Wilderness

Despite the shifts that take place in the lives and relationships of the characters in the story of Michal and David, grace continues to work in the midst of all that occurs in the political and relational dimensions of interpersonal conflict. Michal has the grace and the courage to stand by her man in the face of her father's irrational behavior. Despite the struggles he had with Michal and the physical and geographical distance between them, David attempts to make amends with Michal indirectly by offering her an olive branch. He returns to bless his household but is met instead with disdain from Michal, who has her own struggles to bear. Thus, this story shows us where grace is active and where grace still needs to water the dry areas of people's lives.

Reflection Questions: Can You Now...?

1. Understand how the story of Michal and David, while unique, can offer lessons that transfer to contemporary relationships?

2. Compare Michal's lack of forgiveness with Joseph's ability to forgive? What do you think accounts for the differences?

3. Pick a relationship in your own life and see the stages of formation and deterioration?

4. Think of a relationship you have observed where one or more of the Four Horsemen contributed to deterioration?

5. Remember a time when a family member made "a bid for emotional connection" after a conflict, and the bid was rejected?

6. Think of ways that mulling about a conflict might lead to productive outcomes rather than, as research suggests, worsen the conflict?

7. Think about whether maintenance behaviors can be effective if they are tried "deliberately" rather than spontaneously? That is, a conflict where you decided not to participate in escalation but rather chose to improve the interaction?

8. Identify "dialectical tensions" in your own life that may have contributed to conflict?

9. Identify the extent to which mediated-communication (e-mail, texting, IM, Facebook, MySpace etc.) helped or hurt relationships?

Additional Resources

- Coming together and falling apart is a common theme in the movies. Watch either *The Story of Us* or *Breaking Up*. Can you identify:

    a. the stages of relationship formation and deterioration,

    b. the Four Horsemen,

    c. maintenance behaviors that reverse deterioration?

Additional Reading

Gottman, John. *Seven Principles for Making Marriages Work.* New York: Three Rivers Press, 1999.

———. *What Predicts Divorce? The Relationship between Marital Processes and Marital Outcomes.* Hillsdale, N.J.: Lawrence Erlbaum Associates, 1994).

11

SOCIAL CONFLICT
IN THE GOSPELS
(*Matthew 5–7*)

Blessed are the poor in spirit, for theirs is the kingdom of heaven.

Blessed are those who mourn, for they will be comforted.

Blessed are the meek, for they will inherit the earth.

Blessed are those who hunger and thirst for righteousness, for they will be filled.

Blessed are the merciful for they will receive mercy.

Blessed are the pure in heart, for they will see God.

Blessed are peacemakers for they will be called children of God.

Blessed are those who are persecuted for righteousness' sake, for theirs is the kingdom of heaven.

Blessed are you when people revile you and persecute you and utter all kinds of evil against you falsely on my account. Rejoice and be glad, for your reward is great in heaven, for in the same way they persecuted the prophets who were before you.

You are the salt of the earth, but if salt has lost its taste, how can its saltiness be restored? It is no longer good for anything, but is thrown out and trampled underfoot.

You are the light of the world...let your light shine before others, so that they may see your good works and give glory to your Father in heaven.

Do not think that I have come to abolish the law of the prophets; I have come not to abolish but to fulfill. For truly I tell you, until heaven and earth pass away, not one letter, not one stroke of a letter, will pass from the law until all is accomplished. Therefore, whoever breaks one of the least of these commandments, and teaches others to do the same, will be called least in the kingdom of heaven; but whoever does them and teaches them will be called great in the kingdom of heaven. For I tell you unless your righteousness exceeds that of the scribes and Pharisees, you will never enter the kingdom of heaven. (Matt. 5:3–20)

A Biblical Interpretation of Matthew 5–7

One of the most powerful passages in the synoptic Gospels is the Matthean Sermon on the Mount (Matt. 5:1–7:29), which contains the often quoted and poetic "Beatitudes" (Matt. 5:3–16). Matthew's Sermon on the Mount features Jesus addressing a crowd of listeners and instructing them on how they should live their lives. The lessons take place on a mountain that has a long tradition of being "sacred space" in both the Torah and the New Testament.[1] Although the sermon appears to be straightforward, the social climate is not. Matthew's Gospel as a whole, and the Sermon on the Mount in particular, represents a community in transition that had many factions.

The Historical and Social Background of Matthew's Gospel

Although the facts about dating, authorship, the fabric of Matthew's community, and the setting for the Gospel cannot be firmly established, some historical reconstruction has been possible, even though biblical scholars tend to disagree over the precision of details.

When and where Matthew wrote his Gospel is important to understanding the social climate and conflicts reflected in the Gospel. Accepting the two-source theory that Mark is the earliest Gospel, and that Matthew and Luke drew on Mark and another document, known as Q, to write their Gospels, we can assume that Matthew wrote his Gospel toward the mid- to late 80s C.E. This date is based on the supposition that Mark wrote his Gospel shortly before or after 70 C.E.

With respect to where Matthew wrote the Gospel, certain linguistic clues provide evidence that the place of composition was perhaps in the region of Syria, just north of Palestine. This area was a central point of meeting for both Jews and Greeks, between Jewish Christians and Gentile Christians. Such a conclusion is based on the fact that in the first century C.E., the language of most Jews and Jewish Christians who lived in Palestine was Aramaic, yet Matthew's Gospel was written in Greek. Thus, Matthew was writing for a church as a whole that included Christians who spoke Greek as their first or second language.

Within the Gospel, various words and phrases indicate Jewish and Semitic influences and, in particular, specific rabbinic influences with respect to points of argumentation and debate within the Gospel narratives and discourses. Matthew seems to be writing within Jewish and Gentile circles of culture and social influence, perhaps in Antioch. Biblical scholar John Meier argues that the Gospel of Matthew was "meant to be a public lectionary, catechism, and manual of order to be proclaimed in and read by [Matthew's] entire church."[2] Finally, the actual author of the Gospel assigned to "Matthew" remains unknown, and whether or not the author was a Jew or a Gentile is a point of debate among biblical scholars.[3]

If we assume that Matthew wrote his Gospel in the mid to late 70s C.E., then we can assert that the Gospel was a response to or at least influenced by the destruction of Jerusalem's temple by the Romans. The temple was the central unifying institution for Judaism; with its destruction, the Jewish people were left grappling about their future. Jerusalem, God's Holy City, was also in the hands of the Romans.

New Testament scholar Warren Carter notes that "Rome typically ruled by favor and fear."[4] He adds that "rule by 'favor' meant alliances with local elites, those with wealth, power, and high status in Antioch."[5] Rule by fear "involved awareness of the military consequences of noncooperative acts such as the refusal to pay taxes."[6] Carter also points out:

> Life in the Roman-controlled social and economic world was precarious. For most of it did not seem divinely blessed at all. Heavy taxes usually paid in goods, limited access to resources, overwork, little margin for natural disasters resulting from bad weather or poor returns or seed and livestock, dependence on elite patrons, and anxiety meant a harsh life. Moreover, living areas were densely populated. Apart from the impressive mansions of the elite, most people lived in crowded multistoried tenement buildings. Streets were narrow, functioning as both the communal living room and open waste-disposal areas. Where piped water was absent, water was carried in jars and stored. Disease, filth, and foul smells from decaying matter were pervasive. With inadequate nutrition, uneven food supply, and limited medical knowledge and treatment, it is no wonder that sickness and physical deformities were evident everywhere. With its frequent scenes involving numerous sick and deformed people, Matthew's Gospel accurately reflects the reality of Rome's world (see [Matt.] 4:23–25).[7]

Finally, Carter states that the "societal order was frequently threatened by personal, social, economic, religious, and ethnic conflicts."[8] In the midst of such a situation, the people of Matthew's community were "faced with the huge task of defining [their] identity and way of life in a large city that did not share its particular orientation and commitment, or its new pattern of social relationship."[9] Thus, the Jewish people of Matthew's time and community faced not only many uncertainties but also many transitions under Roman rule.[10]

During this time of transition, many competing groups within the community came to the fore who, in the absence of both a temple (the central place of worship) and political power, now asserted themselves with respect to how life should be lived. The first group, the *Pharisees,* were divided about how accommodating they should be toward the government. They advocated strict observance of the Torah, especially the keeping of the Sabbath, ritual purity regulations, and tithing. They believed in angels, the general resurrection of the dead, and the coming of the Messiah. They argued for free will and the idea that God could play a role in human lives; they preached judgment that focused on rewards and punishments.

The *Sadducees* were a priestly, aristocratic group among the Palestinian Jewish people. They were the descendants from the old Zadokite family, and most of the priests from Jerusalem belonged to the Sadducees. This group of people rejected any development or modernization of the Torah. They rejected the Pharisees' ideas on eschatology and also differed from the Pharisees on matters of ritual. The Sadducees were quick to defend the status quo and were more willing to cooperate with the Romans than were the Pharisees.

The *Zealots*, who led a revolt against Rome, helped the Pharisees eradicate a large number of the Sadducees. After the temple was destroyed, the Sadducees lost power to the Pharisees, who became a dominant presence and who also began imposing a normative Jewish orthodoxy after 70 C.E.

The *scribes* were entrusted to write out the Torah scrolls. Well-educated and conversant in the law, they were also the keepers and interpreters of the Jews' religious tradition.

All of these people paved the way for the early rabbis to begin to formulate a type of Judaism that was not focused on the temple or political control of land. Thus, after 70 C.E., Judaism was in transition, and movements such as the early rabbis, which included the Pharisees and scribes, and the early Christians, which included Matthew's community, began to claim that they had the authentic way of carrying on the Jewish tradition. Matthew's Gospel, then, could be seen as one of several Jewish responses to the temple's destruction in 70 C.E. Similarly, the Matthean community needs to be seen as one group in tension with other Jewish groups, most notably, in tension with the early rabbinic movement. The Matthean Sermon on the Mount reflects, responds to, and challenges the thinking and attitudes of all the various groups present at the time when the Gospel was first written and proclaimed. Matthew's portrait of Jesus is also influenced by and responds to the culture of the day.

The Matthean Portrait of Jesus

The main character in Matthew's Sermon on the Mount is Jesus, who delivers a lengthy instruction/narrative discourse to a crowd gathered around him. Matthew's Jesus speaks with great authority. Daniel Harrington points out that "Matthew presents Jesus as the authoritative interpreter of the Torah."[11] He states further:

The Matthean Jesus not only expresses opinions about the early rabbinic traditions designed to protect against infringement of the Torah

(23:1–39), but he also emerges as the interpreter of the Torah itself, able to play one part off against another as in the cases of the disputes about Sabbath observance (12:1–9) and divorce (19:3–9). The point is that if you want a sure guide to understanding and practicing the Torah, look to the teaching of Jesus.[12]

In his commentary on Matthew, R. T. France sketches a portrait of what Jesus' world was like when he lived:

> *Racially* the area of the former Northern Kingdom of Israel had had, ever since the Assyrian conquest in the eighth century B.C., a more mixed population, within which more conservative Jewish areas (like Nazareth and Capernaum) stood in close proximity to largely pagan cities, of which in the first century the new Hellenistic centers of Tiberias and Sepphoris were the chief examples. *Geographically* Galilee was separated from Judea by the non-Jewish territory of Samaria, and from Perea in the southeast by the Hellenistic settlements of Decapolis. *Politically* Galilee had been under separate administration from Judea during almost all its history since the tenth century B.C. (apart from a period of "reunification" under the Maccabees), and in the time of Jesus it was under a (supposedly) native Herodian prince, while Judea and Samaria had since A.D. 6 been under the direct rule of a Roman prefect. *Economically* Galilee offered better agricultural and fishing resources than the more mountainous territory of Judea, making the wealth of some Galileans the envy of their southern neighbors. *Culturally* Judeans despised their northern neighbors as country cousins, their lack of Jewish sophistication being compounded by their greater openness to Hellenistic influence. *Linguistically* Galileans spoke a distinctive form of Aramaic whose slovenly consonants (they dropped their aitches!) were the butt of Judean humor. *Religiously* the Judean opinion was that Galileans were lax in their observance of proper ritual, and the problem was exacerbated by the distance of Galilee from the temple and the theological leadership which was focused in Jerusalem.[13]

France notes further that "when Jesus arrives at Jerusalem, it is only Matthew who comments on the reaction not only of the accompanying crowds but also of the people of the city (21:10–11), and the two rival 'teams' of Galileans and Judeans are seen starkly opposed in their attitudes to the northern prophet [Jesus]."[14]

Following the thought of France, Carter highlights Jesus' person and works within Judaism:

> The Mosaic tradition was a central concern among the Pharisaic circles. Within this matrix Matthew's community makes claims about

encountering God's forgiving, saving presence in Jesus and in the community committed to him. Hence Matthew explicitly identifies Jesus as being greater than the temple (12:6), Jonah (12:41), and Solomon (12:42). Commitment to him and not claims of privilege based on descent from Abraham (3:9) provides the basis of membership in the people of God (cf. 12:50; 21:43; 22:7).[15]

Finally, Carter observes:

The leaders of the synagogue are presented in the Gospel as finding such claims to be unacceptable. The religious leaders declare Jesus' forgiveness of sin to be "blasphemy" (9:3). They attribute his manifestations of the reign of God to the working of the devil (9:34; 10:25; 12:24). They say his associations with "tax collectors and sinners" indicate he is a "glutton and a drunkard" (11:19). They view his breaking of Sabbath traditions as deserving of death (12:14). They question his authority and its source (21:23–27). In turn, Matthew's Jesus cited the religious leaders for rejecting God's work (21:33–46), for knowing "neither the Scriptures nor the power of God" (22:29), and for being "hypocrites" who "shut up" the reign of God (23:13). This describes a situation of rising antagonism and hostility. Each group refuses to recognize the legitimacy of the other. This eventually leads to the separation of Matthew's group from the synagogue.[16]

Thus, the world of both Matthew and Jesus is complex, with competing parties and voices, all of which led to social conflict that Jesus' Sermon on the Mount subtly addresses.

The Interpretation of Matthew 5–7

Chapters 5 through 7 of Matthew, typically called the "Sermon on the Mount," is part of the teaching sections in the Gospel. Matthew 5–7 is also the first of five major speeches found in the Gospel as a whole (see Matt. 5–7, 10, 13, 18, and 24–25). These discourses came from Q, Mark, and special M (Matthean) material. The Sermon on the Mount is the longest of the five speeches that Jesus addresses to all who have gathered to hear him, especially members of the Jewish community. Its basic theme is that Jesus came not to abolish the Law and the prophets but to fulfill them (Matt. 5:17). Furthermore, the sermon presents hearers then and now with an understanding that "Jesus' words are eternal (24:35) and continue as authoritative teaching for the community (28:20). In the post-70 era the Matthean community understands that in Jesus, not in Moses or in Jewish traditions or in the claims of other revealer figures, is the definitive and authoritative manifestation of God's will."[17] For the Jewish religious leaders of Jesus' day, this profile of Jesus was hard to accept and was met with resistance.

From a literary perspective, Matthew's Sermon on the Mount can be divided into five units:

5:1–20	An introduction
5:21–48	Six antitheses
6:1–18	Three statements about piety
6:19–7:12	Various sayings and teachings
7:13–29	Warnings about judgment

Each unit contains significant lessons and words of wisdom for all who desire to follow God's ways as embodied and proclaimed by Jesus.

An Introduction (Matthew 5:1–20)

This opening unit to the Sermon on the Mount consists of four sections: (1) the setting (vv. 1–2); (2) the Beatitudes (vv. 3–12); (3) the description and identity of Jesus' followers (vv. 13–16); and (4) a teaching about the Law (vv. 17–20). Jesus had been ministering to the crowds before he delivered his lengthy sermon (4:23–25), and great crowds followed him. Seeing them, Jesus ascends the mountain, sits down, his disciples come to him, and he begins to teach (vv. 1–2) The fact that Jesus ascended a mountain is significant. In the ancient world, mountains were sacred sites and considered to be the homes of the gods and goddesses. Furthermore, Moses ascended the mountain (Mount Sinai) to receive and then deliver God's Law to the Israelites. In Matthew, Jesus is about to reveal God's vision to the people, with an authority that far surpasses that of Moses.[18]

Upon ascending the mountain, Jesus sits down. Here Matthew casts Jesus in the role of a rabbinic teacher. Sitting was a posture of authoritative teaching (Matt. 13:2, 24:3, 26:55). After he sits down, his disciples come to him. Clearly Jesus is the one with authority; he gives the teaching instead of receiving it. His address, however, is not just for his disciples; it is for all of the crowds that have gathered near.

Verses 3–11 include his first teaching: the Beatitudes. Beatitudes were common in the wisdom books (see, for example, Ps. 1:1, 32:2, 40:4; Prov. 3:13, 28:14), but unlike the Tanach (beatitudes that assume a reward to be already present), the reward of the New Testament Matthean beatitudes is future and eschatological. Each one of the beatitudes addresses a different group of people and promises them a future reward. The "poor in spirit" (v. 3) are those who possess the virtue of humility and who have either little or no status or who are not caught up with status. They recognize that all is gift, and that all comes from God. They depend on God for protection in the face of oppression from those who exert power over them, namely, the wealthy Roman rulers or even some of their own Jewish leaders. The reward for the "poor in spirit" is the kingdom, which refers to God's reign and sovereignty and implies justice and righteousness.[19]

In the second beatitude, those who mourn will be comforted (v. 4). This beatitude is intended for those whose situation is wretched. Oppression will not be the final word. Here Matthew appeals to Isaiah 61:2–3 where the prophet comforted the people after the devastation of their first temple's destruction in 587 B.C.E. (see Sir. 48:24).

The third beatitude, addressed to the meek (v. 5), promises that they will inherit the earth. Here Matthew appeals to Psalm 37:11. The meek are those whose attitudes are not arrogant and oppressive like some within the culture of their day. Daniel Harrington notes that "the 'land' is not necessarily limited to the land of Israel. In apocalyptic literature (1 Enoch 5:7) the promise is widened to include the gift of the whole world to the just."[20]

In the fourth beatitude (v. 6), those who hunger and thirst for righteousness will be filled. The backdrop for this beatitude is Psalm 107:5, 8–9, in which the psalmist describes God satisfying the hungry and the thirsty. Righteousness refers to divine justice and the establishment of right relationships so badly needed in the time of Jesus and Matthew.

Those who are merciful will receive mercy in the fifth beatitude (v. 7). Matthew depicts Jesus teaching about the spirit and principle of reciprocity. Mercy is a characteristic of God, a virtue that God desires (Hos. 6:6), and that is central to Matthew's preaching as uttered by Jesus (Matt. 9:13, 12:7). Matthew features Jesus upbraiding the Pharisees because they lack mercy (Matt. 23:23). For this beatitude Matthew appeals to Proverbs 14:21, 17:5 (LXX).

The sixth beatitude comments on the pure of heart who will see God (v. 8). The background for this beatitude is Psalm 24:3–4. Only those who have clean hands and a pure heart can ascend God's holy mountain. With this beatitude, Matthew seems to have Jesus sending a message to first-century Judaism, namely, that ritual purity with its emphasis on outward purity is not sufficient for godliness and, in fact, this kind of external purity is condemned by Jesus in Matthew 23:25–28. Here the emphasis is on single-minded and single-hearted devotion to God and God's ways as lived out and taught by Jesus.

Those who are peacemakers will be called children of God in the seventh beatitude (v. 9). Peace, or *shalom*, is the goal and fulfillment of right relationship (Lev. 23:96; Ps. 85:10, 119:165; Isa. 32:17). Peace is the fullness of God's gifts given to those who embrace a life of right relationship. In a time of Roman occupation and in a time of political, social, religious, and economic tension and conflict, Jesus encourages his listeners to be peacemakers instead of persons who take sides and thereby add to the factions, divisions, and tensions that already exist within and outside of the community. To those not part of his immediate community, this beatitude becomes a great challenge especially to the Roman regime and its leadership and ruling class. The peacemakers will be called children of God. One of the attributes of God is peace (see Rom. 15:33, 16:20; 1 Thess. 5:23), and thus one of the characteristics of God's people and a sign that someone is of God is to "seek peace and pursue it" (Ps. 34:14). France observes:

> This beatitude goes beyond a merely peaceful disposition to an active attempt to "make" peace, perhaps by seeking reconciliation with one's

own enemies, but also more generally by bringing together those who are estranged from one another. Such costly "peacemaking" which involves overcoming the natural desire for advantage and retribution, will be illustrated in the extraordinary demands of 5:39–42 which overturn the natural human principle of *lex talionis*.[21]

This beatitude, then, is central to the social fabric of Jewish life as lived in the time of Jesus and Matthew.

The eighth beatitude is a consoling word to those who suffer persecution for righteousness' sake; theirs is the kingdom of heaven (v. 10). The reference to "righteousness" recalls the fourth beatitude (v. 6), and the reference to "the kingdom of heaven" links this beatitude with the first one. Undoubtedly those within Jesus' community and Matthew's community suffered because of their choice to live and act righteously in the midst of societal pressures and conflicts. God's reign will bring justice to their situation, and that reign will be the end of their suffering and the gift of enduring peace.

The last beatitude, the ninth (vv. 11–12), picks up on and expands themes introduced in the one immediately preceding it. This time, however, words of consolation are extended to those who are reviled and suffer all kinds of persecutions and false accusations on account of being followers of Jesus. Here Jesus' discourse shifts from a general to a specific address to the audience in front of him, signaled by the second person pronoun "you." The people's response to being reviled, persecuted, and slandered is to be one of rejoicing because such circumstances place them in the prophetic tradition and will gain them a reward in heaven, a reward that is eschatological and to be hoped for. The phrases "revile you," "persecute you," and "utter all kinds of evil against you falsely" suggest that conflict was active within the communities of Jesus and Matthew. This beatitude addressed specifically to Jesus' listeners sets the tone for the teachings that follow, all of which are addressed to the gathered crowd.

Following the beatitudes, Matthew has Jesus define the identity of his followers (vv. 13–16). They are the salt of the earth (v. 13) and the light of the world (vv. 14–16). Jesus' followers are to be different from other people so that God may be known and glorified (v. 16). In the ancient world, salt was used to flavor food (Job 6:6) and to preserve it; salt was also used to purify and was an ingredient in sacrifices (Lev. 2:13; Ezek. 43:24). The metaphor serves to remind the disciples that they are to participate in life around them, adding flavor to their culture while helping to purify and transform it. The metaphor is also a strong indictment against those disciples who have lost their distinctiveness and thus no longer make a significant contribution to their society.

With respect to the metaphor of light, the disciples are to embody and symbolize the new hope characteristic of the reign of God. Here Matthew draws on Isaiah (Isa. 2:2–5, 42:6, 49:6). Israel is invited to walk in the light of the Lord, and Israel's vocation is to be "a light to the nations." The reference to the city built on a hill inadvertently pertains to the disciples as well. They are to be the New Jerusalem, God's holy city that gives light to the world and welcomes all peoples as well. The imagery also picks up on Isaiah 2:2–5, which contains an allusion to Jerusalem built upon Mount Zion, the place where all nations will come to learn Torah, to live in peace, and to be at home with God. Thus, Jesus' followers and those within Matthew's community to whom these words are addressed and who are listening in general are challenged not to engage in the various conflicts of their day. Instead, they are to be the preservative and transformer of life within their culture and a beacon of hope, especially to those who are suffering from injustice and oppression hinted at in the beatitudes.

Verses 17 through 20 conclude the introduction. These verses establish a relationship between Jesus' teaching and the Torah. Even though Jesus speaks with authority unlike anyone else, except perhaps Moses, and even though he is giving his listeners new instructions, he is not telling them to abrogate the Torah. Matthew makes clear that Jesus is reinterpreting the Law and the teachings of the prophets and not establishing a new law; Jesus is fulfilling the Law and not dismissing it. In sum:

> The sayings about the abiding validity of the Torah as interpreted by Jesus (5:17–20) serve as a further reminder of the organic relation between Judaism and Matthean Christianity. They remind us that at least some Christians in the late first century A.D. found no contradiction in following both the Torah and Jesus' teaching.[22]

The key point here, however, is in Jesus' reinterpretation of the Law that begins in the six antitheses that follow the introduction to the Sermon on the Mount. Finally, Jesus tells his listeners that their righteousness needs to exceed that of the scribes and the Pharisees if they wish to enter the kingdom of heaven. This instruction anticipates Matthew 23, where Jesus upbraids the scribes and Pharisees for not practicing what they preach (23:3) and for being concerned about external expressions of piety instead of practicing the weightier things of the Law: justice and mercy and faith (23:23). Thus, Matthew depicts Jesus telling his followers neither to judge the scribes or Pharisees nor to follow their ways. Instead, the disciples are to exercise a righteousness that goes to the heart of establishing right relationship, which, in turn, will put them at odds with the religious sects of their day and may become a source of persecution for the disciples (see Matt. 5:10).

Six Antitheses (Matthew 5:21–48)

The second unit of the Sermon on the Mount consists of six antitheses concerning: anger (vv. 21–26), adultery (vv. 27–30), divorce (vv. 31–32), oaths (vv. 33–37), retaliation (vv. 38–42), and loving one's enemies (vv. 43–48). In each of these units, Matthew features Jesus juxtaposing the Law to his teaching of it. These antitheses also demonstrate that Jesus came to fulfill and not abolish the Law and the teachings of the prophets.

In verses 21–26, concerning anger, Matthew appeals to Exodus 20:13 and Deuteronomy 5:18, the commandment not to murder. The second part of the statement that stresses liability to judgment may originate from Exodus 21:12, Leviticus 24:17, and Numbers 35:16. Here Matthew portrays Jesus explaining that murder is the result of something deeper going on within the person who commits the crime. For Jesus, anger is the root emotion that can lead to and result in the heinous act of murder; even if anger does not result in murder, anger is an inward, culpable attitude that causes division and either a breach or break in right relationship. This breach or break in right relationship can have ill effects on all parties involved. Thus, while murder violates right relationship, so do the outward manifestations of anger directed toward another.

This unit addresses the many different kinds of social conflict that existed among the ordinary people of Jesus' and Matthew's day, and it informs those who follow Jesus that they are not only to keep the commandment but also to be on guard about their own attitudes concerning others. Important to note here is that the anger being spoken about is not righteous anger that is often given verbal expression by the prophets on account of rampant injustices. The prophets' anger called for change and the reform of one's ways. The anger here is the kind that leads to division or harm among people.

The second antithesis (vv. 27–39) pertains to adultery. Here Matthew draws on Exodus 20:14 and Deuteronomy 5:18. In the ancient world, anyone having sexual relations with someone either married or engaged is guilty of adultery. Punishment was death for both parties (Deut. 22:22–24). As in the case of murder, Matthew depicts Jesus taking the original commandment a step further to consider the condition of one's heart. Not only is the act of adultery itself wrong, so is the inordinate desire for a woman who is otherwise unavailable. If a man looks with lust at a woman, then that man has, according to Matthew, already committed adultery in his heart (see Exod. 20:17). Thus the desire is tantamount to the deed itself. For Matthew and the Matthean Jesus, anger is the root of murder, and lust is the root of adultery. Once again, the concern here is for right relationship within the community. The mention of self-mutilation as a form of chastisement is drastic, but it was a well-known metaphor and custom in the ancient world. The metaphor functioned to strengthen the impact of the saying.

The third antithesis focuses on divorce (vv. 31–32). It expands the theme of marriage and adultery found in Matthew 5:27–28. This antithesis summarizes Deuteronomy 24:1, which outlines the divorce process. Interestingly, this process was always initiated by the husband. At stake is the point that "both here and in 19:9 [Matthew] apparently blurs the stark opposition between Jesus' teaching and that of all Jewish tradition by inserting the clause [except on the ground of unchastity], which appears to allow a single cause for divorce."[23] Traditionally, divorce could occur for any number of reasons.

Verses 33–37 are an antithesis concerning oaths. The background for this fourth teaching is Leviticus 19:12, which forbids swearing falsely by God's name. As with the other antitheses, Jesus, as depicted by Matthew, takes the commandment a step further and advocates that no one should swear at all. Thus, Jesus' expanded teaching that forbids swearing safeguards against false swearing. Harrington notes that "this move has the consequences of rendering the Torah passages about oaths useless."[24] Furthermore, this teaching sharpens what "Matthew understood as fulfillment."[25]

The fifth antithesis, concerning retaliation (vv. 38–42), recalls the law of retaliation known as *lex talionis,* first heard in Exodus 21:24, Leviticus 24:20, and Deuteronomy 19:21. This law was meant to be humane. For example, a life could not be required if someone violated the property of another, but if a life were taken, only then could a life be required. Jesus' words speak of no retaliation whatsoever. The instance of turning the cheek is not meant to be an act of passivity; rather, "the specification indicates the blow comes from the assailant's left hand, and therefore constitutes an insult rather than a violent assault."[26] Jesus' teaching is shocking. He calls for no resistance and no retaliation. Again, the focus is on establishing peace and right relationship instead of engaging in social conflict.

The last antithesis in verses 43–48 takes the love of neighbor (Lev. 19:18) one step further to include the love of enemies. Whether Jesus is talking about one's personal enemies or the Roman occupation and its leadership is uncertain. Given the vision of right relationship expressed thus far, the instruction could umbrella both groups. Jesus' teaching is radical: his followers are told to love their enemies and to pray for their persecutors. The reason is twofold: first, so that Jesus' disciples might become "children" of God, metaphorically addressed as "Father," and second, because God's grace is bestowed upon both the righteous and the unrighteous. God's love embraces all kinds of people (v. 45).

A series of rhetorical questions accents Jesus' instruction (vv. 46–47). Finally, the love that the disciples must have for all people is to surpass that of the Gentiles (v. 47). The disciples are to be "perfect" as God is perfect (v. 48). For Matthew and for the Matthean Jesus, love is not only the greatest commandment but also the fulfillment of the Law and the prophets (Matt. 22:34–40; see 1 Cor. 13:1–13; Gal. 5:14; 1 John 4:7–12). Perfection, then, is not doing everything meticulously. Perfection is associated with holiness (see Lev. 19:2, 20:26, 21:8), a characteristic of which is benevolence toward everyone just as God acts benevolently toward all creation (see Ps. 104).

Finally, the context of these six antitheses is the debate within Judaism about the authoritative interpretation of the Torah. Matthew and other Jewish Christians viewed the Torah as divine revelation that outlined the appropriate response to the God of the covenant, and not as something obsolete and burdensome. Their concern was to show how Jesus came *to fulfill* rather than to *abolish* the Law. Even if the framework appears strained from time to time, it ought not to be abandoned in favor of the sharp contrasts between (Jewish) legalism and the (Christian) gospel of love.[27] Thus, Jesus focuses on the interior life and attitudes of a person and challenges listeners to go one step beyond the Law so that right relationship can be firmly grounded in something more than the Law alone.

Three Statements about Piety (Matthew 6:1–18)

Having given an instruction on the Law by means of six antitheses, Matthew next portrays Jesus teaching about three acts of piety: almsgiving (vv. 1–4), prayer (vv. 5–15), and fasting (vv. 16–18). This discourse warns against the wrong kind of righteousness, often practiced by the scribes and the Pharisees (see Matt. 6:1, 26). In this regard, Matthew 6:1–18 develops the thought in Matthew 5:20. Both the religious and ethical practices of Jesus' disciples are to be distinct from those of the scribes and Pharisees, who are concerned with outward appearance and outward holiness.

Almsgiving, the first pious practice, is the sharing of one's resources with those who are in need. The needs of the poor are addressed in the Deuteronomic Code (Deuteronomy 12–26) and the Holiness Code (Leviticus 17–26). In ancient Israel, community members were to provide for those who were less fortunate within their community. In Matthew 6:2–4, Jesus encourages his followers to continue the practice of almsgiving. Thus, Matthew makes clear that this practice is as important to Christianity as it was to Judaism. The emphasis is to be on the almsgiving itself and not on how this deed will benefit or enhance the reputation of the giver in the midst of various social and religious circles.

The second practice, *prayer,* is to be done in a way similar to that of almsgiving. Prayer is to be done without drawing attention to oneself. Prayer is an ongoing dialogue with God that takes the form of praise, petition, thanksgiving, lament, and just ordinary conversation. This dialogue with God is meant to be personal, intimate, and honest, and not something to be done for show to prove one's holiness, righteousness, or outward piety.

In verses 7–14, Matthew depicts Jesus teaching his followers how to pray. With this prayer, Jesus welcomes all into the covenant and a familial relationship with God. The foundation for this type of relationship can be found in 1 Samuel 7:1–17, especially verse 14, where God promises to be as a father to David and David to be as a son to God. This covenant and sonship extends to the entire Davidic lineage and to Jesus, and in this Matthean passage Jesus welcomes God's people into this wonderful bond.

The remainder of the prayer focuses on right relationship with God and with one another so that God's reign will be made manifest on earth as it is in heaven — the reign of justice and righteousness whose fruit is peace. Embedded in this prayer is the vision of Isaiah 65:17–25, the new heavens and the new earth — the new order — which John echoes in Revelation 21:1–6. The reference to "the time of trial" in verse 13 does not imply trials often thought to be imposed by God to "test" one's faith (see Ps. 11:5, 26:2).

Rather, the trials are "the experiences which are the normal lot of disciples who try to live according to the principles of the kingdom of God in a world that does not share those values" (see Matt. 5:11–12).[28]

Although the instruction on forgiveness seems conditioned, the emphasis here is not meant to be punitive. Rather, what Matthew stresses is reciprocity. As you forgive, so shall you be forgiven, with the understanding that God's forgiveness is without measure (see Mic. 7:18–20).

The third practice, *fasting*, is to follow the discipline of the other two pious practices. Fasting is to be done without calling attention to oneself. The only fast required by Torah was on the day of Atonement (Lev. 16:31, 23:26–32). All other fasts were either private or public in remembrance of national disasters, as petitions in times of great need, as signs of lament (see, for example, Joel 2:12–14; Jonah 3:1–5). The better fast is not to abstain but to live uprightly as the prophet outlined in Isaiah 58:6–14.

In sum, these three lessons are not a criticism against acts of piety nor are they statements against public manifestations of piety. The three statements concern private acts of piety done for the sole purpose of gaining public recognition. Thus, these three lessons stress right intention and indirectly inveigh against those members of the scribes and Pharisees and against any other members of any other religious sects who perform pious deeds for self-serving purposes.

Various Sayings and Teachings (Matthew 6:19–7:12)

Following the three instructions on piety, the Matthean Jesus continues teaching those gathered around him. The first lesson concerns treasures (Matt. 6:19–21). The emphasis here is on trust in God and not in earthly possessions. Implied is also a single-hearted focus on God and not on material possessions. The followers of Jesus are called to a certain simplicity of lifestyle, but more importantly, to a certain spirit of detachment from material goods so that their energies can be directed toward living and carrying out Jesus' mission and ministry.[29]

The second lesson, Matthew 6:22–23, is somewhat enigmatic in its use of the contrast between light and darkness and the image of the eye as the metaphorical lamp of the body. How one sees and perceives life will color how one lives life. Followers of Jesus are called to have the eyes of God, who does not look on outward appearances but instead looks on the heart (see, for example, 1 Sam. 16:7).

The third lesson, Matthew 6:24, builds on the first. Again, Jesus' followers are called to single-minded and single-hearted devotion to God and God's ways, and to the mission and ministry entrusted to Jesus in which they have been invited to participate by virtue of their discipleship.

The fourth lesson, Matthew 6:25–34, draws out the theme of trust in God first heard in Matthew 6:19–21. This passage is one of the most endearing and popular passages of the entire Gospel. Images from the natural world — the birds of the air, the lilies of the field, the grass of the field — all serve as models for God's benevolent care. This divine care extends to those splendid dimensions of creation that do not sow, reap, gather into barns, toil, spin, or have longevity. This care also extends to all humankind. Jesus' listeners are reminded that this God of benevolence knows what is needed and provides richly for those in need. The people's focus should be on the reign and righteousness of God and not on worrying about one's future needs. The key phrase in this passage is verse 32. Here Jesus instructs his listeners that their trust must surpass that of the Gentiles who are worrying about their needs. Thus, Jesus' followers are to be different from the Gentiles.

The fifth lesson concerns passing judgment (Matt. 7:1–5). Again the emphasis is on reciprocity and right relationship: "Do not judge, so that you may not be judged" (v. 1). Verse 2 continues the theme introduced in verse 1. Verses 3 and 4 feature two rhetorical questions that strike at the heart of the matter concerning judgment: one should not draw attention to another's failings when one's shortcomings are greater, and one should not offer to help another when one has not dealt with one's own problems or issues. Both instances admit of a certain insincerity on the part of one who would sit in judgment on another. Jesus is quick to cast aspersions on such a person, "You hypocrite..." and he then states what needs to be done: "first take the log out of your own eye, and then you will see clearly to take the speck out of your neighbor's eye" (v. 5; see also Lev. 19:17). The listeners are reminded that the person being "judged" is a "neighbor" (v. 5). Matthew continues to be concerned about sustaining good and right relationships within and among community members.

The sixth lesson, Matthew 7:6, is an odd saying as dogs and swine are both considered to be "unclean" animals by the Jewish community. That which is "holy" refers to meat sacrificed in the temple. The saying suggests that Jesus' followers be discriminating with respect to what is shared so that they do not come into harm's way unnecessarily so for living, teaching, and preaching the Gospel message.

The seventh lesson, Matthew 7:7–11, reflects the themes of trust and God's benevolence heard earlier in 6:9–13, 19–21, and 25–34. Here the Matthean Jesus stresses that God will indeed hear and answer prayer, a theme found in the writings of the prophets (see, for example, Isa. 30:19; 58:9, 65:24; Jer. 29:12, 14; Hos. 2:23, among others). Jesus encourages his listeners to have a dynamic relationship with God, one that is expectant and anticipatory of good things.

The eighth and last lesson is often called "the Golden Rule" (7:12).[30] The root of this teaching is Leviticus 19:18: "You shall love your neighbor as yourself" (see also Tobit 4:15). Jesus informs his listeners that they are to respect one another, a respect that flows from a spirit of mutuality rooted and grounded in love. Jesus concludes by saying "for this is the law and the prophets" (see also Matt. 22:34–40). Jesus has now summarized and reinterpreted the Law and the prophets for his listeners, reminding them that the Law and the prophets are about right relationship and not about legalisms. Jesus' teaching helps to provide direction for the Torah; it does not nullify it.

In summary, each of these lessons provides Jesus' listeners with a deeper understanding of God, God's ways, and how people should live their lives. The sayings focus on the love that God has for all of them and the love that they, in turn, should have for one another. In a culture and society ripe with conflict, Jesus' listeners and followers are to be "counter-cultural."

Warnings about Judgment (Matthew 7:13–29)

Earlier in Matthew 7:1–5, Jesus warned the crowd not to judge others. In this concluding section of the Sermon on the Mount, Jesus sets up sharp contrasts between two groups of people and intimates that both groups are liable, in the end, to God, who will act accordingly toward each group.

In verses 13 and 14, Jesus encourages his listeners to choose the way not often taken by others: "Enter through the narrow gate; for the gate is wide and the road is easy that leads to destruction, and there are many who take it. For the gate is narrow and the road is hard that leads to life, and there are few who find it."[31]

The "gate" is most likely the city gate, the main entrance into the city itself. The specific city to which the passage refers is obscure; it allows for multiple interpretations, inclusive of the metaphorical image of the New Jerusalem as a city and as a people within the reign of God (see Matt. 5:14; Rev. 21:1–2; Isa. 60–62, 2:1–4). Jesus instructs his listeners that discipleship carries with it a cost: even though the mission of evangelization that includes teaching, healing, and preaching God's inclusive love for all people can be rewarding, the mission can also have its difficulties that stem from having to love and respect all people in the midst of conflict, adversity, and even rejection by those who feel threatened by the good news being proclaimed.[32] This passage reflects traditional Jewish teaching that speaks of two ways. Here the two ways are set up as contrasts that lead into the next warning.

In verses 15 through 20, Jesus, as depicted by Matthew, warns his listeners about false prophets and uses the imagery of good and bad trees and good and bad fruit to illustrate his lesson. Jesus puts his listeners on notice about duplicitous, false prophets who come in sheep's clothing — seemingly innocent, gentle, harmless, but who inwardly are ravenous wolves (v. 15). False prophets are a recurring theme in the writings of the prophets (see, for example, Jeremiah 28). No evidence exists to indicate that Jesus' community had to deal with false prophets, but Matthew indicates that Jesus was aware of the potential hazard of false prophets (Matt. 24:11, 24), the likes of which begin to appear in early Christian community circles. Two trees and their respective fruits characterize true and false prophets, and the latter will meet their demise like the rotten tree.

The imagery of contrasts heard in verses 13–14 and verses 15–20 continues in verses 21–23. Here two groups of people are juxtaposed: one who does God's will and one who does not. Verbal homage paid to Jesus, specifically, "Lord, Lord" that acknowledges Jesus as a Holy One is not enough if one wishes to enter the kingdom of heaven. Additionally, even if a person prophesies, casts out demons, and performs many powerful deeds all in Jesus' name, the kingdom of heaven is not guaranteed. Only those who do God's will can enter the kingdom of heaven. What is God's will? The question has been answered throughout the entire Sermon on the Mount. Only those who have and live a life of deep love for God, self, and neighbor can enter the kingdom of heaven, whose foundation is right relationship and whose cornerstone is peace.

Again, Jesus reminds his listeners that worship and deeds are secondary to how one lives one's life in community and in the world. Those who wish to follow Jesus are not meant to be a clan unto themselves. They must interact with others who are not like-minded or of the same religious, social, or political persuasion, inclusive of the Roman guard and leadership as well as the leadership of the various Jewish sects within the rabbinic movement. This lesson is, indeed, a challenge to Jesus' listeners and to all the Matthean community as well as to those who hear the Gospel.

The Sermon on the Mount draws to a close in verses 24 through 29, where Jesus presents one final contrast — one house is built on rock and the other on sand — to explain his main point. The person who hears and acts on Jesus' words will be like a house built on a rock and able to endure the storms of the times. The person who hears and does not act on Jesus' words will be like a house built on sand and destroyed by storms because of its unstable and weak foundation. The lesson here is for Jesus' people to trust in Jesus' teachings, to live by them, and to put them into practice. Jesus' word is sure, steadfast, and life-giving because it flows from God, who is the source of Jesus' authority and his authoritative teaching and preaching (see Matt. 28:18, 9:2–8).

Such teaching astonishes the people because it is delivered with an authority that is quite different from their experience with the scribes. Jesus, the one baptized by water and the Spirit, now stands in stark contrast to the religious leaders of his day. Those who follow his teachings will stand in the same vein but with the command not to write off or do harm to any opponents but rather to embrace, engage, and try to live in right relationship with others who are not like-minded, without compromising their own inner God-given authority (see Matt. 28:16–20). Those listeners among the crowd who will become followers of Jesus may be astounded at first by his teaching, but they have no idea what they are in for later on if they choose to follow.

With such teaching proclaimed, the threat that Jesus poses to the Roman and Jewish leaders of his day becomes ever greater and unfolds as the Gospel of Matthew itself unfolds. The Gospel features Jesus living out the law of love through his mission and ministry while remaining fully yet wisely engaged nonviolently with all who oppose him.

Looking through the Communication Lens

The text that precedes the Sermon on the Mount above tells us that Jesus' "fame spread throughout all Syria" and that "great crowds followed him from Galilee, the Decapolis, Jerusalem, Judea, and from beyond the Jordan" (Matt. 4:24–25). We know that the preaching of Jesus placed him in peril because John the Baptist had already been arrested. Jesus lived and preached during a time of social conflict.

People disagreed then and still do today on whether Jesus was a reformer or a revolutionary.[33] According to Matthew's portrait of Jesus, Jesus clearly had an agenda he wanted to put forward, but whether he wanted to reform Judaism or replace Judaism is not clear. He lived during a time of great ideological variety. Among the Jews, the Sadducees, Pharisees, and Essenes competed for followers. Each sect had its own approach to Judaism and vied for the allegiance of the Jewish people.[34] While they all believed in the Torah, they disagreed about the details of observance. Aside from the Jewish population, various representatives of the Roman government strived for power. Priests collected tithes and, as representatives of the Roman government, also collected taxes. The party of Zealots wanted to throw off the yoke of Rome. Clearly, Jesus was not the only voice speaking against the status quo. However, this text in Matthew known as the Sermon on the Mount was tantamount to a mission statement for the religious organization Jesus inspired.

What Is Social Conflict?

Earlier, we defined interpersonal conflict as "a struggle between at least two interdependent parties who perceive incompatible goals, scarce resources, and interference from others in achieving their goals."[35] Social conflict bears all the markings of interpersonal conflict with an added dimension: the parties involved are groups with goals that deviate from the status quo, and in order to prevail groups need to surpass their rivals for the allegiance of their targeted audience.[36] Social conflict can make use of noncoercive or coercive methods.[37] A leader who tries to attract followers from rival groups or ideologies might use persuasion and positive sanctions as part of a noncoercive campaign, emphasizing the positive benefits that would result from changing behaviors and adopting the leader's values. Coercive methods could include threats, attacks, and physical attempts to injure opponents.[38]

Looking at the text of the Sermon on the Mount in isolation might raise questions about its involvement with social conflict. However, as the history section above demonstrated, the Sermon on the Mount was intended to win over the hearts and minds of people who might otherwise continue to accept the status quo. Jesus tries to persuade his audience to change the way they live by using his considerable rhetorical skills, as did Daniel when he faced a situation of conflict (see chapter 5). In Israel at this time, while no one is yet fighting, conflict smolders between Rome, the occupier, and the Jewish people. As the various Jewish sects struggle among themselves, differences between their positions, including those of Jesus and his followers, gradually unfold.

The Stages of Emerging Conflict

Researchers have identified five stages of conflict: a latent period, a perceived feeling, a triggering event, its manifestation, and finally the aftermath. In the *latency stage* incompatibilities exist but have not yet been confronted. Gradually, the parties begin to *perceive a threat* to their goals; they assess their sources of power and plan a strategy. Eventually, a *triggering event* changes the climate and the conflict escalates. As the conflict *manifests* itself, moves and countermoves unfold as participants marshal their sources of power. The *aftermath* may yield a clear winner and loser, it may set the stage for the next episode, or it may leave participants right where they were before the event.[39]

According to Matthew's narrative, the teaching of Jesus was well received by the people: "Now when Jesus had finished saying these things, the crowds were astounded at his teaching, for he taught them as one having authority, and not as their scribes" (Matt. 7:28–29). Eventually, however, the chief priests and Pharisees pushed back: "Then some of the scribes said to themselves, 'This man is blaspheming'" (9:3), and very soon Matthew reports that "the Pharisees went out and conspired against him, how to destroy him" (12:14). We can observe the conflict moving from a latent stage to a perceived threat and ultimately to the marshaling of power.

Groups and Conflict

What happened at the time of Jesus is generally true of groups: groups, numbers of people, coalesce to enact change. Usually, one or more people claim to represent larger numbers of people such as classes, ethnic communities, or governments. Typically, issues of economic and political identity become salient, and moral values may fuel the conflict.[40] The groups believe their objectives are incompatible and that one group stands to gain if the other is defeated.[41]

Conflict is less likely to occur when ample resources, balanced power, trust, shared norms, and compatible aspirations exist.[42] When we have wide acceptance of certain goals, rules of conduct, role definitions, procedures for decision making, and authority, we are less likely to experience group conflict.[43] By contrast, when resources are scarce, when power imbalances emerge, when norms conflict, and people's aspirations clash with each other, social conflict can spark. The historical narrative that we have reconstructed points to all of these conditions.

Theologians, historians, and biblical scholars have spent much time during the previous century and this one constructing scenarios describing the life and times of Jesus. Clearly economic and political issues form a backdrop to the Sermon on the Mount. Comparable to the Sermon on the Mount in our own country's recent history is Martin Luther King's "I have a Dream Speech." Dr. King advocated better economic and social conditions for African Americans and equal access to the political process. Although his speech was welcomed by many in the country, it was also rejected by others. As a result, however, many groups of people came together to form coalitions to bring about change and to increase the equality of opportunity in the United States.

Going beyond economic and political issues, however, we need to explore how the nature of groups contributes to social conflict. Groups are defined not only by what they stand for, but also by what they are against. At times, one's own story denies the other's story, so "truth" can be very different for different groups. In the Sermon on the Mount, Jesus focused on the values and behaviors he stood for, with a suggestion of whom and what he was against. "Christians" as a group did not yet exist.[44] After his death, other leaders helped shape Christianity's identity.

The Importance of Narrative

Group identity consists of its beliefs, history, institutions, and values.[45] In social conflict, each group must create a *narrative* that tells what binds them together and what separates them from others.[46] Once narratives are grounded in a social system and culture, they can be very resistant to change. The power to enforce a narrative is one of the strongest forms of social control.[47]

A major component of a group's narrative is its *collective memory*. It is not surprising that controlling *collective memory* is a key feature of social conflict.[48] A group's collective memory selectively assembles facts and interpretations of events to serve the interests of the group. Dominant groups try to shape the collective memory of other groups, and this is how history gets revised. Throughout the Gospels, history and memory were shaped to create a clearer Christian group identity.[49]

We have seen that economic, political, and moral issues contribute to social conflict as well as group narratives. Actual conflict between or among groups usually emerges when three conditions exist: (1) a conscious sense of being a member of a collective entity; (2) a sense of dissatisfaction relative to another group; and (3) the belief that this dissatisfaction will be relieved by changing the relationship with the other group.[50]

Jesus, the disciples, and the ordinary people who rallied behind his teachings gradually began to see themselves as a group apart from those who adhered to the teachings of the Sadducees, the Pharisees, the scribes, and the priests. They heard the appeal of Jesus for social justice and righteousness and, as a result, some began to differentiate their identity as Jesus-followers from those who were not.

Social Conflict and Religion

The social conflict in Matthew revolved around religion, both in beliefs and practices. Generally, religions use three elements to imbue followers with religious attachment: compliance, identification, and internalization.[51] *Compliance* requires an individual to conform to the teachings and demands of the religion. Children learning a religion, or adults contemplating conversion to a religion, typically learn to obey the demands and rules of the religion. After a time, however, initiates follow the group because it helps them *identify* with the group. When *internalization* occurs, adhering to the norms ("doing the right thing") contributes to the individual's positive self-concept. Being part of the group may require a high level of personal commitment and meeting group norms, values, and ideals may take precedence over the self. During the time of Matthew, these processes were at work, but not yet solidified.

A Group's Perceptions and Conflict

The perceptions, even distorted perceptions, a group has of itself and the other party or parties strongly impact any conflict. Although research on perceptual distortions was originally done on international conflict, it also applies generally to social conflict.[52] The term "mirror image" describes how each group sees itself as representing truth, justice, and good, while the other group does not. Hence, followers of Jesus will see themselves as good, and competing groups as lacking or sinful. The same is true for the Romans, the Pharisees, the scribes, the Essenes, the Zealots, and so on. It is easy to see all the evil and underhanded things the opposing group does, while being completely blind to those same behaviors in one's own group.[53] Another distortion of perception is when a group makes use of a double standard to justify its position. Even if "we" admit to acting in ways that are not perfect, we have good reasons! Finally, one of the worst distortions is that of polarization: everything our group does is right and good, and everything the other group does is wrong and bad.

Pulling It All Together

At one level, the Sermon on the Mount appears to be a talk in which Jesus inspires his listeners to do good deeds, to live simply, and to behave honorably. When we view the oration in the context of its times, however, we can understand how it also forms a part in social conflict. Historians tell us that at that time political and economic conditions were oppressive and, as has been pointed out, when resources are scarce, when power imbalances exist, and when values are being challenged, conditions are ripe for social conflict.[54] Many sects were trying to win the hearts, minds, and loyalties of "the people";[55] many Jewish leaders were cooperating with their Roman rulers; and a variety of Jewish sects were rivals for power and influence. Social conflict simmered. Even among the followers of Jesus, there were disagreements on the extent to which followers needed to adhere to the laws of the Torah.

Group identity consists of beliefs, values, and the history of a group, and the teachings of Jesus as laid out in the Sermon on the Mount helped forge an identity for his followers. In Matthew 5:3–11, Jesus identifies behaviors and values to which his followers should subscribe. Thus the Sermon on the Mount created a narrative that outlined what type of person he wanted in his flock. After his death, his apostles continued shaping the group's narrative through its collective memory. For Christians today, the four Gospels and other readings in the New Testament demonstrate how that group identity and group memory were forged.[56]

Theological Reflection on Matthew 5–7

The Sermon on the Mount, one of the most famous passages in the Gospel of Matthew and the synoptic Gospels as a whole, presents Jesus' and Matthew's community with an entirely different way of living and of responding to life. In a world fraught with tension caused by many different types of social conflicts, the Sermon on the Mount calls listeners then and now to espouse a new way of dealing with difficult situations. The Sermon also serves as a word of consolation and encouragement for those who have encountered hardship because of oppression.

Ultimately, Jesus' discourse deals with the state of one's inner being and heart and focuses on right relationship. Keeping the Law is not enough; one must go deeper than the Law to live a life of radical love, and to live that life authentically in a spirit of humility.

Those listeners who would become followers of Jesus are assured of God's steadfast love. They are also reminded that just as God's love is extended to all people regardless of their difficulties, attitudes, and states of life, so must their love be extended to all in an effort to transform social conflict into mutual respect so that peace may abide in the hearts of all and in the world of all.

The lesson of the Sermon on the Mount is not only for Jesus' listeners. Its message was also intended for the Romans and the Jewish leaders of Jesus' and Matthew's day. Hence, the Sermon on the Mount presents hearers of the word then and now with a dynamic vision and challenge for living nonviolently. Jesus' listeners are encouraged to be catalysts of change and to teach by example so that others can learn by example how to turn their swords into plowshares and their spears into pruning hooks in order to sow and cultivate seeds of justice and righteousness with peace as its fruit.

In Sum: Grace in the Wilderness

Living in a world of social conflict and surrounded by expressions of hostility, Matthew and Jesus could easily have instructed their listeners in ways that would help them defend themselves according to the principle of *lex talionis*. Instead, Jesus and Matthew offer the people of their respective communities a way to handle social conflict that preserves the dignity and well-being of all while establishing and sustaining peace in the land. The Sermon on the Mount functions as a polemic against the ways and attitudes of the Roman Empire. The Sermon is also an invitation to personal and communal transformation for all, where differences are honored and the true exercise of power leads not to conflict and division but to unity and peace.

Reflection Questions:
Can You Now...?

1. Think of a speech of the last hundred years that has had a mobilizing effect on its listeners? To what extent was that speech part of a social conflict? What, if anything, did the speech do to forge group identity?

2. Read and interpret the Gospel of Matthew through the lens of the Sermon on the Mount?

3. Explain the "Sermon on the Mount" as a stage in conflict?

4. Explain the various ways that one can respond to conflict as outlined by the Sermon on the Mount?

5. Explain where the audience of Jesus stood with respect to compliance, identity, and internalization of his message at the time the Sermon on the Mount was delivered?

6. Identify any distorted perceptions in a personal conflict you have had, a group conflict of which you have had a part, or in a current international conflict?

7. Identify the various social groups and their differences that could be sources of conflict for each other?

8. Explain how one's own inner attitudes can lead to conflict and what needs to be transformed if social conflict is not to be the "order of the day"?

Additional Resources

- View the movie *King,* which tells the story of Martin Luther King Jr.'s leadership of the nonviolent civil rights movement. What parallels can you draw with the experience of Jesus at the time of the Sermon on the Mount?

12

"WHAT'S LOVE GOT TO DO WITH IT?"

Transforming Conflict:
A Look at Pauline Literature

*Let love be genuine; hate what is evil, hold fast to what is good;
love one another with mutual affection; outdo one another in showing
honor. Do not lag in zeal, be ardent in spirit, serve the Lord. Rejoice
in hope, be patient in suffering, persevere in prayer. Contribute to the
needs of the saints; extend hospitality to strangers.*

*Bless those who persecute you; bless and do not curse them. Rejoice
with those who rejoice, weep with those who weep. Live in harmony
with one another; do not be haughty, but associate with the lowly; do
not claim to be wiser than you are. Do not repay anyone evil for evil,
but take thought for what is noble in the sight of all. If it is possible, so
far as it depends on you, live peaceably with all. Beloved, never avenge
yourselves, but leave room for the wrath of God; for it is written,
"Vengeance is mine, I will repay says the Lord." No, "if your enemies
are hungry, feed them; if they are thirsty, give them something to drink;
for by doing this you will heap burning coals on their heads." Do not
be overcome by evil, but overcome evil with good.* (Rom. 12:9–21)

*If I speak in the tongues of mortals and of angels, but do not have
love, I am a noisy gong or a clanging cymbal. And if I have prophetic
powers, and understand all mysteries and all knowledge, and if I have
all faith, so as to remove mountains, but do not have love, I am nothing. If I give away all my possessions, and if I hand over my body so
that I may boast, but do not have love, I gain nothing.*

*Love is patient; love is kind; love is not envious or boastful or
arrogant or rude. It does not insist on its own way; it is not irritable or
resentful; it does not rejoice in wrongdoing, but rejoices in the truth. It
bears all things, believes all things, hopes all things, endures all things.*

*Love never ends. But as for prophecies, they will come to an end; as
for tongues, they will cease; as for knowledge, it will come to an end.
For we know only in part, and we prophesy only in part; but when the
complete comes, the partial will come to an end. When I was a child, I*

spoke like a child, I thought like a child, I reasoned like a child; when I became an adult, I put an end to childish ways. For now we see in a mirror, dimly, but then we will see face to face. Now I know only in part; then I will know fully, even as I have been fully known. And now faith, hope, and love abide, these three; and the greatest of these is love. (1 Cor. 13:1–13)

Having looked at conflict from many perspectives in the preceding chapters, in this last chapter we focus on the apostle Paul's addresses to the people in Rome (Rom. 12:9–21; 14:1–12; 15:1–13) and in Corinth (1 Cor. 12:12–13:1–13).

A Biblical Interpretation
of Romans 12:9–21, 14:1–12, and 15:1–13 and 1 Corinthians 12:12–13:1–13

The most dynamic and charismatic itinerant preacher of the first century C.E. after the time of Jesus was Paul of Tarsus, who untiringly instructed, exhorted, admonished, encouraged, and graced the people of various communities in Asia Minor, Macedonia, and Greece. As founder of these communities, Paul knew the people's strengths and weaknesses and the areas in need of ongoing growth. One of the ways that Paul communicated with these communities that he founded was through letters. They were another form of preaching, especially since Paul himself could not always be physically present to the communities because of his extensive missionary journeys and his periodic imprisonment.

Two such letters that Paul wrote were to the community at Rome and to the community at Corinth. This chapter focuses on passages from these letters, emphasizing how conflict was transformed and how these passages set the tone for this experience so needed in our world today. We yearn for peace and an end to the many faces of conflict that scar all communities of life on the planet.

Paul the Apostle

Born sometime between 4 B.C. and 10 C.E. in Tarsus, the capital of the Roman province of Cilicia in Asia Minor, Paul was raised in a small minority Jewish community at some distance from Palestine. Paul was well educated, receiving his early education in Tarsus, whose schools were far superior to those found in Alexandria and Athens. Tarsus was a center for Hellenistic culture, philosophy, and education. In school, Paul was well trained in Greek and philosophy and was also taught a Hellenistic view of religion, all of which influenced his thought and writings. One of the common characteristics of Hellenistic thought was its emphasis on dualism, which is often found throughout Paul's writings.

Paul, however, was also convinced that he was "of the race of Israel, of the tribe of Benjamin, a Hebrew of Hebrew parentage" (Phil. 3:5). Like other observant Jews of his time and community, he attended synagogue on the Sabbath and observed the Mosaic Law — Torah — which was more important to the Jewish diaspora community than observing the various temple sacrifices and other forms of ritualistic worship.

Paul was also trained and educated as a Pharisee with a mission to teach and interpret the Mosaic Law. He followed a strict interpretation of the Law to the point of persecuting Christian-Jews because they seemed to be a threat to the Law (Gal. 1:13; 1 Cor. 15:9; Phil. 3:6). Not until about 35 C.E., when Paul had an experience of the risen and glorified Christ, which caused a deep conversion in him, did his focus and religious emphasis change. He shifted from persecution to salvation, realizing that God intended to save the world in and through the risen and glorified Christ. He then moved from being a zealous observant of Jewish Law to one seeking complete conformity to and unity with Christ. He now sought a righteousness not based on the Law but on faith in Christ (see Phil. 7–11).

In the end, Paul was shaped by his formal Greek and Hellenistic education, his Jewish family and community lifestyle, and his profound religious experience. Paul's religious experience and his conversion as a result of it was a singular life-changing event in his life. After his experience, he shifted his allegiance from the Pharisees to a messianic Jew. These influences made him an appropriate person to preach to the Gentiles. As a result of Paul's preaching, many Gentiles shifted their allegiances to Christ and the God of Israel. However, there continued to be many dichotomies in Paul's writings and thinking, revealing to the modern reader that deep integration of the teachings of Jesus was still needed in the apostle himself.

After his conversion experience (see Acts 9:1–19), Paul began his missionary activity: to preach Jesus Christ to the Gentile world and to found communities in Asia Minor, Macedonia, and Greece. As a preacher, he worked for three years around Damascus and the area southeast of it (Gal. 1:17), and then he went to Jerusalem, where he met up with Peter (Gal. 1:19–20). While establishing the first churches in Europe, he also traveled to Jerusalem where he settled disputes about the Mosaic Law, and to other parts of Asia Minor and Macedonia, where he wrote letters to the various churches as he continued his missionary activities. Many of the letters disclose the many different kinds of controversies with which Paul had to deal with respect to religious beliefs and practices and everyday life issues. Paul's witness to Jesus Christ also involved imprisonments, house arrest, and eventually martyrdom.

Paul's World

Paul was writing and preaching during the time of the diaspora, a time when the Jews were living outside of Judea. Paul's world was not too different from that of Jesus. Paul lived during the time of Roman rule and Roman occupation. Tatha Wiley notes:

> The Jewish world of Palestine and the Diaspora — in fact, what was considered the known world — was dominated by the Roman Empire. Roman control originated with and was sustained with violence. Rome's standing armies kept subject peoples subdued, and its exploitative economic system kept people poor or, if elite and wealthy, kept them in collaboration with the oppressors. Its oppressive politics trumped the rule of law as well as revolutionary attempts to restore independence.[1]

Additionally, as in the time of Jesus, many Jewish sects existed that included the Sadducees, Essenes, Zealots, Pharisees, and messianc Jews, among others. Wiley notes:

> Jewish parties disagreed on the levels of conformity or resistance to Roman rule that they should maintain. But if they were elite and wealthy, collaboration was the only way to retain their lifestyle. Most people did not have wealth to protect, and they undertook various strategies of resistance: anticolonial actions. Dispossessed peasants resisted increased taxation and occupation by foreign troops through "social banditry."[2]

Resorting to social banditry, the dispossessed would organize into bands and raid and steal from the local and imperial elite. Because of all of these forces at work, Paul, like Jesus, engaged in strategies of resistance that were nonviolent in nature. Most of these strategies included the use of rhetoric to express themes that would offset or present alternative views and possibilities to the ones offered to the people by the Roman occupation. One such example is Paul's teaching on the peace of Christ, which was meant to counter the *Pax Romana*. Wiley notes that "the Romans described the Pax Romana as 'salvation,' what saved nations from the bloodshed of ongoing war. But salvation seen from on top meant loss of freedom and independence, and subservience to Rome from the bottom."[3] At times, Paul also found himself at odds with other evangelists as well, in particular, over the issue of circumcision and the Gentiles.

Authorship, Audience, and the Nature of Paul's Letters

The question of authorship is a major one with regard to the many books of the Bible, and Paul's letters are no exception. Of the thirteen letters termed "Pauline," the authorship of seven remains relatively undisputed. These seven include: 1 Thessalonians, Philemon, Philippians, 1 and 2 Corinthians, Galatians, and Romans. The authorship of the other six letters is disputed. These letters include Colossians, Ephesians, and 2 Thessalonians, and the pastoral epistles of 1 and 2 Timothy and Titus.

While Paul's preaching was directed primarily to the Gentiles, his letters were intended primarily for the communities that he founded. The letters offered words of encouragement and advice but they also offered much more. Most of the letters were instructional. Paul often presented a new question, problem, or concern within the community and then offered a rich theological, ethical, and personal response to the questions posed or the issues raised. Many of the communities struggled with a sense of identity and the issue of belonging since many factions and many expressions of mission existed within the various communities. Paul always stressed unity and inclusivity. For Paul, differences were not to be seen as a source for division, but they did have to be resolved among the community members so that the community could function as a whole.

One characteristic of Paul's writing was his great rhetorical skill and his power to persuade. As each of his letters addressed different areas of concern, the material is rich and varied. The two letters of focus here are Romans and First Corinthians. Paul's letter to the Romans, the last one that he wrote, can be dated around 58 C.E. It is addressed to the Christians who reside in Rome, the capital city of the Roman Empire. This letter, however, treats the Christian community as a "mixed" community, one with a predominately Gentile background. In this letter Paul "addresses a number of problems, offers unsolicited ethical direction, and issues various admonitions about disharmony, tensions between the 'strong' and the 'weak,' those who cause dissensions and offenses, and other difficulties."[4] Paul also addresses topics such as the Law, sin, salvation, humanity in Christ, faith, love and charity, hope, baptism, the Body of Christ, and what is meant by "church." In addition, he lays out what is appropriate Christian conduct, what is meant by living "in Christ," and appropriate attitudes toward civil authorities. The letter also contains teaching about God, Jesus, and the Spirit. Thus, Paul's letter has a theological, Christological, pneumatological (dealing with Spirit), anthropological, and ethical dimension to it.[5]

Paul's First Letter to the Corinthians is also specifically admonitory, instructing the community in what they should know and do and what they should not do. Raymond F. Collins notes:

> The letter should be read as an extended exhortation. It is addressed to the Christians at Corinth, urging them in the name of the Lord Jesus to have no divisions among them. Rather they ought to be in agreement with one another. At issue is the nature of the Christian community itself. Concern for the community as a community called to be holy pervades the entire letter.[6]

The people of Corinth were struggling with identity issues, namely, what unified them and what made them distinct from others. Collins adds:

> Paul's choice of the image of the human body in 12:12–26 graphically represents the situation. In developing his reflection on the image of

the body, identified as the body of Christ (12:12, 27), Paul focuses on the unity-in-diversity and diversity-in-unity of the community.[7]

Wiley outlines additional problems within the Corinth community:

* Divisions; factions
* Exclusionary behavior of members at liturgical meals
* Status distinctions in spirituality
* Sexual immorality
* Court suits against one another
* Continued participation in other religious rites
* Questions about marriage, divorce, celibacy[8]

Wiley's final observation is that "all of these problems touch upon a basic one of belonging."[9]

Paul's words to the communities at Rome and Corinth are rich and inspiring. They present us with an ideal way to live life in solidarity and communion with one another. They also present us with an ideal way to handle conflict, and, in many ways, the themes presented in Romans 12:9–12, 14:1–12, 15:1–13, and 1 Corinthians 12:12–13:13 echo many of the themes heard earlier in Matthew's Sermon on the Mount (Matt. 5–7). Although Paul's message may seem idealistic, we need to hold on to the vision that Paul offers, knowing that transformation is possible with human effort and divine grace. Conflict does not have to be the order of the day.

The Nature of a Christian Life (Romans 12:9–21)

Having instructed the Christian community in Rome about the unity that exists among them despite their diverse gifts (Rom. 12:1–8), Paul now offers a series of twenty-nine exhortations. The Christians are to:

let their love be genuine
hate what is evil
hold fast to what is good
be ardent in spirit
serve the Lord
rejoice in hope
be patient in suffering
persevere in prayer
contribute to the needs of the saints
extend hospitality to strangers
bless those who persecute them
   bless and not curse them
rejoice with those who rejoice
weep with those who weep
live in harmony with one another
not be haughty

love one another with mutual affection
outdo one another in showing honor
not lag in zeal
associate with the lowly
not claim to be wiser than they are
not repay anyone evil for evil
take thought for what is noble in the sight
   of all
live peaceably with all
leave room for the wrath of God
never avenge themselves
feed enemies if they are hungry
give enemies something to drink if they
   are thirsty
not be overcome by evil
overcome evil with good (vv. 9–21).

This impressive and challenging list of counsels describes the demands that Christian life makes on those who profess to be Christian. They are also the virtues that will allow for peaceful living within the community and right relationships among community members. The first counsel, "Let your love be genuine" (v. 9), governs and directs all of the other counsels.

In sum, in verses 10 through 13 Paul outlines the basic Christian obligations. Verses 14 through 21 focus on the Christians' obligations toward enemies or persecutors. Brendan Byrne comments that the persecutors are not likely to be believers, and thus they are probably outside the Christian community.[10] With respect to vengeance,

> the meaning is not that believers should refrain from seeking to inflict punishment upon adversaries in the hope that this will mean the more severe punishment for them later on at the hands of God. Rather, the appeal comes out of a longstanding biblical and post-biblical prohibition against human beings taking vengeance into their own hands. Vengeance is entirely a prerogative of God. In line with this tradition, given classic statement in Deuteronomy 32:35 (quoted v. 19b), what is required of human beings is a trust and confidence that God will see to the restoration of the order of justice that has been disturbed.[11]

Finally, the passage serves as an instruction to the Christian community, and as such the instruction becomes a polemic against the Roman Empire and its lack of values.

The Practice of Tolerance (Romans 14:1–12)

Paul continues his exhortation to the Christian community at Rome in chapter 14:1–12. In this passage Paul advocates tolerance when dealing with certain contentious areas of Christian life, specifically the eating of meat and the reckoning of holy days. Fitzmyer points out that the passage "deals with the age-old problem of scrupulous versus the enlightened conscience, or the conservative versus the progressive."[12] Fitzmyer also suggests that "Paul seems to have heard something about such a problematic group in the Roman church...and in this part of Romans he addresses the problem."[13] The passage also picks up on the debt of love and charity (see Rom. 13:8) but now the duty to love is to be extended to the weak in the community. The " 'weak' are probably Jewish Christian members of the Roman community; the 'strong,' the gentile Christian members."[14]

With respect to the eating of meat, no prohibition against eating meat existed in Judaism. The practice of abstaining from it among Jewish Christians may have come into existence because of the people's fear that the meat was "unclean" or that it had once been offered to idols (see 1 Cor. 8). Paul makes clear that whether or not one eats meat or abstains from it is not essential to Christian faith; however, the obligation to mutual charity is.

With respect to observing the holy days, Sabbaths, new moons, feasts, and jubilee years were practiced by Palestinian Jews (see Zech. 7:5, 8:19).

The "weak" Christians in Rome continued to distinguish these holy days from ordinary days, but the "strong" were not concerned about them at all. Here Paul stresses that people can have different religious convictions and should not be judged by another because of one's convictions.

Throughout the passage Paul emphasizes that within the Christian community room exists for those who are different from one another and who make different choices. Paul warns that mutual charity is to be practiced toward all, and those within the community are not to criticize or pass judgment on another. All are welcomed and respected in God's house and all have a place at the table, and so it must be within Christian communities as well. Paul reminds everyone that all are accountable to God (v. 12).

Good News for Both Jews and the Gentiles (Romans 15:1–13)

This next passage from Paul's letter to the Romans can be divided into two units, verses 1 through 6 and verses 7 through 13. In the first unit, Paul stresses "the mutual acceptance of Jews and Gentiles in the Christian community that is governed by the rule of Christ."[15] For Paul, Christ is the model for righteous living. Fitzmyer comments that "Christ's giving of his life was motivated by his love for human beings" (8:32–35). Love, then, should motivate Christians to please others and "to contribute to the upbuilding of all."[16] Paul ends this first section with a prayer: "May the God of steadfastness and encouragement grant you to live in harmony with one another, in accordance with Christ Jesus, so that together you may with one voice glorify the God and Father of our Lord Jesus Christ" (15:5–6). Paul realizes that such unanimity within the community is a divine gift (v. 5), and when such unanimity exists, God is glorified (v. 6).

The second unit, verses 7–13, stresses "the mutual acceptance of Jews and Gentiles in the Christian community that is governed by the rule of Christ."[17] Hospitality is a Christian virtue, and Paul wants the Christians to move beyond tolerating or acting civil toward one another. He desires that they accept one another as family members of a household — God's household — and that their love for one another be that of brothers and sisters. For Paul, both the Jews and the Gentiles share in God's promises (see Rom. 11:13–24). The confirmation of the promises given to the patriarchs is the basis for unity among Jewish and Gentile Christians, even though both groups have diverse ethnic backgrounds. This unity would be the motivation for the Gentiles to praise God. In order to bolster the impact of his exhortation, Paul uses a rhetorical device in his appeal to Scripture:

> As it is written,
> > "Therefore I will confess you among the Gentiles,
> > > and sing praises to your name";
> and again he says,
> > "Rejoice, O Gentiles, with his people";
> and again,

> "Praise the Lord, all you Gentiles,
>   and let all the peoples praise him";
> and again Isaiah says,
>   "The root of Jesse shall come,
>   the one who rises to rule the Gentiles;
>   in him the Gentiles shall hope." (15:9–12)

The background for Paul's scriptural quotation is Psalm 18:50, Deuteronomy 32:43, Psalm 117:1, and Isaiah 11:10. For Paul, unity within the church is paramount.

All three passages from Romans studied thus far are meant to help the Christian community then and now to strive for this unity even though it may seem elusive or unattainable at first.

1 Corinthians 12:12–13:13

One of the most often quoted passages from Paul's letters is 1 Corinthians 12:12–13:13, on unity and love. Here Paul provides the Christians of Corinth with an extraordinary vision of who they truly are meant to be (1 Cor. 12:12–31) and the virtue that is central not only to their transformation but also to right relationships (1 Cor. 13:1–13). The passage calls Paul's listeners then and now to a new way of living. Ultimately, the way to transform conflict is through radical love, the kind that Paul alluded to in selected passages from Romans and that Jesus called for in his Sermon on the Mount (Matt. 5–7). First Corinthians 12:12–13:13 offers not only a vision but also a challenge and a word of hope. Within the human spirit and the human community rests the possibility for a new world order symbolized by the one body whose heart will contain an enduring love.

In 1 Corinthians 12:12–26, Paul uses the metaphor of the body to present the church at Corinth with a vivid picture of who they are meant to be as a community. The use of the body as a metaphor for a social or political group was common in ancient literature, and the metaphor was commonly used to symbolize unity. Collins outlines how Paul uses the metaphor in a way that was both typical and atypical:

> Paul's exhortation to the Christian assembly at Corinth is the classic Christian use of the metaphor of the body as a symbol of social unity (cf. Rom. 12:4–5; cf. Eph. 1:23; 2:16; 3:6; 4:1–16; Col. 1:18–24; 2:17–19; 3:15). The topos of the human body was commonplace among rhetoricians, philosophers, moralists, and historians contemporary with Paul.... Paul's use of the body image was, nonetheless, different from that of the classical topos insofar as Paul attributes the diversity of the various members of the body and the order among them to God (*theos*, vv. 18, 24) rather than to nature (*physis*). Another difference is that Paul used the metaphor to urge all members to utilize their gifts for the common good (12:7; cf. Rom 12:3–8) rather than

to urge the subordination of some members to others for the good of the whole. He employed the image to advocate the interdependence of all bodily members (vv. 21, 25–26). He states that it is the supposedly weaker (and presumably less honorable) members of the body that are to be honored and that this is in accordance with the divine ordinance in arranging the body (vv. 22–25).[18]

Paul's use of the metaphorical image of the body underscores both the unity and the diversity of the community as a body (vv. 14–26). Paul emphasizes that "in the one Spirit we were all baptized into one body — Jews or Greeks, slaves or free — and we were all made to drink of one Spirit" (v. 13). For God's people once separated by various traditions, beliefs, cultures, and races, this is good news, but for some who want to be "distinct" from others, the message can be threatening.

In the last part of 1 Corinthians 12:12–31, specifically verses 27 through 31, Paul takes the metaphor of the body one step further and tells the Corinthians that they are the body of Christ. Here Paul celebrates both the unity and diversity that exists within the community. Verses 28 through 31a consist of two lists of charisms. The first list (v. 28) names eight different charisms: those of apostles, prophets, teachers, deeds of power, gifts of healing, forms of assistance, forms of leadership, and various kinds of tongues. Following this list, Paul creates another list in which he poses seven rhetorical questions to his listeners to point out that while all of these gifts are bestowed upon the body of the community as a whole, not all of its individual members possess all of these gifts (vv. 29–30). In order to make the body function effectively, the individual members must work together to complement each other. Again, Paul stresses unity and the function of diversity within unity.

Paul concludes this first part of his address to the Corinthians with a simple exhortation, "But strive for the greater gifts" (v. 31a). After all the gifts that Paul has listed, he now tells his audience that they have to work toward greater gifts. His final statement is, "And I will show you a still more excellent way" (v. 31b). This last sentence leads directly into the next section of Paul's letter, 13:1–13.

In 1 Corinthians 13:1–13, the prologue to this part of his letter, Paul highlights the primary quality of Christian life: love. His vision of love flows from the tradition of Hellenistic Judaism. In verses 1 through 3 Paul focuses on a number of the charismatic gifts as well as robust efforts of self-sacrifice, but then he delivers the punch line: without love all of these gifts and efforts are worthless.

In the following verses (4–7), the body of 1 Corinthians 13:1–13, Paul picks up on the keyword "love" and describes the qualities of love: "Love is patient; love is kind; love is not envious or boastful or arrogant or rude. It does not insist on its own way; it is not irritable or resentful; it does not rejoice in wrongdoing, but rejoices in the truth. It bears all things, believes all things, hopes all things, endures all things." Paul's description of love consists of two positive affirmations about love (v. 4a), a series of statements about what love is not (vv. 4b–6), and four more affirmations of what love does do (vv. 6b–7). Through the use of comparisons embedded in these verses, Paul instructs his listeners on the virtue of love and offers a lesson on how they should live their lives not only in the midst of the Christian community but also in the midst of Roman occupation.

The last section of Paul's instruction on love (1 Cor. 13:8–13) begins with the simple phrase, "Love never ends." This statement of affirmation joins verses 4–7 with 8–13 and continues the thought begun in verses 4–7. Paul makes clear how many of the gifts will come to an end, namely, prophecy, the gift of tongues, and knowledge. He also emphasizes that these gifts are not complete gifts in and of themselves, and that we only have partial use of them. For Paul, the greatest of all gifts is, ultimately, love (v. 13), and for him, "love is not so much a virtue as it is eschatological power, the gift of God poured out into the very depths of one's being (Rom. 5:5)."[19]

Paul's understanding of love is also different from that of the synoptic tradition, which tends to view love in relation to ethics and ethical responses. Love for Paul is a virtue, a gift, a divine quality, and his discourse on love is more theological than ethical. Paul concludes his discourse with the familiar Christian triad: "And now faith, hope, and love abide, these three; and the greatest of these is love." This triad appears in 1 Thessalonians 1:3 and 5:8, giving expression to the greater gifts for which Christians must strive (see 1 Cor. 12:31). It gives expression to the authentic Christian life, and love, the last virtue in the triad, is the greatest of all virtues and gifts. Love is the transformative element for one's life. Love is also the virtue that binds the Christian community together, and humankind with one another and all of life. Love is an enduring gift, a gift of the Spirit, and it is the essence and expression of who God is.

Thus, Paul's teaching on love brings Matthew's Sermon on the Mount full circle and deepens it. An ethical way of life has now moved into the way of the heart, and for Christians and for Jews alike, the heart is the central organ, the seat of intelligence, and how God relates to the people (see Deut. 7:7–8). The way of love, the way of the heart, is, then, the way of life in and with God and with one another. In 1 Corinthians 13:1–13, Paul has given the Corinthians a firm foundation on which to build their community life and their life in a world fraught with hostility and conflict. By doing so, however, he has also established a polemic against the Roman Empire that knows only violence as a way of life.

Looking through the Communication Lens

The letters of the apostle Paul, with their clashing messages, reveal much about the nature of conflict, and they bear witness to the social conflict described in the Gospel of Matthew.[20] On the one hand, we see Paul's messages about love and harmony and, on the other hand, when we look at all the letters written under Paul's name, we note his very polemical views of how people should practice Christianity (see, for example, Col. 3:18–24 and 1 Tim. 2:11–12).

As indicated in the biblical analysis, in many ways the whole of Paul's letters fueled conflict. Many problems and quandaries surfaced as people in a variety of communities began to grapple with the teachings of Jesus. The apostles themselves differed in their approaches. For example, James, the brother of Jesus, held the position that converts needed to go through circumcision, follow the laws of the Torah, and embrace the divinity of Jesus. Paul, on the other hand, provided leadership for Christ-followers outside of Jerusalem, and his position contradicted that of James. He did not believe Gentiles needed circumcision, and he abrogated James's insistence that Gentile followers needed to observe the laws of the Torah.[21] Some commentators argue that Paul was more egalitarian regarding who should be included in the nascent religion.[22]

Within Paul's letters, however, while there is strong support for egalitarianism in the early letters, the later letters advocate rather oppressive power structures. In Timothy 2:11–12, for example, Paul is said to have written, "Let a woman learn in silence with full submission. I permit no woman to teach or to have authority over a man; she is to keep silent." And regarding slavery, the text of Colossians 3:22–24 reads: "Slaves, obey your earthly masters in everything, not only while being watched and in order to please them, but wholeheartedly, fearing the Lord. Whatever your task, put yourselves into it, as done for the Lord and not for your masters, since you know that from the Lord you will received the inheritance as your reward; you served the Lord Christ."

The letters of Paul seen in their historical context show the complexity of the times in which they were written and the evolution of thought among the followers of Jesus and, over time, those contradictions fueled quarrels among believers. Paul's advocacy of authority in some of his letters was used throughout history to support the domination of women, anti-Semitism (1 Thess. 2:15), and slavery. As noted earlier, most biblical scholars maintain that the later letters were not written by Paul and thus such inconsistencies do not in fact exist. Another interpretation is that Paul's thinking itself changed over time.

In addition to conflicts within the emerging Christian community, Paul also needed to address threats from the Roman rulers. In asserting the kingship of Jesus, Paul directly confronted the Roman authorities. We cannot overlook that Paul wrote his letters in a time of great conflict both within and without the emerging community. We also must acknowledge that over two thousand years our understandings of conflict and change have greatly broadened. Despite all the political, social, and religious clashes that surrounded Paul, however, he did proclaim, "And now faith, hope, and love abide, these three; and the greatest of these is love" (1 Cor. 13:13).

We too have hope, and we would like to focus on the communication abilities that contribute to the flourishing of love and peace. More specifically, what knowledge and ability can help turn around the negative spirals of destructive interactions and conflict? This chapter further develops some of the ideas presented earlier, but it probes more deeply into how we can transform conflict.

Transforming conflict does not mean eliminating it altogether. John Paul Lederach, a professor of peace-building at Notre Dame, has pointed out that because conflict is sometimes the only way to address egregious wrongs and generate change, conflict can have a positive goal.[23] Transforming conflict means using skills that reduce the chances of negative escalation and impasse, skills that help participants look for collaborative means to address their differences. To transform conflict we need knowledge of the many factors that contribute to a given situation and communication skills that can work to implement the goal of change.[24] Transforming conflict also means that we attend to what we do and how we do it in our interpersonal, group, community, or international settings, working always toward transforming embittered conflict into a relationship with the possibility of renewed connection for the participants.

What We Know So Far

Paul urges his followers, "Let love be genuine; hate what is evil, hold fast to what is good; love one another with mutual affection" (Rom. 12:9). Conflict often makes these goals elusive. In previous chapters, we have described how conflict exists at multiple levels, and how participants themselves are often not aware of all the complexities. People build up narratives in which they cast themselves as heroes or victims and the other party as villain. Strong emotions of hurt, anger, and revenge may flood both parties. Mulling over hurt and anger and telling one's own side of the story to others may exacerbate self-absorption and obscure the other side's version of events.

Conflict can be handled in many different ways. Sometimes our skills and knowledge allow us to improve the way we manage conflict. Other times, however, the dynamics and patterns are so complicated that outside help is needed. In many cultures, communities routinely rely on third parties to mediate conflict and negotiate peace in an effective manner.[25] Regardless of whether one is trying to manage one's own conflict or acting as a third party to facilitate resolution of the conflict of others, a grasp of the skills of understanding emotion, deep listening, and reframing are fundamental to changing the quality of interaction from negative and destructive to positive and constructive.[26]

Parties to a conflict in which the history of grievances runs long and deep may also try coercive methods, including physical, financial, or legal approaches. When this happens, neither party can recognize the injuries inflicted on the other, and both parties may feel helpless. Given the realities of conflict, how can we avoid such coercive means and, instead, open up opposing narratives that may be grounded in the past to begin to approach the ends described by Paul?

The Function of Emotion

Researchers have indicated that negative emotion is a common link to most definitions of conflict.[27] Andrea Bodtker and Jessica Jameson agree, noting that "human conflict does not exist in the absence of emotion."[28] Hence, any transformation of conflict must address emotion. Bodtker and Jameson, along with other experts in mediation and conflict resolution, use the term "emotional experience" to convey the idea that conflict involves physiological, cognitive, and behavioral components.[29] When our goals are thwarted, our primitive brain and body undergo *physiological arousal* and our brain sends out messages that put us in what has been termed a fight or flight mode. Then a *cognitive component* that engages higher brain functions to determine how we appraise the conflict moderates or exacerbates our *behavioral response*. At times our behavioral response occurs as a reflex action, in what has been called *emotional hijacking*.[30] When our brain is hijacked by emotion, we behave without thinking. Road rage provides an example of how people will at times react "from the gut" without considering the consequences of a rash act. At other times, we think carefully about how we want to respond. Clearly, if we are to transform conflicted relationships, the emotions associated with conflict need to be addressed.

Basic Tenets for Handling Emotions with Competence

While many skills are involved in handling emotions, researcher Tricia Jones identifies four underlying tenets to emotional competence.[31] The first tenet is the need for *emotional awareness*. Often we may be unaware of our own physiological arousal. We may not immediately realize that we are hurt, that the hurt generates anger, and that anger contributes to defensiveness. An awareness of feelings and a vocabulary to talk about them is essential.

The second tenet Jones pinpoints is emotional perspective-taking. In addition to becoming aware of our own feelings, we also need an awareness of feelings aroused in *other* people. We have already discussed cognitive perspective-taking and the need to understand other points of view. *Emotional perspective-taking* means an awareness of how *other* people feel about a situation. Emotional perspective-taking, also termed "recognition," is a shift in thinking that participants in a conflict can make to transform conflict.[32] A clear or new understanding of the other's emotional perspective helps move parties from their self-absorption.

The third tenet returns to principles discussed in chapter 2 of this book. Emotional competence also means the ability to *consider how customs and rules of a culture* we are interacting with might be different from our own. For example, in many Western cultures, making eye contact is a sign of respect, but that is not true for all cultures. If we interact with a culture that shows respect by averting the eyes, we can easily misinterpret any interaction.

The last tenet relates to what Jones calls strategic expression.[33] This involves *curbing impulsive responses* to emotional surges. For example, if a colleague delays in getting work done on time, a vitriolic confrontation may let him or her know how upset you are, but such animosity may deteriorate the relationship, making future work together even more difficult. Attacking another person's identity does little in the long run to improve conflict. Emotional competence is facilitated with deep listening to others and to ourselves.

The Skills of Listening

The words of the apostle James in his letter to the early churches are helpful: "Let everyone be quick to listen, slow to speak, slow to anger" (James 1:19b). While good listening may not be reciprocal at the beginning of a conflict, listening should improve on all sides. Reciprocity, however, is unlikely under some circumstances. People who are narcissistic may lack the ability to see another's perspective even in ordinary circumstances, even when they are not embroiled in conflict. People who are sociopaths may lack the ability to empathize. Some people's need for dominance and power is so great that the playing field will never be even; winning is always paramount for such individuals. Most of the time, however, we are not dealing with such extreme situations and, at the very least, good listening should clarify the conflict so, even if such circumstances are in play, our options will be clearer.

Deep Listening

Ordinarily, we assume that listening is automatic. *Deep listening,* however, requires listening with intentionality.[34] Even in relationships founded on love, without mindful attention we can lapse into "hearing," in other words, hearing the other person with the goal of refutation, hearing only to validate our preconceived beliefs about the conflict, or hearing focused solely on our needs without questioning how both parties might meet their needs. To listen deeply, requires that we acknowledge our own feelings (anger, hurt, defensiveness) and then set them aside to connect with what the other is trying to communicate. Deep listening means temporarily putting our own issues on hold in order to grasp what the other person is saying about the issues, how the other person's identity is impacted by our differences, and how the power relationship of the situation affects ongoing interaction. Deep listening may be the process by which we are able to heed Paul's directions in his letter to the Romans, "Bless those who persecute you; bless and do not curse them. Rejoice with those who rejoice, weep with those who weep" (Rom. 12:14–15).

Listening, however, does not mean that we must yield our perspective on the conflict. Rather we want to foster mutual understanding as a way forward to joint problem solving. John Stewart describes specific skills that he calls *dialogic listening* to facilitate good listening in conflict without abandoning our own goals.[35]

Dialogic listening builds on a skill noted in chapter 8, that of *active listening*. Active listening reflects an attempt to empathize with the feelings of the other party and verbally verify that we have correctly understood the other person's position and perspective. Active listening itself can be very validating for the other person. It assumes that we set aside our critical thoughts about the other person or group and that we attempt to determine what emotion is generating heat in the conflict. We must set aside our reflex to immediately rebut the other person. Dialogical listening begins with active listening, and it assumes that our identity is not bound up with being right.

Dialogical listening works if parties in a conflict can replace an attitude of "I know I am right" with an attitude of curiosity. While we may be committed to our own ideas and solutions, we can also be curious about how the other person's ideas and solutions work, and we can be interested in how he or she has experienced our interaction. John Stewart describes these skills as "paraphrase plus": first paraphrase the other person's content and emotion to their satisfaction; respond with your own point of view; and then invite a response to what was said.[36] Inviting a response means verifying that the other party has also understood our perspective: "I'm not sure I've been clear. What have you gotten out of what I've been saying?"

Several rounds of this technique may be required. When mutual comprehension appears in hand, ask the other person, gently, to share his or her understanding of what is going on. For example, "Just to make sure we're on the same page, could you tell me what you think we've agreed to so far?"

It should be obvious by now that an open attitude is especially important in dialogic listening. Generally, attitude is conveyed by our tone of voice, facial expression, and body language. Since nonverbal behaviors are typically deeply entrenched habits, we need to do more than merely "go through the motions."

Open-ended Questions

A second skill involved in listening is the use of open-ended questions. These are questions that cannot be answered by a simple "yes" or "no." They solicit more than a one-word answer. Whether one is a party to a conflict or one is mediating a conflict, open-ended questions can be used to promote deep listening and emotional competence.

Reframing

Another skill that contributes to deep listening is the skill of reframing, a concept that was introduced in chapter 8. Recall that frames are the cognitive structures that we use to organize experience and to "name the situations in

An Exercise in "Paraphrase Plus"

With a partner and a third-party observer role play the use of "paraphrase plus" in the following situations. The observer should record and give feedback on the extent to which the three steps of paraphrase plus are included: (1) paraphrase the other person's content and emotion to their satisfaction; (2) respond with your own point of view; and (3) invite a response to what was said.

Situation 1. Your significant other has made arrangements to get together with friends for the last two Friday nights but Friday night is "date night" for you. Your partner says, "I need to be able to spend time with my friends, and I see you other times."

Situation 2. Your coworker has not met the benchmarks you jointly set for a large project due in a month. You are worried about not getting the project done on time, which goes against your personal ethics, and you are also worried that your reputation will be tarnished because you will be blamed jointly for the missed deadline. Your coworker says, "How I structure my work is my business!"

Situation 3. Following an incident in which a gunman opened fire on a college campus, you and a friend begin arguing about carrying guns. One of you adamantly believes carrying concealed weapons on campus increases safety and prevents or at least limits destruction from a rogue gunman; the other believes that carrying concealed weapons decreases everyone's safety.

Examples of Open-ended Questions
That Help Transform Conflict

- ◆ *How has this situation impacted you?*
- ◆ *How did that event affect you?*
- ◆ *What would help you?*
- ◆ *If you could change anything about what happened, what would it be?*
- ◆ *What information, if any, was new to you in this conversation?*

which we find ourselves."[37] The metaphor of a photograph may be useful in understanding this concept. In the same way that we can crop photographs to emphasize what is important, we can use verbal frames to "crop" experience. Some elements in a picture are central and some elements may be "cropped out."[38] When communicating with others, our frames help us select the words we use to make some elements of a situation stand out and other elements of a situation recede into the background. Such selectivity may help resolve a conflict but it may also feed the conflict as each party develops its own narrative, making it difficult to heed the other's perspective. Effective use of reframing skills can help reduce the impact of emotional language and name-calling.

When describing the issues, it is possible to *deconstruct* or take apart the story, so that parties can see the values or cultural norms involved. It is also possible to *reconstruct* the narrative to help participants modify the way they view a situation.[39] For example, a family who ran a business together sought mediation. An adult daughter initiated the meeting. Concerned about her father's erratic behavior and lack of communication, she felt it would be sensible to take away his control. Her younger brother had worked closely with their father; he not only perceived her father differently, but also felt very threatened by his sister's usurping the market they had jointly developed.

The mediator might have concentrated the conversation on whether or not the father should lose control of the business, with the risk of locking the parties into their positions. After listening carefully to all of the family members talk about the reasons for their behavior, the mediator observed, "Each of you has expressed a fear caused by the behavior of the other. How might you each communicate so the other will feel safe?" In this example, the mediator focused on "safety," a value all parties shared. By offering a new way to think about the conflict, they found ways to transform the discussion from conflict to a positive approach to running the family business.

The use of language can also help parties detoxify conflict.[40] The words people use express the depth of their feelings, which should not be minimized. At the same time, the way an individual names a situation can be polarizing. The challenge in detoxifying a person's emotional expression is to do it in such a way that the intensity of feelings and breadth of concerns are reflected, but the inflammatory emotional language and accusations are eliminated.

In long entrenched conflicts, emotional competence, listening skills, and reframing skills are vital, but certainly not sufficient in themselves to move toward conflict transformation. Conflicts with long history require an integrated and holistic program for *peace education*. Similarly, in social conflicts where adversaries with religious, ethnic, racial, or national differences have been subjugated and persecuted, difficult historical memories, mutually exclusive narratives, debilitating inequities, and clashes over deeply held emotional and symbolic grievances must be addressed.

Consider, for example, the difficulties involved in situations of conflict after the end of apartheid in South Africa and struggles for power in the Balkans, Ireland, Israel/Palestine, Rwanda/Burundi, and North and South Korea, to name but a few. Designing such a program involves an array of types of communication that can be mobilized into a communication campaign, including media projects that carefully construct messages.[41] For example, in Rwanda, following the genocide, a media campaign was conducted that referred to all people in the country as "Banyarwanda" instead of referring to the two dominant ethnic groups of Tutsi and Hutu.[42] Alone, such a change only papers over differences. The government's intent, however, was to reduce divisions in the country and reverse the media campaign waged during the genocide that told Hutu to destroy Tutsi. The media can be used to promote both war and peace.

Detoxifying Language

A landlord and a tenant were upset with each other. The landlord said, "I would never write that jerk a decent reference. He's been an arrogant idiot in trying to settle the damage deposit."

A third party detoxifies and reframes the comment: "You resent that the tenant sent you an angry letter demanding his damage deposit be returned."

Pulling It All Together

Despite the tremendous pressures that Paul faced in reaching out to both Jews and non-Jews, he inspired others with his words, "And now faith, hope, and love abide, these three; and the greatest of these is love" (1 Cor. 13:13). However, we know that there are challenges and conflicts in which differences don't yield to love. Perhaps at sometime in the future, a conflict resolution formula will be discovered that prevents conflicts from becoming so destructive. While to dream such a dream is tempting, a more grounded approach is sensible. Having the tools to analyze situations of conflict and having a repertoire of responses increases the likelihood of pursuing a path that avoids an impasse and the escalation of conflict.

Theological Reflection on Paul

In these selected passages from Romans and Corinthians, Paul has provided the Christian communities in Rome and Corinth with a vision of what the Christian life and community should look like and how both should function. Paul has also given Christians in both of these major locations a word of encouragement. He has informed them about what is essential to Christian life and what is not, thereby quelling some of the religious and social disputes among them. By enumerating the various gifts of the Spirit, he has helped his listeners to realize that the entire community is gifted, that each member is gifted, but that no one member possesses all of the gifts. Paul has tried to foster a spirit of interdependence among community members and to bolster their self-confidence in the midst of oppressive times under the regime of the Roman Empire. Paul has also tried to inform his listeners about the many other virtues they need to practice so that life in the Christian communities can flourish without unnecessary discord. Striking in his address to the Romans is the hope that he extends to the Gentiles. Indeed, they are included in God's vision of salvation and promise of life.

Finally, Paul has waxed eloquent on the primary virtue that roots and binds the entire Christian community together — love — without which nothing has any real purpose or true meaning. For Paul, love is at the heart of and key to transformation into the body of Christ. The Christian community is called to embody and mirror this body of Christ for all peoples, which, in turn, will make them countercultural "lights of the world" and the "city on the hill," of which the Matthean Jesus speaks in the Sermon on the Mount (see Matt. 5–7). As the Christian community is transformed, as individual lives are transformed, so will the community and its members effect transformation within its own culture and throughout the world. Paul's vision is magnificent and his teaching remains a daunting challenge not only for the communities of his day but also for contemporary communities in today's world.

In Sum: Grace in the Wilderness

Paul and the communities of believers whom he addressed lived in turbulent times politically, socially, religiously, and culturally. Tensions also existed within the various Christian communities to which Paul was writing. Despite these hard and challenging times, grace did exist for God's people. This grace was given to them by means of Paul's preaching and teaching.

Paul's letters to the Romans and the Corinthians helped to focus the communities on what was essential and important with respect to life and to inform them about what they needed to be and do so that they could embody and reflect the life of wholeness and holiness to which they were called. The same is true today. Paul helps Christian communities understand what is essential for the common good and the right relationships that need to exist among all parties. Paul has also given his readers a way to deal with the Roman occupation and has provided hope for the Gentiles. Finally, Paul's focus on love reminds all that love is the only enduring gift and power undergirding and effecting true and lasting transformation. From Paul, the Christians learn that love is to be the fire in their hearts, the center of their lives, and the light by which they walk. Paul's vision of love is the same fire and light by which people can walk today.

In our contemporary lives, however, inspiration is not sufficient. Love is a beginning, but attaining peace requires more than an ideal of love. We need transformative communication to make real the ideal. Some understanding of emotion, some understanding of how to listen deeply to the other, some understanding of how to reframe and diffuse toxic messages are needed. Right relationship does not happen because we wish it to be so.

In a world of pain and suffering, we must begin by improving our interactions with each other, with the groups with whom we differ, and with the global community. Such work requires a journey through the wilderness. May the journey begin, may the journey continue, and may we one day walk into that new heaven and that new earth that has been promised so long ago (see Isa. 65:17–25): "For now we see in a mirror, dimly, but then we will see face to face" (1 Cor. 13:12).

Reflection Questions:
Can You Now...?

1. Recall a conflict in which you had a completely different account than another person of an incident and in which you were eventually able to see the other side's version? How did that transformation come about? Was the other party able to accept the validity of your version of events?

2. Recall a time when you or someone close to you was emotionally hijacked? At what point did you or the other person realize you had acted without thinking? Can you think of an example where emotional hijacking might benefit an individual?

3. Understand how deep listening involves not only *aural* skills but also good *oral* communication skills (summarizing content, reflecting back feelings, paraphrasing plus, reframing, and the use of open-ended questions)?

4. Recall a time when someone else's deep listening was transformative?

Additional Resources

- Read Paul's address to the people in Athens (Acts 17:16–33) and analyze it as an example of reframing.

- Two films, *Good Will Hunting* and *Antwone Fisher*, attest to the power of deep listening to transform. View one of these and watch for instances of deep listening.

EPILOGUE

In the Hebrew Scriptures, we find these timeless poetic words of the prophet Isaiah:

> *In days to come*
> *the mountain of the* LORD's *house*
> *shall be established as the highest of the mountains,*
> *and shall be raised above the hills;*
> *all the nations shall stream to it.*
> *Many peoples shall come and say,*
> *"Come, let us go up to the mountain of the* LORD,
> *to the house of the God of Jacob;*
> *that he may teach us his ways*
> *and that we may walk in his paths."*
> *For out of Zion shall go forth instruction,*
> *and the word of the* LORD *from Jerusalem.*
> *He shall judge between the nations,*
> *and shall arbitrate for many peoples;*
> *they shall beat their swords into plowshares,*
> *and their spears into pruning hooks;*
> *nation shall not lift up sword against nation,*
> *neither shall they learn war any more.* (Isa. 2:1–4)

The vision and hope for lasting peace continue to burn in the hearts of many people today. Living in a world graced and glorious in possibilities, we continue to strive for right relationships with one another and with all of creation. Many swords have not yet been turned into plowshares, and many spears have not yet been turned into pruning hooks. Nations continue to lift up sword against nation, and wars have not yet come to an end. Despite all of our knowledge, all of our intelligence, all of our experience down through the ages, we continue to struggle with conflict.

Perhaps the greatest lesson we can learn is how to deal with conflict in ways that are creative, honest, and transformative so that as a human community living among so many other communities of life on our planet we can turn the swords into plowshares and the spears into pruning hooks. Our goal should be to sow seeds of peace and not of war; seeds of life, not of death; seeds of hope, not of despair; seeds of understanding, not of intolerance; and seeds of compassion, not of disdain.

We are the history-makers, story-tellers, and poet-prophets of a new day. What song shall we sing? What poem shall we write? Or will we allow history to repeat itself, taking us further away from the vision of peace and hope instead of closer to it? Dare we acknowledge differences and celebrate them while discovering and cherishing all that we have in common? Can we live as one people on one planet, in the midst of one Sacred Presence whose abiding love continues to sustain and nurture all of us in spite of our weaknesses and shortcomings? Because relationships are not always easy to negotiate, learning how to deal with conflict positively is perhaps the greatest lesson we can learn. Learning how to deal with conflict is indeed one inroad to the way of right relationship and peace.

As we draw this study to a close, we wish we could conclude with the words "and they lived happily ever after." Our hope, however, must be more modest. By studying this text and considering the biblical case studies, we hope that readers might live happier ever after, that they will be able to avoid some of the pitfalls in handling conflict, and that through positive practices conflictive encounters will end more productively. We hope that readers will be able to see "the grace" in times of conflict.

Our hope also is that readers understand more fully their choices when encountering conflict. Every biblical story included here offers lessons to be learned. What was true for the characters in the stories is true for us: We must do the best we can with what we know. In the millennia that have passed, we have learned more about conflict, and yet we still make some of the same mistakes. People still opt for win-lose scenarios, and they lock themselves into positional fighting rather than exploring how mutual interests can best be served. They fall prey to polarized thinking and attribute personal failures to others or to circumstances. Lastly, some people, rather than developing skills in understanding emotion, listening, and reframing, believe that love is enough and "doing what comes naturally" is best.

Once readers have finished this book, they need to recognize that the journey is not over: learning about conflict is a lifelong endeavor. Every roadblock offers an opportunity to problem solve, to consider the variables that a particular scenario offers, to consider the perspectives of others, and to consider how another's culture, family, or goals might contribute to the current impasse.

We also hope that readers will think carefully and deeply about their own goals in a given situation and about all the options available to accomplish a particular goal. Most of all we hope readers will continue using life's lessons to continue developing skills to transform conflict and to serve willingly to mediate the conflicts of others.

We close now with the words of an ancient Gaelic blessing:

Deep Peace
  of the running wave to you.
Deep Peace
  of the flowing air to you.
Deep Peace
  of the shining stars to you.
Deep Peace
  of the gentle night to you.
Moon and stars
  pour their healing light on you.
Deep peace to you.

NOTES

Introduction

1. All biblical references and passages are taken from the New Revised Standard Version of the Bible.

2. Joseph P. Folger, Marshall S. Poole, and Randall K. Stutman, *Working through Conflict: Strategies for Relationships, Groups, and Organizations*, 5th ed. (Boston: Pearson Education, 2005).

3. Aaron Beck, *Love Is Never Enough: How Couples Can Overcome Misunderstandings, Resolve Conflicts, and Solve Relationship Problems through Cognitive Therapy* (New York: Harper & Row, 1988).

4. Gary Petersen, *Communicating in Organizations: A Casebook* (Scottsdale, Ariz.: Gorsuch Scarisbrick, 1994).

5. Joanne Keyton and Pamela Shockley-Zalabak, *Case Studies for Organizational Communication: Understanding Communication Processes,* 2nd ed. (Los Angeles: Roxbury Publishing Company, 2006).

6. Julie C. Kunselman and Kathrine A. Johnson, "Using the Case Method to Facilitate Learning," *College Teaching* 52 (2004): 87–92.

7. Mary A. Lundeberg, Barbara B. Levin, and Helen L. Harrington, "Reflections on Methodologies and Future Research," in *Who Learns from Cases and How? The Research Base for Teaching and Learning with Cases,* ed. Mary A. Lundeberg, Barbara B. Levin, and Helen L. Harrington (Mahwah, N.J.: Lawrence Erlbaum Associates, 1999), 231–40.

8. Michiel R. Leenders, A. Mauffette-Leenders, and Louise and James Erskine, *Writing Cases,* 4th ed. (London, Ontario: Richard Ivey School of Business, 2001).

9. Ibid.

10. The content for this discussion on case studies has been published. For a more comprehensive discussion of the use of biblical stories as case studies for teaching conflict see Elayne Shapiro, " 'Ye Shall Be as Gods Knowing Good and Evil': Using the Bible to Teach Conflict," *Religious Education* 104, no. 5 (2009): 527–38.

11. Selma Wasserman, *Introduction to Case Method Teaching: A Guide to the Galaxy* (New York: Teachers College Press, 1994).

Chapter 1: The Bible and Conflict

1. Mary A. Lundeberg, Barbara B. Levin, and Helen L. Harrington, "Reflections on Methodologies and Future Research," in *Who Learns from Cases and How? The Research Base for Teaching and Learning with Cases,* ed. Mary A. Lundeberg, Barbara B. Levin, and Helen L. Harrington (Mahwah, N.J.: Lawrence Erlbaum Associates, 1999), 231–40.

2. For further study, see Carol J. Dempsey, "Creation and Covenant," in *Hope amid the Ruins: The Ethics of Israel's Prophets* (St. Louis: Chalice Press, 2000), 19–34; see also Dempsey, "Creation, Revelation, and Redemption: Recovering the

Biblical Tradition as a Partner to Ecology," in *The Wisdom of Creation*, ed. Edward Foley and Robert Schreiter (Collegeville, Minn.: Liturgical Press, 2004), 53–64.

3. Henri Barki and Jon Hartwick, "Conceptualizing the Concept of Interpersonal Conflict," *International Journal of Conflict Management* 15, no. 3 (1994): 216–44.

4. William W. Wilmot and Joyce L. Hocker, *Interpersonal Conflict*, 7th ed. (Boston: McGraw-Hill, 2007), 9.

5. Douglas Stone and his colleagues suggest that the parties reframe the question rather than blaming each other. Rather than ask, "Who is to blame?" we should ask, "What have we each contributed?" (See Douglas Stone, Bruce Patton, and Sheila Steen, *Difficult Conversations, How to Discuss What Matters Most* (New York: Viking, 1999).

6. Paul Watzlawick, Janet H. Beavin, and Don D. Jackson, *Pragmatics of Human Communication* (New York: W. W. Norton, 1967).

7. Robert A. Baruch Bush and Joseph P. Folger, *The Promise of Mediation: The Transformative Approach to Conflict*, 2nd ed. (San Francisco: Jossey-Bass, 2005).

8. Fritz Heider, *The Psychology of Intergroup Relations* (New York: Wiley, 1958).

9. Harold H. Kelley and Jon L. Michaela, "Attribution Theory and Research," *Annual Review of Psychology* 31 (1980): 457–501.

10. Edward E. Jones and Keith E. Davis, "From Acts to Disposition: The Attribution Process in Person Perception," in *Advances in Experimental Social Psychology*, ed. Leonard Berkowitz, 2 (1965): 219–66.

11. Heider, *The Psychology of Intergroup Relations*.

Chapter 2: Joseph at Seventeen

1. John Bright, *A History of Israel*, 4th ed. (Louisville: Westminster John Knox, 2000), 92.

2. See Thomas L. Thompson, *The Historicity of the Patriarchal Narratives*, Beihefte zur Zeitschrift für die alttestamentliche Wissenschaft 133 (Berlin: Walter de Gruyter, 1974); John Van Seters, *Abraham in History and Tradition* (New Haven: Yale University Press, 1975).

3. See W. F. Albright, *From the Stone Age to Christianity: Monotheism and the Historical Process* (Baltimore: Johns Hopkins University Press, 1957); W. F. Albright, *Archaeology and the Religion of Israel* (Baltimore: Johns Hopkins University Press, 1968); G. E. Wright, *Biblical Archeology* (Philadelphia: Westminster, 1962).

4. Victor H. Matthews, *A Brief History of Ancient Israel* (Louisville: Westminster John Knox, 2002), 4.

5. Ibid.

6. Ibid.

7. Carol Meyers, "The Family in Early Israel," in *Families in Ancient Israel*, ed. Leo G. Perdue, Joseph Blenkinsopp, John J. Collins, and Carol Meyers (Louisville: Westminster John Knox, 1997), 19.

8. Ibid., 37.

9. Ibid., 29.

10. See the analysis of the Joseph stories by Barbara Green in *"What Profit for Us?" Remembering the Story of Joseph* (Lanham, Md.: University Press of America), esp. 35.

11. Victor Hamilton, *The Book of Genesis: Chapters 18–5,* New International Commentary on the Old Testament (Grand Rapids: Eerdmans, 1995), 409.

12. Ibid.

13. See, for example, Genesis 20:3, where God warns Abimelech in a dream not to take Sarah as a wife. In Genesis 31:24, Laban is warned in a dream not to harm Jacob. In a dream, Jacob is assured that he will return to the land (Gen. 46:1–4). At Gibeon, Solomon and God have a wonderful conversation, and Solomon comes to the realization that this wondrous exchange all happened in a dream (1 Kings 3:5–14). For further study of dreams, see Betty Jane Lillie, "Dreams," in *The Collegeville Dictionary of Pastoral Theology,* ed. Carroll Stuhlmueller (Collegeville, Minn.: Liturgical Press, 1996), 226–29; see also Leland Ryken, James C. Wilhoit, and Tremper Longman III, eds., "Dreams," in *Dictionary of Biblical Imagery* (Downers Grove, Ill.: InterVarsity Press, 1998), 217–19.

14. Interestingly, Joseph's mother, Rachel, was deceased prior to Joseph receiving these two dreams (see Gen. 35:19).

15. The terms "Ishmaelites" and "Midianites" are interchangeable. These people were nomads, primarily in southern Palestine.

16. The mention of "daughters" in Gen. 37:35 is surprising since only one daughter, Dinah, is mentioned thus far (see Gen. 34). Perhaps Jacob's daughters-in-law are to be included in the reference to "daughters," though no concrete evidence is given to tell us how we are to understand the term as stated in the text.

17. Edward T. Hall, *Beyond Culture* (New York: Doubleday, 1976).

18. Geert Hofstede, "National Cultures in Four Dimensions," *International Studies of Management and Organization* 13, no. 2 (1983): 53–73.

19. Ibid.; Stella Ting-Toomey, Ge Gao, Paula Trubisky, Z. Yang, H. Kim, S. Lin, and T. Nishida, "Culture, Face Maintenance, and Conflict Styles of Handling Interpersonal Conflict: A Study in Five Cultures," *International Journal of Conflict Management* 2 (1991): 275–91; M. Kamil Kozan, "Cultural Influences on Styles of Handling Interpersonal Conflict: Comparisons among Jordanian, Turkish, and U.S. Managers," *Human Relations* 42 (1989): 787–99; Sayed M. Elsayed-Ekhouly and Richard Buda, "Organizational Conflict: A Comparative Analysis of Conflict Styles across Cultures," *International Journal of Conflict Management* 7 (1996): 71–80.

20. Hofstede, *National Cultures in Four Dimensions,* 53–73.

21. Leslie A. Brody, Anne P. Copeland, Lisa S. Sutton, Dorothy R. Richardson, and Margaret Guyer, "Mommy and Daddy Like You Best; Perceived Family Favouritism in Relation to Affect, Adjustment and Family Process," *Journal of Family Therapy* 20 (1998): 269–91.

22. Grania Sheehan and Patricia Noller, "Adolescents' Perceptions of Parental Favouritism," *Family Matters* 49 (Autumn 1998): 17–19.

23. Alan C. Mikkelson, "Communication among Peers: Adult Sibling Relationships," in *Widening the Family Circle,* ed. Kory Floyd and Mark T. Morman (Thousand Oaks, Calif.: Sage Publications, 2006), 21–35.

24. Victor G. Cicirelli, "Sibling Relationships in Cross-Cultural Perspective," *Journal of Marriage and Family* 56, no. 1 (1994): 7–20.

25. Joseph P. Folger, Marshall S. Poole, and Randall K. Stutman, *Working through Conflict: Strategies for Relationships, Groups, and Organizations,* 5th ed. (Boston: Pearson Education, 2005); Richard E. Walton, *Interpersonal Peacemaking: Confrontations and Third-Party Consultation* (Reading, Mass.: Addison-Wesley, 1969);

Morton Deutsch, *The Resolution of Conflict* (New Haven: Yale University Press, 1973); Roger Fisher and William Ury, *Getting to Yes: Negotiating Agreement without Giving in* (Boston: Houghton Mifflin, 1981); Dean G. Pruitt and Peter J. Carnevale, *Negotiation in Social Conflict* (Pacific Grove, Calif.: Brooks/Cole, 1993); and Kenneth W. Thomas, "Conflict and Conflict Management," in *Handbook of Industrial Psychology*, ed. Marvin Dunnette (Chicago: Rand McNally, 1975).

26. William W. Wilmot and Joyce L. Hocker, *Interpersonal Conflict*, 7th ed. (Boston: McGraw-Hill, 2007).

27. Folger et al., *Working through Conflict.*

28. Pruitt and Carnevale, *Negotiation in Social Conflict.*

Chapter 3: Joseph and Potiphar's Wife

1. Christiana De Groot, "Genesis," in *The IVP Women's Bible Commentary*, ed. Catherine Clark Kroeger and Mary J. Evans (Downers Grove, Ill.: InterVarsity Press, 2002), 26.

2. For further study, see J. Vergote, *Joseph en Egypte* (Louvain: Publications Universitaires, 1959), 147–48.

3. See also Gen. 30:27, 30, where God blessed Laban because of Jacob.

4. Victor P. Hamilton, *The Book of Genesis: Chapters 18–50*; New International Commentary on the Old Testament (Grand Rapids: Eerdmans, 1995), 461.

5. Ibid., 467.

6. Kathy Domenici and Stephen Littlejohn, *Facework: Bridging Theory and Practice* (Thousand Oaks, Calif.: Sage Publishers, 2006).

7. William R. Cupach and Sandra Metts, *Facework* (Thousand Oaks, Calif.: Sage Publishers, 1994).

8. Joseph P. Folger, Marshall S. Poole, and Randall K. Stutman, *Working through Conflict: Strategies for Relationships, Groups, and Organizations*, 5th ed. (Boston: Pearson Education, 2005).

9. Penelope Brown and Stephen Levinson, *Politeness: Some Universals in Language Usage* (Cambridge: Cambridge University Press, 1987).

10. Sally Planalp, *Communicating Emotion: Social, Moral, and Cultural Processes* (Cambridge: Cambridge University Press, 1999).

Chapter 4: Joseph Encounters His Brothers

1. For a detailed study on the relationship between forgiveness, compassion, peace, and right relationship, see Carol J. Dempsey, *Justice: A Biblical Perspective* (St. Louis: Chalice Books, 2008), 87–109.

2. Victor P. Hamilton, *The Book of Genesis, Chapters 18–50* (Grand Rapids: Eerdmans, 1995), 515.

3. Ibid., 519.

4. Walter Brueggemann argues that underneath Joseph's "cool front" are "two further facets of Joseph's person which are important for this narrative." Brueggemann states that Joseph "is presented as ruthless, cunning, and vengeful. He is prepared to return to his brothers some of the grief caused him. He has forgotten nothing. There is nothing noble about him. There is no hint that he has any awareness of a larger vocation" (*Genesis*; Interpretation [Atlanta: John Knox, 1982], 340). I (Carol Dempsey) do not entirely agree with Brueggemann's reading of the text nor his analysis of Joseph. I would argue that Joseph is merely giving his brothers a "run

for their money" after they had sold him into slavery. What the brothers did to Joseph was malicious, while no malice exists in what Joseph is asking of his brothers. His "trick" will eventually reunite the family, whereas the brothers' ploy separated the family. Sol Schimmel notes that the brothers' "crime involved vicious cruelty toward their brother as well as the most callous insensitivity to their father's anguish — anguish that they themselves had brought upon him" ("Joseph and His Brothers: A Paradigm for Repentance," *Judaism* 37, no. 1 [Winter 1988]: 62). Schimmel also states that Joseph tries "to produce an analogous situation" to what had happened to him but that Joseph's intention is different. He is trying to see if his brothers repent of their previous behavior; he is not acting out of jealously or revenge.

5. Hamilton, *The Book of Genesis*, 555.

6. Ibid., 570.

7. Steven Erlanger, "Freed Colombian Grapples with Recalling and Releasing Pain, and Resuming Life," *New York Times*, July 11, 2008.

8. Roy F. Baumeister, Julie J. Exline and Kristin L. Sommer, "The Victim Role, Grudge Theory, and Two Dimensions of Forgiveness," in *Dimensions of Forgiveness, Psychological Research and Theological Perspectives*, ed. Everett L. Worthington Jr. (Philadelphia: Templeton Foundation Press, 1998), 79–104; Everett L. Worthington Jr., *Forgiveness and Reconciliation: Theory and Application* (New York: Routledge, 1999); Kathleen A. Lawler-Row, Cynthia A. Scott, Rachel L. Raines, Meirav Edlis-Matityahou, and Erin W. Moore, "The Varieties of Forgiveness Experience: Working Toward a Comprehensive Definition of Forgiveness," *Journal of Religion and Health* 46, no. 2 (2007): 233–48.

9. Worthington, *Forgiveness and Reconciliation*, 386.

10. Everett L. Worthington Jr. and Nathaniel G. Wade, "The Psychology of Unforgiveness and Forgiveness and Implications for Clinical Practice," *Journal of Social and Clinical Psychology* 18 (1999): 385–418.

11. Ibid.

12. Robert E. Enright and Catherine T. Coyle, "Researching the Process Model of Forgiveness within Psychological Interventions," in *Dimensions of Forgiveness: Psychological Research and Theological Perspectives*, ed. Everett L. Worthington Jr. (Philadelphia: Templeton Foundation Press, 1998), 139–61.

13. Vincent R. Waldron and Douglas L. Kelley, *Communicating Forgiveness* (Los Angeles: Sage Publications, 2008).

14. Cory Flintoff, "U.S. Military Admits Killing Iraqi Commuters" (NPR.org, July 28, 2008), *www.npr.org/templates/story/story.php?storyId=93006656* (accessed July 29, 2008).

15. Cynthia L. Battle and Ivan W. Miller, "Families and Forgiveness," in *Handbook of Forgiveness*, ed. Everett L. Worthington Jr. (New York: Routledge, 2005), 227–42.

16. Ibid.

17. Steven J. Sandage and Ian Williamson, "Forgiveness in Cultural Context," in *Handbook of Forgiveness*, ed. Everett L. Worthington Jr. (New York: Routledge, 2005), 45.

18. Lydia R. Temoshok and Prabha S. Chandra, "The Meaning of Forgiveness in a Specific Situational and Cultural Context: Persons Living with HIV/AIDS in India," in *Forgiveness: Theory, Research, and Practice*, ed. Michael E. McCullough, Kenneth I. Pargament, and Carl E. Thoresen (New York: Guilford Press, 2000), 48.

19. Mark S. Rye, M. Amir Ali, Guy L. Beck, Elliot N. Dorff, Charles Hallisey, Vasudha Narayanan, and James G. Williams, "Religious Perspectives on Forgiveness," in *Forgiveness: Theory, Research, and Practice,* ed. Michael E. McCullough, Kenneth I. Pargament, and Carl E. Thoresen (New York: Guilford Press, 2000), 18–39.

20. Ibid., 20.

21. Ibid. Steve M. Easterbrook, Eevi Beck, James S. Goodlet, Lydia Plowman, Mike Sharples, and Charles C. Wood, "A Survey of Empirical Studies of Conflict," in *CSCW: Cooperation or Conflict?,* ed. Steve M. Easterbrook (London: Springer-Verlag, 1993), 1–68.

22. Rye et al., "Religious Perspectives on Forgiveness," 18–39; Easterbrook et al., "A Survey of Empirical Studies of Conflict," 1–68.

23. Douglas Kelley, "The Communication of Forgiveness," *Communication Studies* 49, no. 3 (1998): 255–71.

24. Ibid.

25. Vincent R. Waldron and Douglas L. Kelley, "Forgiving Communication as a Response to Relational Transgressions," *Journal of Social and Personal Relationships* 22, no. 6 (2005): 723–42.

26. Andy J. Merolla, "Communicating Forgiveness in Friendships and Dating Relationships," *Communication Studies* 59, no. 2 (2008): 114–31.

27. Wanda Malcolm and Leslie S. Greenberg, "Forgiveness as a Process of Change in Individual Psychotherapy," in *Forgiveness: Theory, Research, and Practice,* ed. Michael E. McCullough, Kenneth I. Pargament, and Carl E. Thoresen (New York: Guilford Press, 2000), 179.

28. Waldron and Kelly, *Communicating Forgiveness,* 135.

29. Ibid., 135–42.

30. Baumeister et al., "The Victim Role, Grudge Theory, and Two Dimensions of Forgiveness," 79–104.

31. Ibid.

32. Waldron and Kelley, *Communicating Forgiveness,* 136–43.

33. Worthington and Wade, "The Psychology of Unforgiveness and Forgiveness and Implications for Clinical Practice," 392.

34. Baumeister et al., "The Victim Role, Grudge Theory, and Two Dimensions of Forgiveness," 86.

35. Julie J. Exline, Roy F. Baumeister, Anne L. Zell, Amy J. Kraft, and Charlott V. O. Witvliet, "Not So Innocent: Does Seeing One's Own Capability for Wrongdoing Predict Forgiveness," *Journal of Personality and Social Psychology* 94, no. 3 (2008): 495–515.

Chapter 5. Tamar and Judah

1. Judah had originally been in the mountainous area of eastern Canaan. Now he goes down to Adullam, about sixteen miles southwest of Jerusalem. Today the area would most likely be identified with Tell esh-Sheikh Madhkur in the Shephelah, lying southwest of Bethlehem and northwest of Hebron.

2. In this verse the grammar of both the Hebrew and English texts seems ambiguous. Some commentators, for example, David W. Cotter (Berit Olam, *Genesis* [Collegeville, Minn.: Liturgical Press, 2003], 280) understand Shua to be the name of the Canaanite man whom Judah encountered; thus the woman would then

be nameless. See also Victor P. Hamilton, *The Book of Genesis: Chapters 18–50* (Grand Rapids: Eerdmans, 1995), 433. Other commentators understand Shua to be the name of the Canaanite woman whom Judah married. See Susan Niditch, "Genesis," in *Women's Bible Commentary: Expanded Edition with Apocrypha*, ed. Carol A. Newsom and Sharon H. Ringe (Louisville: Westminster John Knox, 1998), 25. In *Women in Scripture*, ed. Carol Meyers, Toni Craven, and Ross S. Kraemer (Grand Rapids: Eerdmans, 2000), Alice Laffey notes that Shua is the name of a woman (see 156). Genesis 38:12, however, sheds light on Genesis 38:2: "In the course of time the wife of Judah, Shua's daughter." Thus, Judah's wife is nameless; her father is Shua.

3. See W. Sibley Towner, *Genesis*, Westminster Bible Companion (Louisville: Westminster John Knox, 2001), 250.

4. Nowhere else does the name Chezib appear in the Hebrew Scriptures.

5. See Hamilton, *The Book of Genesis*, 436.

6. In Hebrew Timnah means "allotted portion." Its exact location is obscure. Timnah was either on the border of Judah, a little more than four miles northwest of Beth-shemesh, and identified with Tell el-Batashi, or Timnah could have been Khirbet Tibneh, two miles south and southwest of Beth-Shemesh (see Josh. 15:57).

7. Towner, *Genesis*, 251. Hamilton adds further that "the Middle Eastern laws state that free Assyrian women, their daughters, and concubines must veil themselves when they go out on the street. In addition, a married 'sacred prostitute' must veil herself when she goes outside. Those who must not be veiled when they are outside are (1) an unmarried sacred prostitute; (2) a harlot; (3) female slaves. Those who must be veiled in public were married women and women of upper classes, whether married or not. Also a concubine was to be veiled when traveling with the chief wife in any public area.... Anybody who sees a prostitute or an ordinary slave girl veiled in a public place must turn her over to the authorities or be subject to a heavy penalty" (*The Book of Genesis*, 442).

8. Hamilton, *The Book of Genesis*, 441.

9. In ancient Israel, the giving and taking of pledges was common, and the Torah governed the procedures as to how the exchanges were to be done (see Exod. 22:26; Deut. 24:6, 10–13). Interestingly, a pledge to a prostitute is found only in Genesis 38:17–18, with Amos 2:7–8 being a possible exception.

10. William W. Wilmot and Joyce L. Hocker, *Interpersonal Conflict*, 7th ed. (Boston: McGraw-Hill, 2007), 9.

11. Kenneth Boulding, *The Three Faces of Power* (Newbury Park, Calif.: Sage Publications, 1990), 15.

12. Joseph P. Folger, Marshall S. Poole, and Randall K. Stutman, *Working through Conflict: Strategies for Relationships, Groups, and Organizations*, 5th ed. (Boston: Pearson Education, 2005).

13. Ibid.

14. John R. P. French and Bertram Raven, "Bases of Social Power," in *Studies in Social Power*, ed. Dean Cartwright (Ann Arbor: University of Michigan Press, 1959), 150–67.

15. Folger et al., *Working through Conflict*.

16. Wilmot and Hocker, *Interpersonal Conflict*.

17. Ibid.

18. John W. Thibaut and Harold H. Kelley, *Social Psychology of Groups* (New York: Wiley, 1959).

19. Allan R. Cohen and David L. Bradford, *Influence without Authority*, 2nd ed. (New York: John Wiley & Sons, 1995), 20.

20. G. Marwell and D. R. Schmitt, "An Introduction," in *Seeking Compliance: The Production of Interpersonal Influence Messages*, ed. J. P. Dillard (Scottsdale, Ariz.: Gorsuch Scarisbrick, 1990), 3–5.

Chapter 6: Susanna

1. Much scholarly consensus exists for the case to be made that the elders tried to "seduce" Susanna, but Jennifer A. Glancy has argued convincingly that the elders' advance is not seduction but attempted rape. I concur with Glancy's reading of the text. See Jennifer A. Glancy, "The Accused: Susanna and Her Readers," in *A Feminist Companion to Esther, Judith and Susanna*, ed. Athalya Brenner (Sheffield: Sheffield Academic Press, 1995), 288–302.

2. Amy-Jill Levine argues rightly that the story of Susanna is also about the threatened exiled covenant community and that Susanna is a "projection" of the community and serves as a "warning to those who would enjoy social privileges in foreign settings: no garden is safe." See Levine, " 'Hemmed in on Every Side': Jews and Women in the Book of Susanna," in *A Feminist Companion to Esther, Judith and Susanna*, ed. Athalya Brenner (Sheffield: Sheffield Academic Press, 1995), 312.

3. The NRSV states that Susanna "feared" the Lord. In ancient Israel and in this story's context, "fear of the Lord" is synonymous with "love" of the Lord.

4. For more on "elders," see Lawrence Boadt, C.S.P., and Elaine M. Wainwright, "Elders," in *The Collegeville Pastoral Dictionary* (Collegeville, Minn.: Liturgical Press, 1996), 244–47.

5. For more on "judges," see Leslie J. Hoppe, O.F.M., "Judges," in *The Collegeville Pastoral Dictionary*, 503–4.

6. The NRSV reads that Susanna's "heart trusted in the Lord." In ancient Israelite anthropology, the central organ of the body is the heart. The heart is the seat of all emotion and intelligence and governs one's actions.

7. William W. Wilmot and Joyce L. Hocker, *Interpersonal Conflict*, 7th ed. (Boston: McGraw-Hill, 2007), 190.

8. Judee K. Burgoon, Michelle L. Johnson, and Pamela T. Koch, "Nature and Measurement of Interpersonal Dominance," *Communication Monographs* 65 (1998): 316.

9. Dominic A. Infante and Andrew S. Rancer, "Argumentativeness and Verbal Aggressiveness: A Review of Recent Theory and Research," in *Communication Yearbook*, 19th ed. (Thousand Oaks, Calif.: Sage Publications, 1996), 319–51.

10. Dominic A. Infante and Charles J. Wigley III, "Verbal Aggressiveness: An Interpersonal Model and Measurement," *Communication Monographs* 53 (1986).

11. Ibid.

12. Burgoon et al., *Nature and Measurement of Interpersonal Dominance*, 318.

13. James C. McCroskey and Jason J. Teven, "Goodwill: A Reexamination of the Construct and Its Measurement," *Communication Monographs* 66, no. 1 (1999): 90.

14. Ibid.

15. Ibid.

16. James Kouzes and Barry Posner, *Leadership Challenge* (San Francisco: Jossey-Bass, 1993).

17. Robert Cialdini, *Influence, Science and Practice,* 4th ed. (Boston: Allyn and Bacon, 2001).

18. Wilmot and Hocker, *Interpersonal Conflict.*

Chapter 7: Judith

1. Benedikt Otzen, *Tobit and Judith,* Guides to Apocrypha and Pseudepigrapha (Sheffield: Sheffield Academic Press, 2002), 81.

2. Ibid.

3. Ibid. For a simple yet detailed chronological listing of the historical events represented in the book of Judith, see Otzen's discussion on p. 82.

4. Ibid., 83.

5. Carey Moore, *Judith,* Anchor Bible 40B (Garden City, N.Y.: Doubleday, 1985), 203.

6. In ancient times, a tent often had several sections or "rooms" (see Jud. 13:1–3, 14:14–15; Isa. 54:2).

7. Judith now stands in the tradition of the great male warriors of her past. For example, Jael bashed in General Sisera's head on the plain of Esdraelon (Judg. 5:26), and David overpowered the mighty Goliath and decapitated him with his sword (1 Sam. 17:51).

8. Ironically, Holofernes now rests at the feet of Judith, dead, but completely derailed of his power over Judith and over her people.

9. The memory of Judith and her famous accomplishment will rest in the people's hearts. For the ancient Israelite community, the heart was the central organ of the body. All emotions, choices, and memories resided in the heart (see Prov. 3:3). Furthermore, the heart was the main instrument of thought (see, for example, Gen. 6:5; 1 Chron. 29:18; Prov. 16:9) and the primary place where commitments were made (for example Deut. 6:4–6, 7:7, 10:12–13, 30:6) and lives transformed (Deut. 10:16, 30:2–3, 6, 10; Jer. 4:4).

10. Achior's circumcision and his joining the house of Israel contradicts Deuteronomy 23:3, which states that "no Ammonite or Moabite shall enter the assembly of the Lord; even to the tenth generation none belonging to them shall enter the assembly of the Lord forever." Scholars offer various suggestions on Achior joining the house of Israel. See Moore (*Judith,* 235–36) for a sampling of interpretations.

11. Suzanne McCorkle and Janet L. Mills, "Rowboat in a Hurricane: Metaphors of Interpersonal Conflict Management," *Communication Reports* 5, no. 2 (Summer 1992): 57–66.

12. Robert Blake and Jane S. Mouton, *Managerial Grid* (Houston: Gulf Publishing, 1964); Kenneth W. Thomas and Ralph H. Kilmann, *Thomas-Kilmann Conflict Mode Instrument* (Tuxedo, N.Y.: Xicom, 1974); and M. Afzalur Rahim, "A Measure of Styles of Handling Interpersonal Conflict," *Academy of Management Journal* 26 (1983): 368–76.

13. Joseph P. Folger, Marshall S. Poole and Randall K. Stutman, *Working through Conflict: Strategies for Relationships, Groups, and Organizations,* 5th ed. (Boston: Pearson Education, 2005).

14. William W. Wilmot and Joyce L. Hocker, *Interpersonal Conflict,* 7th ed. (Boston: McGraw-Hill, 2007).

15. Associated Press, "Video Is Said to Be Polish Hostage's Beheading in Pakistan," *New York Times,* February 2, 2009.

16. Richard A. Oppel and Pir Zubair Shah, "In Pakistan, Radio Amplifies Terror of Taliban," *New York Times,* January 25, 2009.

17. Deborah Brunswick and LaNeice Collins, "Founder of Islamic TV Station Accused of Beheading Wife," CNN.com, *www.cnn.com/2009/CRIME/02/16/buffalo .beheading/index.html?iref=mpstoryview* (accessed February 17, 2009).

18. George Lakoff and Mark Johnson, *Metaphors We Live By* (Chicago: University of Chicago Press, 1980).

19. John Haynes, "Metaphors and Mediation" (1999), *http://mediate.com/articles/ metaphor.cfm.*

20. Wilmot and Hocker, *Interpersonal Conflict.*

Chapter 8: Moses and God

1. In *Exodus* (New York: Cambridge University Press, 2005) Carol Meyers points out that the calf was "actually, a young bull or ox (see Ps. 106:19–20) — from jewelry donated by both men and women" (259). She comments further that "the bull was a symbol of divine strength, energy, fertility, and even leadership in the biblical world. In Ancient Near Eastern art, gods sometimes are depicted standing on bulls and frequently wear horned headdresses" (see ibid.); see also Meyers's note 73 on 259.

2. Ibid.

3. Ibid.

4. J. Gerald Janzen argues that the calf "is a replacement for Moses, a visible reassurance of God's presence and activity in their midst." See *Exodus,* Westminster Bible Companion (Louisville: Westminster John Knox, 1997), 228.

5. Ibid. See also Thomas B. Dozeman, *Commentary on Exodus* (Grand Rapids: Eerdmans, 2009), 704.

6. Dozeman notes that verses 1 through 6 are all motifs taken from 1 Kings 12:26–32 (ibid., 698).

7. The notion of God having written the law on the front and back of the two tablets is an example of biblical anthropomorphism, whereby living qualities are ascribed to God. Here God is envisioned as a person capable of writing, which can lead us to speculate on which language God used to write the Law on the tablets!

8. Janzen, *Exodus,* 237.

9. This formula, as it appears in the text, is considered by biblical scholars to be a secondary and later addition to the text.

10. The notion of a heavenly record book (vv. 32, 33) is, according to Meyers, "part of a general Near Eastern belief in heavenly ledgers" (*Exodus,* 261). For an excellent discussion on this topic, see 261–62.

11. Adam Curle, *Making Peace* (London: Tavistock Publications, 1971).

12. Roy Lewicki, Bruce Barry, and David M. Saunders, *Essentials of Negotiation,* 4th ed. (Burr Ridge, Ill.: McGraw-Hill, 2007).

13. William W. Wilmot and Joyce L. Hocker, *Interpersonal Conflict,* 7th ed. (Boston: McGraw-Hill, 2007), 245.

14. Leon Festinger, *A Theory of Cognitive Dissonance* (Palo Alto, Calif.: Stanford University Press, 1957).

15. Roger Fisher, William Ury, and Bruce Patton, *Getting to Yes: Negotiating Agreement without Giving In,* 2nd ed. (New York: Penguin Books, 1991).

16. Randall G. Rogan and Mitchell R. Hammer, "Crisis Negotiations: A Preliminary Investigation of Facework in Naturalistic Conflict Discourse," *Journal of Applied Communication Research* 22, no. 3 (1994): 216.

17. Fisher et al., *Getting to Yes*, 85.

18. See Lewicki et al., *Essentials of Negotiation*.

19. Ibid.

20. Robert Gardner, "Identity Frames, Beyond Intractability," Conflict Research Consortium, *www.beyondintractability.org/essay/framing* (accessed June 29, 2010).

21. S. C. Gwynn, *Empire of the Summer Moon: Quanah Parker and the Rise and Fall of the Comanches, the Most Powerful Indian Tribe in American History* (New York: Scribner, 2010).

22. See Donald G. Ellis, *Transforming Conflict: Communication and Ethnopolitical Conflict* (Lanham, Md.: Rowman & Littlefield, 2006).

23. Deborah Shmueli, Michael Elliott, and Sanda Kaufman, "Frame Changes and the Management of Intractable Conflict," *Conflict Resolution Quarterly* 24, no. 2 (2006): 207–18.

24. William Ury, Jeanne M. Brett, and Roger Fisher, *Getting Disputes Resolved: Designing Systems to Cut the Costs of Conflict* (San Francisco: Jossey-Bass, 1988).

25. Laura E. Drake and William A. Donahue, "Communicative Framing Theory in Conflict Resolution," *Communication Research* 23, no. 3 (1996): 297.

26. John Paul Lederach, *Preparing for Peace: Conflict Transformation across Cultures* (Syracuse: Syracuse University Press, 1995), 13.

27. For further reading and discussion, see Carol J. Dempsey, "Justice and Liberation Attained through Violence: An Ancient Reality — A Contemporary Dilemma," in *Justice: A Biblical Perspective* (St. Louis: Chalice Press, 2008), 9–43; see also Carol J. Dempsey, *The Prophets: A Liberation-Critical Reading* (Minneapolis: Fortress, 2000); Deuteronomy 28.

Chapter 9: Jeremiah

1. For a comprehensive literary study of the book of Jeremiah, with an explanation of the multilayered historical backdrop to the book, see Carol J. Dempsey, *Jeremiah: Preacher of Grace, Poet of Truth* (Collegeville, Minn.: Liturgical Press, 2008).

2. Historically, Nebuchadnezzar captured Jerusalem in 597 B.C.E. Jehoiachin, who reigned as king of Judah at that time, was exiled to Babylon.

3. Coniah is a shortened form of "Jehoiachin." Whether or not Zedekiah reigned over Judah instead of Jehoiakim is a point debated among scholars because the Septuagint (LXX) omits the phrase "Coniah son of." Thus, Zedekiah would have reigned in place of Jehoiakim. For further reading on the debate, see Jack R. Lundbom, *Jeremiah 37–52*; Anchor Bible 21C (New York: Doubleday, 2004), 53–54.

4. Jack R. Lundbom, *Jeremiah 37–52*; Anchor Bible 21C (New York: Doubleday, 2004), 55.

5. Verse 5 refers to the Chaldeans, another name for the Babylonians. John M. Bracke notes that historical evidence does support the point that the Egyptians did send an army into the region around 588 B.C.E., which disrupted the Babylonian attack on Jerusalem. The reigning pharaoh would have been Apries, known for his ambition but also his incompetence. See John M. Bracke, *Jeremiah 30–52 and*

Lamentations, Westminster Bible Companion, ed. Patrick D. Miller and David L. Bartlett (Louisville: Westminster John Knox Press, 2000), 64.

6. The use of the prophetic messenger formula is a secondary and later addition to the text. The phrase functions as a way of lending authority and credibility to the prophetic/divine word that follows.

7. The general assumption is that one of Jeremiah's relatives has died, and he must take care of a land apportionment that would be associated with his right of redemption. This transaction was eventually settled when one of Jeremiah's cousin's approached him in the court of the guard (see Jer. 32:6–15). The redistribution of land would be in keeping with the Jubilee laws (see Lev. 25). The tenth year of Zedekiah was a Jubilee year (cf. Jer. 34:8–9).

8. The Benjamin Gate was a northern city gate leading to Benjamin and Anathoth. Often the gate has been identified as the Ephraim Gate (2 Kings 14:13; Neh. 8:16), the Muster gate (Neh. 3:31); the People's Gate (Jer. 17:19). The Benjamin Gate is also mentioned in Jeremiah 38:7 and Zechariah 14:10.

9. Jeremiah is no longer a stranger to harsh treatment as a prophet. The people of his day, particularly those of his own community, were forever looking for ways to put end his life. See, for example, Jeremiah 11:18–20, 15:10–21, 18:18, and 20:1–18. At this time, private residences, including royal palaces, were often used for prisons. Imprisonment was often a way of holding people until a further decision could be reached; those imprisoned could be freed, put to death, or left to die.

10. Bracke, *Jeremiah 30–52 and Lamentations*, 65.

11. See Lundbom, *Jeremiah 37–52 and Lamentations*, 62.

12. The text of Jeremiah 38:6 states that Jeremiah is thrown into the cistern of Malehiah, the king's son. Historically, Malechiah is not one of Zedekiah's sons. Zedekiah was no more than thirty-two years old when he reigned over Judah (cf. 2 Kings 24:18). Lundbom notes further that "water cisterns nearly empty have wet mud in the bottom (Ps. 40:3) [Eng 40:2]). A cistern of this description is what we might expect in July, the month the city was taken (Jer. 39:2). The water had been used up, and under normal circumstances the cistern would not begin to fill up again until the winter rains came, which would be about November." See Lundbom, *Jeremiah 37–52*, 68).

13. Typically eunuchs were high-ranking governmental officials and in the military. Here Ebed-melech is a palace eunuch at the service of the king.

14. Most commentators and modern versions of the Bible read "three men" but the New International Version of the Bible as well as the New Jerusalem Bible read "thirty men." The Septuagint, Targums, and Latin Vulgate all read "thirty." Only one Hebrew manuscript reads "three." Whether or not three or thirty men did the job of rescuing Jeremiah is relatively unimportant. What is important, though, is the fact that the king effectively countered the princes who usurped his power.

15. In antiquity, a common punishment for slaves was to blind them, but only one eye was blinded so that the slave could continue on with the work of the day.

16. Jeremiah 52:29 cites that only 832 persons were exiled this time, a much smaller number than the first exile in 597 B.C.E.

17. Gary Harper, *Joy of Conflict Resolution: Transforming Victims, Villains and Heroes in the Workplace and at Home* (Gabriola Island, B.C.: New Society Publishers, 2004), 4.

18. Robert A. Baruch Bush and Joseph P. Folger, *The Promise of Mediation: The Transformative Approach to Conflict*, 2nd ed. (San Francisco: Jossey-Bass, 2005), 49–51.

19. Bush and Folger, *The Promise of Mediation*, 49.

20. Harper, *Joy of Conflict Resolution*, 5.

21. Ibid.

22. Ronald D. Gordon, "The Difference between Feeling Defensive and Feeling Understood," *Journal of Business Communication* 25, no. 1 (1988): 53–64.

23. Ibid., 53.

24. Glen Stamp, Anita L. Vangelisti, and John A. Daly, "The Creation of Defensiveness in Social Interaction," *Communication Quarterly* 40, no. 2 (1992): 177–90.

25. Jack Gibb, "Defensive and Supportive Communication," *Journal of Communication* 11 (1961): 141–48.

26. Waldron et al., "Coding Defensive and Supportive Communications," 197–203.

27. Ibid., 198.

28. Jean Poitras, "A Study of the Emergence of Cooperation in Mediation," *Negotiation Journal* 211, no. 2 (2005): 293.

29. Holly B. Waldron, Charles W. Turner, James F. Alexander, Cole Barton, "Coding Defensive and Supportive Communications: Discriminant Validity and Subcategory Convergence," *Journal of Family Psychology* 7, no. 2 (1993): 197–303.

30. Ibid.

31. Ibid.

32. Jennifer A. H. Becker, Barbara Ellevold, and Glen H. Stamp, "Creation of Defensiveness in Social Interaction II: A Model of Defensive Communication among Romantic Couples," *Communication Monographs* 75, no. 1 (2008): 95.

33. Gibb, *Defensive and Supportive Communication*, 141–48.

34. Douglas Stone, Bruce Patton, and Sheila Steen, *Difficult Conversations: How to Discuss What Matters Most* (New York: Viking, 1999), 167.

35. Ibid.

Chapter 10: Michal and David

1. David Toshio Tsumura, *The First Book of Samuel*, New International Commentary on the Old Testament (Grand Rapids: Eerdmans, 2007), 482.

2. See Eugene H. Peterson, *First and Second Samuel*, Westminster Bible Companion (Louisville: Westminster John Knox, 1999), 151.

3. Lillian R. Klein, "Michal, the Barren Wife," in *Samuel and Kings: A Feminist Companion to the Bible* (second series), ed. Athalya Brenner (Sheffield: Sheffield Academic Press, 2000), 42.

4. Ibid., 41.

5. See Danna Nolan Fewell and David M. Gunn, *Gender, Power, and Promise: The Subject of the Bible's First Story* (Nashville: Abingdon Press, 1993), 157.

6. Klein, "Michal, the Barren Wife," 42.

7. Ibid., 43.

8. Robert Alter, *The Art of Biblical Narrative* (New York: Basic Books, 1981).

9. Joseph P. Folger, Marshall S. Poole, and Randall K. Stutman, *Working through Conflict: Strategies for Relationships, Groups, and Organizations*, 5th ed. (Boston: Pearson Education, 2005).

10. Willard Waller, *The Family: A Dynamic Interpretation* (Oxford: Cordon, 1938.

11. Susan Sprecher, Maria Schmeeckle, and Diane Felmlee, "Principle of Least Interest," *Journal of Family Issues* 27, no. 9 (2006): 1255–80.

12. Ibid.

13. Ibid.

14. Ibid.

15. Mark Knapp, *Social Intercourse: From Greeting to Goodbye* (Boston: Allyn and Bacon, 1978).

16. Ibid.

17. Denise H. Cloven and Michael E. Roloff, "Sense-Making Activities and Interpersonal Conflict, II: The Effects of Communicative Intentions on Internal Dialogue," *Western Journal of Communication* 57 (Summer 1993): 309–29.

18. William R. Cupach and Daniel J. Canary, *Competence in Interpersonal Conflict* (New York: McGraw-Hill, 1997).

19. Larry A. Erbert, "Conflict and Dialectics: Perceptions of Dialectical Contradictions in Marital Conflict," *Journal of Social and Personal Relationships* 17, no. 4–5 (2000): 638–59.

20. John M. Gottman and Janice L. Driver, "Dysfunctional Marital Conflict and Everyday Marital Interaction," *Journal of Divorce and Remarriage* 43, no. 3 (2005): 63–78.

21. Linda J. Roberts, "Fire and Ice in Marital Communication: Hostile and Distancing Behaviors as Predictors of Marital Distress," *Journal of Marriage and Family* 62 (August 2000): 692–707.

22. Gottman and Driver, "Dysfunctional Marital Conflict and Everyday Marital Interaction," 63–78.

23. Ibid.

24. Daniel J. Canary and Laura Stafford, "Relational Maintenance Strategies and Equity in Marriage," *Communication Monographs* 59 (1992): 243–67.

25. Ibid., 15

26. Gottman and Driver, "Dysfunctional Marital Conflict and Everyday Marital Interaction," 63–78.

27. Daniel J. Weigel and Deborah S. Ballard-Reisch, "Influence of Marital Duration on the Use of Relationship Maintenance Behaviors," *Communication Reports* 12, no. 2 (1999): 59–70.

28. Leslie A. Baxter and Barbara M. Montgomery, *Relating: Dialogues and Dialectics* (New York: Guilford Press, 1996).

29. Ibid.

30. Erbert, *Conflict and Dialectics*, 638–59.

31. Ibid.

32. Jessica J. Cameron and Michael Ross, "In Times of Uncertainty: Predicting the Survival of Long-Distance Relationships," *Journal of Social Psychology* 147, no. 6 (2007): 581–606.

33. Ibid.

34. As mentioned earlier, Michal's childlessness could be the result of her earlier idol worshiping or David's refusal to have relations with her.

Chapter 11: Social Conflict in the Gospels

1. See, e.g., Exod. 3:1, 12; 4:27; 19:20, and so on.

2. See John Meier, *The Vision of Matthew: Christ, Church, and Morality in the First Gospel* (New York: Crossroad, 1991), 14.

3. The majority of scholars maintain that Matthew was a Jewish Christian but John Meier argues that Matthew was a learned Gentile Christian, not a Jewish Christian (ibid., 19).

4. Warren Carter, *Matthew: Storyteller, Interpreter, Evangelist,* rev. ed. (Peabody, Mass.: Hendrickson, 2004), 68.

5. Ibid.

6. Ibid.

7. Ibid., 69.

8. Ibid.

9. Ibid., 70.

10. For a fuller discussion on the events that led up to and that followed the temple's destruction, see Daniel J. Harrington, S.J., *The Gospel of Matthew,* Sacra Pagina series, 1, ed. Daniel J. Harrington, S.J. (Collegeville, Minn.: Liturgical Press, 1991), 10–13.

11. Ibid., 17.

12. Ibid., 17–18.

13. See R. T. France, *The Gospel of Matthew* (Grand Rapids: Eerdmans, 2007), 6.

14. Ibid., 7.

15. Carter, *Matthew,* 76.

16. Ibid., 76–77.

17. Ibid., 76.

18. In Matthew's Gospel, significant events in Jesus' life take place on mountains: his temptation (4:8–10), the feeding of the four thousand (15:29–29), the transfiguration (17:1–9), his arrest (26:30–35), and his final commissioning of the disciples (28:16).

19. Matthew appeals to Isaiah 66:2, among many other sources, for this first beatitude.

20. Harrington, *The Gospel of Matthew,* 79.

21. France, *The Gospel of Matthew,* 169.

22. Harrington, *The Gospel of Matthew,* 84.

23. France, *The Gospel of Matthew,* 208.

24. Harrington, *The Gospel Matthew,* 88.

25. Ibid.

26. Ibid.

27. Ibid., 92.

28. France, *The Gospel of Matthew,* 252.

29. See Ezra 7:77, 8:33, 36; 2 Baruch 14:12, 24:1; and Tobit 4:8–9 for references to treasures in heaven.

30. The designation of this passage as "The Golden Rule" seems to have originated with the Roman emperor Alexander Severus (222–35 C.E.) who was not a Christian but who was said to have been so impressed by this teaching that he had it inscribed in gold on the wall of his calendar.

31. For the background to the notion of the kingdom being hard and only a few entering it, see 4 Ezra 7:20, 47, 8:1, 9:15, 22; 2 Baruch 44:15, 48:33.

32. For further study on the New Jerusalem as a city and a people, see Carol J. Dempsey, "From Desolation to Delight: The Transformative Vision of Isaiah 60–62," in *The Desert Will Bloom: Poetic Visions of Isaiah,* ed. A. Joseph Everson and Hyun Chul Paul Kim (Atlanta: Society of Biblical Literature, 2009), 217–32.

33. Donald A. Hagner, "Matthew: Apostate, Reformer, Revolutionary?" *New Testament Studies* 49 (2003): 193–209.

34. Lawrence H. Schiffman, *From Text to Tradition: A History of Second Temple and Rabbinic Judaism* (Hoboken, N.J.: Ktav Publishing House, 1991).

35. William W. Wilmot and Joyce L. Hocker, *Interpersonal Conflict,* 7th ed. (Boston: McGraw-Hill, 2007), 9.

36. Lewis A. Coser, *Continuities in the Study of Social Conflict* (New York: Free Press, 1967).

37. Louis Kriesberg, *Constructive Conflicts: From Escalation to Resolution,* 3rd ed. (Lanham, Md.: Rowman & Littlefield, 2007).

38. Ibid.

39. Louis R. Pondy, "Organizational Conflict: Concepts and Models," *Administrative Science Quarterly* 127, no. 2 (1967): 296–320; Rudolf J. Rummel, *Understanding Conflict and War: The Conflict Helix,* vol. 2 (Beverly Hills: Sage Publications, 1976).

40. W. Barnett Pearce and Stephen W. Littlejohn, *Moral Conflict: When Social Worlds Collide* (Thousand Oaks, Calif.: Sage Publications, 1997).

41. See Kriesberg, *Constructive Conflicts.*

42. Dean G. Pruitt and Sung Hee Kim, *Social Conflict: Escalation, Stalemate, and Settlement,* 3rd ed. (Boston: McGraw-Hill, 2004).

43. Ibid.

44. Hagner, *Matthew,* 193–209.

45. Herbert C. Kelman, "Building a Sustainable Peace: The Limits of Pragmatism in the Israeli-Palestinian Negotiations," *Journal of Palestine Studies* 28, no. 1 (September 1998): 36.

46. Donald G. Ellis, *Transforming Conflict: Communication and Ethnopolitical Conflict* 2 (Lanham, Md.: Rowman & Littlefield, 2006).

47. Bernard Mayer, *Staying with Conflict: A Strategic Approach to Ongoing Disputes* (San Francisco: Jossey-Bass, 2009).

48. Donald Ellis, *Transforming Conflict.*

49. Schiffman, *From Text to Tradition;* Raimo Hakola and Adele Reinhartz, "John's Pharisees," in *In Quest of the Historical Pharisees,* ed. Jacob Neusner and Bruce D. Chilton (Waco, Tex.: Baylor University Press, 2007), 131–47.

50. Ellis, *Transforming Conflict,* 26.

51. Kelman, "Building a Sustainable Peace," 36.

52. Herbert C. Kelman, "Social-Psychological Dimensions of International Conflict," in *Peace-Making in International Conflicts: Methods and Techniques,* ed. I. William Zartman and J. Lewis Rasmussen (Washington, D.C.: United States Institute of Peace Press, 1997), 191–238.

53. The term used to describe this, "mote-beam mechanism," actually derives from the Gospel of Matthew 7:3 (Kings James translation).

54. Pruitt and Kim, *Social Conflict.*

55. Schiffman, *From Text to Tradition.*

56. Evert-Jan Vledder. "Conflict in the Miracle Stories, A Socio-Exegetical Study of Matthew 8 and 9," *Journal for the Study of the New Testament* Supplement Series 152 (2001): 243–65; Anders Runneson, "Rethinking Early Jewish-Christian Relations: Matthean Community History as Pharisaic Intragroup Conflict," *Journal of Biblical Literature* 127 (2008): 95–132.

Chapter 12: "What's Love Got to Do with It?"

1. Tatha Wiley, *Encountering Paul: Understanding the Man and His Message* (Lanham, Md.: Rowman & Littlefield, 2010), 12–13.

2. Ibid., 13.

3. Ibid., 17.

4. Ibid., 112.

5. For a more detailed and comprehensive study, see Joseph A. Fitzmyer, S.J., *Romans*, Anchor Bible, vol. 33 (New York: Doubleday, 1993), 25–143.

6. Raymond F. Collins, *First Corinthians*, Sacra Pagina 7, ed. Daniel J. Harrington, S.J. (Collegeville, Minn.: Liturgical Press, 1999), 20.

7. Ibid.

8. Wiley, *Encountering Paul*, 100–101.

9. Ibid., 101.

10. Brendan Byrne, S.J., *Romans*, Sacra Pagina 6, ed. Daniel J. Harrington, S.J. (Collegeville, Minn.: Liturgical Press, 1996), 377.

11. Ibid., 382.

12. Fitzmyer, *Romans*, 686.

13. Ibid., 686–87.

14. Ibid., 687.

15. Ibid., 705.

16. Ibid., 702.

17. Ibid., 705.

18. Collins, *First Corinthians*, 460.

19. Ibid., 484.

20. Philip F. Esler, *Conflict and Identity in Romans: The Social Setting of Paul's Letter* (Minneapolis: Fortress Press, 2003).

21. Michael Wyschogrod, "Paul, Jews, and Gentiles," in *Abraham's Promise: Judaism and Jewish-Christian Relations*, ed. R. Kendall Soulen (Grand Rapids: Eerdmans, 2004), 188–201.

22. Wiley, *Encountering Paul*.

23. John Paul Lederach, *Little Book of Conflict Transformation* (Intercourse, Pa.: Good Books, 2003).

24. Ibid.

25. National truth and reconciliation committees come to mind, as do the *gacaca* or traditional courts, put in place in Rwanda after the 1994 genocide.

26. Joseph P. Folger, Marshall S. Poole and Randall K. Stutman, *Working through Conflict: Strategies for Relationships, Groups, and Organizations*, 6th ed. (Boston: Pearson, 2009).

27. Henri Barki and Jon Hartwick, "Conceptualizing the Concept of Interpersonal Conflict," *International Journal of Conflict Management* 15, no. 3 (1994): 216–44.

28. Andrea M. Bodtker and Jessica K. Jameson, "Emotion in Conflict Formation and Its Transformation: Application to Organizational Conflict Management," *International Journal of Conflict Management* 12 (2001): 259–75.

29. Jessica K. Jameson, Andrea M. Bodtker, and Tim Linker, "Facilitating Conflict Transformation in a Workplace Conflict," *Negotiation Journal* 26, no. 1 (2010): 25–48.

30. Daniel Goleman, *Emotional Intelligence,* 2nd ed. (New York: Bantam Books, 2005).

31. Tricia Jones and Ross Brinkert, *Conflict Coaching: Conflict Management Strategies and Skills for the Individual* (Los Angeles: Sage Publications, 2008).

32. Folger et al., *Working through Conflict.*

33. Jones and Brinkert, *Conflict Coaching,* 105.

34. Lisbeth Lipari, "Listening for the Other: Ethical Implications of the Buber-Levinas Encounter," *Communication Theory* 14, no. 2 (2004): 122–41.

35. John Stewart and Carole Logan, "Empathic and Dialogic Listening," in *Bridges Not Walls: A Book about Interpersonal Communication,* ed. John Steward, 8th ed. (New York: McGraw Hill, 2002), 208–29.

36. Ibid.

37. Deborah Shmueli, Michael Elliott, and Sanda Kaufman, "Frame Changes and the Management of Intractable Conflicts," *Conflict Resolution Quarterly* 24, no. 2 (2006): 208.

38. Robert Gardner, "Identity Frames, Beyond Intractability," Conflict Research Consortium, *www.beyondintractability.org/essay/framing* (accessed June 29, 2010).

39. Bernard Mayer, *Staying with Conflict: A Strategic Approach to Ongoing Disputes* (San Francisco: Jossey-Bass, 2009).

40. Bernard Mayer, *Dynamics of Conflict Resolution* (San Francisco: Jossey-Bass, 2000).

41. Donald G. Ellis and Yael Warshel, "Contributions of Communication and Media Studies to Peace Education," in *Handbook on Peace Education,* ed. Gavriel Salomon and Edward Cairns (New York: Psychology Press, 2010), 135–53.

42. Eugenia Zorbas, "Reconciliation in Post-Genocidal Rwanda," *African Journal of Legal Studies* 1, no. 1 (2004): 29–52.

Index